Singapore Ageing

Issues and Challenges Ahead

Other World Scientific Titles by the Authors

Critical Issues in Asset Building in Singapore's Development
ISBN: 978-981-3239-75-3

Collected Readings on Community Development in Singapore
ISBN: 978-981-120-382-4
ISBN: 978-981-120-459-3 (pbk)

Community Development Arenas in Singapore
ISBN: 978-981-120-411-1

Singapore Ageing

Issues and Challenges Ahead

Editors

S Vasoo
Bilveer Singh
Srinivasan Chokkanathan

National University of Singapore, Singapore

World Scientific

JERSEY · LONDON · SINGAPORE · BEIJING · SHANGHAI · HONG KONG · TAIPEI · CHENNAI · TOKYO

Published by

World Scientific Publishing Co. Pte. Ltd.
5 Toh Tuck Link, Singapore 596224
USA office: 27 Warren Street, Suite 401-402, Hackensack, NJ 07601
UK office: 57 Shelton Street, Covent Garden, London WC2H 9HE

Library of Congress Cataloging-in-Publication Data
Names: Vasoo, S., editor. | Singh, Bilveer, 1956- editor. | Chokkanathan,
  Srinivasan, editor.
Title: Singapore ageing : issues and challenges ahead / editors, S Vasoo,
  Bilveer Singh, Srinivasan Chokkanathan.
Description: Hackensack, NJ : World Scientific, 2023. | Includes
  bibliographical references and index. |
Identifiers: LCCN 2022047053 | ISBN 9789811265181 (hardcover) |
  ISBN 9789811265198 (ebook) | ISBN 9789811265204 (ebook other)
Subjects: LCSH: Aging--Social aspects--Singapore. | Aging--Economic
  aspects--Singapore.
Classification: LCC HQ1061 .S5214 2023 | DDC
  305.26095957--dc23/eng/20221025
LC record available at https://lccn.loc.gov/2022047053

British Library Cataloguing-in-Publication Data
A catalogue record for this book is available from the British Library.

First published 2023 (Hardcover)
Reprinted 2024 (in paperback edition)
ISBN 9789811288494 (pbk)

For any available supplementary material, please visit
https://www.worldscientific.com/worldscibooks/10.1142/13109#t=suppl

Desk Editor: Jiang Yulin

Typeset by Stallion Press
Email: enquiries@stallionpress.com

Contents

List of Abbreviations

ACP	Advanced Care Planning
ADLs	Activities of Daily Living
AI	Artificial Intelligence
AIC	Agency for Integrated Care
AIDS	Acquired Immunodeficiency Syndrome
AMD	Advanced Medical Directive
APS	Adult Protective Service
CBIS	Community-based Integrated Service
CDC	Community Development Council
CENSA	Centre for the Study of Ageing
CNS	Community Network for Seniors
CPF	Central Provident Fund
COVID-19	Corona Virus Disease 2019
FCM	Fuzzy Cognitive Map
GMCs	Golden Manpower Centres
HALE	Healthy Life Expectancy
HDB	Housing and Development Board
HIP	Home Improvement Programme
HIV	Human Immunodeficiency Virus
HPS	Housing Pension System
IADLs	Instrumental Activities of Daily Living
IMC	Inter-Ministerial Committee
IoT	Internet of Things

LPA	Lasting Power of Attorney
LTSS	Long-term Services and Support
MCA	Mental Capacity Act
MDW	Migrant Domestic Worker
MG	*Merdeka* Generation
MGP	*Merdeka* Generation Package
MOH	Ministry of Health
MPA	Maintenance of Parents Act
MRT	Mass Rapid Transit
MSF	Ministry of Social and Family Development
NCSS	National Council of Social Service
NHP	National Health Plan
NTUC	National Trades Union Congress
OADR	Old-age Dependency Ratio
PAP	People's Action Party
PG	Pioneer Generation
PGA	Pioneer Generation Ambassador
PGO	Pioneer Generation Office
PGP	Pioneer Generation Package
RHS	Regional Health System
RSVP	Retired and Senior Volunteer Programme
SACs	Senior Activity Centres
SAGE	Singapore Action Group of Elders
SCC	Senior Citizens' Clubs
SCH	SingHealth Community Hospitals
SDT	Self-determination Theory
SEB	Social Exchange Bank
SGA	Silver Generation Ambassadors
SGO	Silver Generation Office
SHARE	Survey of Health, Ageing and Retirement in Europe
SHC	Singapore Hospice Council
SRS	Supplementary Retirement Scheme
SSC	Senior Citizens' Club
SSO	Social Service Office
TAFEP	Tripartite Alliance for Fair and Progressive Employment Practices

TFR	Total Fertility Rate
VAA	Vulnerable Adults Act
VWOs	Voluntary Welfare Organisations
WISS	Workfare Income Supplement Scheme

Acknowledgements

This publication is the result of collaborative efforts by a number of active and experienced contributors, some of whom are researchers, administrators, practitioners, advocates and academics, from varied social service and care sectors. The presenters have been encouraged to share their thoughts and concerns on the future challenges resulting from Singapore's ageing population, which have been examined over the years. However, the arenas covered in this publication are more or less different as the discussions take on a more futuristic dimension, which includes the less romantic aspect of ageing, which can be heart wrenching for younger readers who are yet to face the burdensome aspects of the life course of the very old. The young will eventually have to deal with matters of ageing, which cannot be avoided, as everyone will have to face this tertiary aspect of life, some of which are manageable and pleasant, whilst others can be painful and trying. The contributors in their own domains of interest examine all these key concerns and issues. Readers are reminded that the discussions on each topic are not fully exhaustive but provide a forum for further thoughts and more importantly to find more effective and realistic solutions to deal with the challenges of Singapore ageing.

Dr. S. Vasoo is Emeritus Professor of the National University of Singapore. He obtained his Master's degree and Doctorate of Social Work from the University of Hong Kong and holds a Diploma in Social Studies with distinction from the University of Singapore. He has authored a number of monographs on social issues and has published various articles both internationally and locally. He was awarded the Honorary Life Member of the Singapore Association of Social Workers for his outstanding contributions to social work in Singapore. He was a Member of Parliament from 1984 to 2001 and he served as Chairman of the Government Parliamentary Committee for Community Development. He is Advisor to a number of Voluntary Welfare Organisations in Singapore and is still actively involved in community development work and activities.

In the introductory and first chapters, **Dr. S. Vasoo** explores the **Social and Healthcare Issues of Singapore Ageing** and examines some of the implications and challenges facing Singapore. Some suggestions to strengthen the service delivery will be presented. The future challenges of Singapore ageing are discussed, taking into consideration the lessons learned about the consequences of ageing and ways to reduce the impacts on the vulnerable elderly. The moral and ethical issues on the questions about the end of life are debated. There is an urgency to consider setting up a national body to plan and formulate various policies and coordinate services in preparation to meet the challenges of ageing Singapore. In the concluding chapter, he raises a few critical issues, which have to be addressed by policy makers in concert with Singaporeans to find innovative solutions to help Singapore meet the complex issues of population ageing.

Associate Professor Bilveer Singh, who teaches in the Department of Political Science, National University of Singapore, and is presently the Deputy Head of the Department and is concurrently an Adjunct Senior Fellow at the Centre of Excellence for National Security, S. Rajaratnam School of International Studies, Nanyang Technological University, presents Chapter 2 on Singapore and the Politics of Ageing: An Overview. He received his MA and PhD in International Relations from the Australian National University. His research covers Singapore's politics and foreign policy as well as security issues in the Southeast Asia region with a particular focus on terrorism.

In this chapter by **Prof. Bilveer Singh** on **Singapore and the Politics of Ageing: An Overview**, he argues that politics is essentially about many things but eventually about who gets what resources and how is its essence. When the elderly or seniors were a small proportion of the total population, it was possible to ignore many of the demands of this group of citizens. However, as their numbers and demands increase, as in most developed societies, there will be a need to respond to their demands as they represent an important and critical component of the electorate. Every elder or senior is part of a wider family structure and this represents a powerful vote bank. Partly in view of this dimension, the State as a whole has been extremely proactive in addressing the issues relating to the seniors, especially in the various domains of basic needs from housing to healthcare. This chapter also examines the nexus between responding to the needs of the seniors and national politics.

In Chapter 3 focussing on **Family Policies, Dr. Kalyani K. Mehta** presents **Family Relationships and Older Adults**. Dr. Kalyani K. Mehta was Professor and former Head of the Gerontology Programme, S. R. Nathan School of Human Development at the Singapore University of Social Sciences. Her research on ageing services and policies has been published in international and regional journals, and presented at reputed international and regional conferences. In her various roles as a Consultant to the United Nations' Economic and Social Commission for Asia and the Pacific (ESCAP) and Nominated Member of Singapore Parliament, Professor Mehta has recommended policies and services for the improved quality of life of older persons. Her co-edited volume, *Experiencing Grandparenthood: An Asian Perspective* (2012) added greatly to the literature on the status and roles of grandparents in ageing societies. She has published more than 40 journal articles and more than 30 book chapters, which have been widely cited by scholars. Her publications and research interests include family caregiving, religion and ageing, widowhood, remarriage, mature workers and cross-cultural patterns of ageing.

In this chapter, Professor Mehta focusses on seniors in Singapore, using a strengths perspective, and examines the family policies relating to seniors from a critical gerontology framework. The current cohort of seniors, 65 years and above, consists of the baby-boomer generation alongside seniors 80 years and above who belong to the pre-baby-boomer generation. The latter are often referred to as the pioneer generation. Policies regarding family support, vulnerable seniors, caregiving and grandparenting will be analysed for their social impact as well as influence on positive ageing. Legislations enacted with the intention of protecting vulnerable seniors, will be critically analysed. The chapter, using a macro perspective, will conclude with the identification of social trends in family structures, and how future policies could be shaped.

Chapter 4 which presents **Dr. Kalyani K. Mehta and Dr. S. Vasoo's** views on **Organisation and Service Delivery of Long-term Care in Singapore: Present Issues and Future Challenges** is still relevant today although the paper was first presented in 2006. The ideas and suggestions are still useful for policy makers and administrators as proposed service delivery ideas can still be pursued. Minimal changes have been made except for minor updates on the data. The ideas and suggestions raised can be applied in the Singapore context and other places as well. The community programmes for the elderly can be implemented by agencies operating the various housing estates of Singapore. The delivery of social programmes for the elderly is focussed on those who are less mobile and homebound. It examines the need to review long-term care services for the elderly. It is important to promote ageing in place rather than deploying more resources for institutionalised services. More community-based support services can ensure a cost-effective approach. Challenges of such community-based long-term care services for the elderly are proposed.

Chapter 5 on **Building a Social Network for Older Adults: A Nation-wide Initiative by the Singapore Silver Generation Office** is presented by **Dr. Corinne Ghoh and Mr. Andrew Sim**. It covers community outreach to the elderly in building a support network. Dr. Corrine Ghoh is Senior Consultant with the Ageing Planning Office, Ministry of Health. She is also an Adjunct Associate Professor at the Department of Social Work, National University of Singapore. She has more than 30 years of social work practice in family and child protection, juvenile delinquency and aged care.

The co-author is Mr. Andrew Sim who has 15 years of experience in the Singapore Public Service. He has been serving in the Silver Generation Office, Agency for Integrated Care Pte Ltd. for over five years as a Deputy Head. He is also a senior Combat Medic with over 10 years of military reserve clinical experience.

Chapter 5 touches on the national initiative by the Singapore Silver Generation Office (SGO) in building a social network of support for older adults with the aim to enhance health and social outcomes in a rapidly ageing society. The discussions entail how the SGO seeks to build social capital at both the micro and macro levels to improve social and health-related outcomes of older adults in Singapore, the issues involved in building a support network and the implications moving forward.

Chapter 6 by **Tan Tai Kiat** is on **Issues and Challenges of Digitalisation of Ageing in Singapore**. Tan is Chief Operating Officer (COO) with SingHealth Community Hospitals and COO of Environmental Sustainability at SingHealth Group. He read economics at the National University of Singapore and graduated with an MSc in Public Policy and Administration from the London School of Economics and Political Science (LSE) under the Singapore–LSE Trust Scholarship. Currently, he is a PhD Candidate in Gerontology at the Singapore University of Social Sciences under the Alice Lim Memorial Fund Scholarship. His research interests are caregiving, digitalisation and social prescribing.

This write-up asserts that digitalisation is potentially a new social determinant of health and can affect ageing. From a gerontological perspective, digitalisation can affect ageing biologically, socially and psychologically. Digitalisation covers digital literacy and connectivity and can be an enabler or a disenabler. Enabling and disenabling people from communities can be both physically and virtually, and even from resources like information and services. Using Singapore's case, this chapter discusses how effects of digitalisation can present policy implications in the politics of ageing. This includes implications on future politics of ageing, taking into consideration the political force of ageing coupling with digitalisation as another political force.

Chapter 7 by **R. Jai Prakash** on **Reaching Out to the Elderly Living Alone: Tightening the Nodes**, explores ways to enhance the support network to help the elderly integrate into the community. As Singapore ages, there are increased risks of social isolation among the elderly, worsened, in part, by the recent pandemic. Therefore, it is crucial to strengthen the ecosystem of support networks for elderly living alone. A pragmatic model of community intervention is proposed to augment social connectedness for the lonely elderly.

R. Jai Prakash works in the Singapore Ministry of Social and Family Development and he has the opportunity to review policies for persons with disabilities and families in need. He has discussed social welfare issues at international forums. He pioneered the Social Service Office in Singapore. Jai holds a Master of Social Work degree from Washington University in St Louis. He is a PhD candidate researching community development and systems thinking.

Chapter 8 is by **Dr. Jedi Pan Zhengxiang** on **Information Technology's Role in Ageing and Community Service**. Dr. Jedi Pan Zhengxiang, PBM, was named one of JCI's 10 outstanding young persons of the world in Science and Technology. He is passionate about applying his knowledge, creativity and rallying like-minded youth to enhance residents' lives through age-friendly innovations. He was given top national compliments for his outstanding efforts in technology innovations for our ageing society and is actively involved in carrying out community projects to enhance the lives of seniors. He completed his PhD study in the field of IT Technology and Ageing in Nanyang Technological University (NTU).

Dr. Pan reiterates that information technology has left a mark on society with a plethora of exciting applications. As good as these inventions may sound, the bridge to translate digital technology into social good still depends on how people embrace, utilise and innovate in this rapidly evolving field. The chapter provides an overview on how the Singapore community is bridging its social needs with digital technology. He asserts for an age-friendly silver technology for the ageing population, and states a case for information technology's role in enhancing community service.

Chapter 9 on **Productive Ageing: Examining Conceptual and Empirical Issues** is by **Peter Sun and Professor Nancy Morrow-Howell**. Nancy Morrow-Howell, MSW, PhD, is the Bettie Bofinger Brown Distinguished Professor at Washington University in St. Louis, Missouri, USA, and the Director of the Harvey A. Friedman Centre for Aging. Dr. Morrow-Howell is past President and Fellow of the Gerontological Society of America. Her scholarship focusses on productive engagement in later life, specifically programme and policies to optimally engage older adults in paid and unpaid work, including working, volunteering and caregiving. Peter Sun is a doctoral student at the Brown School of Social Work at Washington University in St. Louis. His research focusses on the productive engagement of older adults in rural contexts.

The authors argue that although population ageing around the globe presents enormous challenges such as economic security and healthcare, the view that older adults are a problem to society is no longer tenable. The productive ageing perspective reorients our view to older adults as assets, "natural resources" that have the potential to offset the demands of population ageing. Recognising and supporting the contributions of older adults may also enhance the quality of life for older adults. To achieve these promises, innovative programme and policy designs that support older people as workers, volunteers and caregivers are necessary.

Chapter 10 is by **Dr. Leong Chan-Hoong and Ms. Angelica Ang Ting Yi** on **Data Management and Analysis in Social Service Sectors**. This paper discusses how data drawn from the ageing sector can be collated, managed and analysed. First, the article starts of by describing the different genres and classifications of databases and how these can be harnessed to make policy or programme decisions. The types of data include information derived from ethnographic research, quantitative surveys, primary versus secondary databases, administrative data and location-based information. Following this, the paper discusses the limitations of data management. It is emphasised that this chapter is not aimed at demonstrating the full range of statistical models and data analytics but to give readers a flavour of the diverse possibilities in the field of data management and analysis, such that readers may be more cognisant of the potential to harness reliable data from their current and future work in the ageing sector.

Leong Chan-Hoong, PhD, is currently the Head for Policy Development, Evaluation and Data Analytics at Kantar Public, a global consulting firm that specialises in the studies of public and non-profit sectors. Prior to this position, he was Associate Professor at the Centre for Applied Research, Singapore University of Social Sciences (2019–2022), and Head of Social Lab at the Institute of Policy Studies, National University of Singapore (2009–2019). He graduated with a PhD in Psychology (Wellington, 2006) and MSc's in Statistics (NUS, 2011) and Applied Geographic Information Systems (NUS, 2019). Presently, his academic interests sit at the intersection of environmental psychology and mental and physical health, specifically how a neighbourhood's conditions shape residents' well-being and spatial vulnerability. Dr. Leong publishes widely, reaching out to both the academic audience and policy makers with evidence-based outcomes derived from a myriad of methodologies and analytical techniques.

Ms. Angelica Ang Ting Yi, a third-year undergraduate student at the National University of Singapore, reading a Double Major in Life Science and Public Health. Her areas of research interests include patient-centric studies seeking to improve health systems, policies and healthcare delivery for the Singapore populace. She is most compassionate about engaging with the community and building platforms for the voices and opinions of different groups and individuals from different facets of society to be articulated.

Chapter 11 covers **Ageing in Singapore and the Asian Context** by **Associate Professor Srinivasan Chokkanathan**. The article highlights that Singapore like many Southeast Asian countries is ageing rapidly. The increase of adults aged 85 years and above, diminishing old-age support ratio, low labour force participation and increasing chronic illness are some challenges associated with the unprecedented growth of elderly in Singapore. Increasing the retirement age, non-discriminatory work environment, equitable access to the healthcare system and creating a favourable social environment devoid of ageist attitudes are some measures to promote an age-inclusive society in Singapore and in other Asian countries.

Dr. Srinivasan Chokkanathan, the article contributor, is an Associate Professor in the Department of Social Work, National University of Singapore. His research interest centres on ageing and well-being, with a special focus on Asian countries. He has conducted research and published extensively on the interaction between resources and adversities and their influence on elder mistreatment and well-being of older people.

Chapter 12 is presented by **Associate Professor Lee Geok Ling and Ms. Chee Wai Yee**, on **Every End Requires Planning — End-of-life Issues Among Older Adults**. The authors examine the access to hospice and palliative care services, healthcare financing and legislations that address end-of-life care, which are three major pillars to provide quality end-of-life care for older adults. Currently, discrepancies are observed in the allocation of resources and availability of hospice and palliative care services. Legislative measures such as Advanced Medical Directive, Advance

Care Planning and Lasting Power of Attorney introduced to empower the older adults with their rights over treatment and care require improvement in their execution. While end-of-life care and death require planning, the plan is far from desired.

Prof. Lee Geok Ling's research interests include loss, grief and bereavement, palliative social work and social work in health. She is a member of the International Work Group on Death, Dying, Bereavement and the Asia-Pacific Hospice Network. She also serves in some committees that promote psychosocial care for patients and their families. She is currently an Associate Professor with the Department of Social Work, National University of Singapore.

Ms. Chee Wai Yee's professional interests include palliative care social work, grief and bereavement. She provides training and contributes to several committees that promote advance care planning, patient and family advocacy, and psychosocial care for patients and their caregivers. Currently, she is a Senior Director with Montfort Care where she started Grief Matters, a programme for the bereaved.

A number of key topics have been covered and these are not exhaustive but substantial as a starting block for further explorations by people interested in finding compassionate ways to enable Singapore or any other society facing the silver tsunami challenge to live to the fullest, not in despair but with dignity. The ways in which we care for our elders decently will demonstrate if we are a notable society, which cares for all people despite their stations, whether young or elderly.

The opinions in the book are not representative of the government and its agencies. Readers should check on latest information or data from official sources.

Editors

Introduction

Singapore Ageing: Some Issues and Challenges Ahead

S. Vasoo

Abstract

This chapter covers an overview of the various discussions advanced by the authors who have contributed engaging thoughts on Singapore ageing. This volume has tapped wide-ranging views from social service practitioners in the field of ageing, researchers on gerontology and academics from the social and political realms to contribute their thoughts, views and suggestions on dealing with the complex social, political and healthcare implications of an acute ageing Singapore society which is unfolding very quickly like climate change in the next three decades. A number of critical decisions about allocation of resources and social policies for the ageing community will have to be made and these are more often than not fraught with controversies as the silver power will gain prominence and is likely to make demands to protect its interest.

In Singapore, which has a low fertility rate,[1] population ageing will increase dramatically if nothing is done to tackle the issue of population

---

[1] TFR, 2019. https://www.channelnewsasia.com/news/singapore/singapore-total-fertility-rate-tfr-falls-historic-low-2020-baby-14288556.

rejuvenation and renewal.[2] The various chapters will provide opportunities for all those involved in the social and health service sectors to voice their views. In particular, those working with the elderly can share ideas on social issues that affect Singapore society as well as offer some realistic proposals for those concerned about Singapore's future to take proactive steps to find innovative solutions to confront the ageing scenario of our society, which is also shared with the ageing world.[3] Not all is doom or gloom if we can bravely face some of the stark realities and tackle them realistically without being limited and holding on to confirmatory bias in our attitudes and actions in dealing with Singapore ageing.[4]

Social policies in Singapore have to contend with the economic uncertainties of capital accumulation, which is an important driver for the delivery of social services, especially when Singapore will be confronting rapid population ageing in the coming decades with a low replacement rate.[5] About at least 25% of our population will be above 60 years of age in 2030 and the healthcare requirements of the ageing sector have been examined at some length.[6] This will mean that productivity can slow down and consumption of social services will increase.[7] More funds will have to be set aside for healthcare and community support services. The societal and family burdens will grow, and therefore it is more prudent

---

[2] Department of Statistics Singapore, *Population Trends 2020*, 2020.

[3] *United Nations Population Report 2019*. United Nation Population Division.

[4] Teoh, Z. W. and Zainal, K. "Successful Aging: Progressive Governance and Collaborative Communities," *Ethos*, Issue 19, 8 July 2018, (Singapore: Civil Service College, 2018).

[5] Ministry of Finance Singapore. Budget 2019; Teoh, Z. W. and Zainal, K. "Successful Aging: Progressive Governance and Collaborative Communities," *Ethos*, Issue 19, 8 July 2018, (Singapore: Civil Service College, 2018); Vasoo, S. *Investments for the Social Sector to Tackle Some Key Social Issues in Collected Readings on Community Development in Singapore*, (World Scientific Publishers, 2019). pp. 601–617.

[6] Ministry of Community Development, "Report of the Inter-Ministerial Committee on the Ageing Population", (Singapore, 1999); Ministry of Health, "Blue Paper on the National Health Plan (NHP)", (Singapore, 1983); Ministry of Health, "White Papers on Affordable Health Care", (Singapore, 1993); and Ministry of Health (1997–1998); (1999), Annual Reports, (Singapore, 1999); and Labour Force Report 2020, Ministry of Manpower, Singapore.

[7] Khalik, S. "Singapore Tops in Life Expectancy at 84.8 Years," *The Straits Times*, 20 June 2019.

now to prepare people to stay healthy and have savings for their retirement.[8]

Another challenge facing social policy makers is to cultivate the capacity to visualise and predict changes in the social and human environment. Many people will retire and we will have a more ageing workforce.[9] We will be confronted by the need to find continuing job opportunities for those who can work. For those who want to retire, they must have adequate savings to live on, and for those with limited savings, they will have to depend on their family members and children to help them. In understanding the socio-economic and demographic changes of our globalising environment, we can then develop a clearer sense of direction in providing relevant services to see that the older workforce and retirees can live life meaningfully and with human dignity.[10]

The acute increase in the number of older workers and retirees will pose various competing demands on the resources of our workplaces, families and communities. Will we have the wherewithal to deal with these changing demographic profiles? Will we have the ability to generate the social and economic resources necessary to support this group of citizens and at the same time deal with the rising expectations and other competing demands of the various social and community groups? What

---

[8] Central Provident Fund Reports, Singapore, 2020; Central Provident Fund; *CPF Contribution and Allocation Rates.* https://www.cpf.gov.sg/employers/employerguides/employer-guides/paying-cpf-contributions/cpf-contribution-and-allocation-rates; Central Provident Fund; *Self-employed Matters.* https://www.cpf.gov.sg/members/FAQ/schemes/Self-Employed-Scheme/Self-Employed-Matters/FAQDetails?category=Self-Employed%20Scheme&group=Self-Employed%20Matters&folderid=12405&ajfaqid=2188316.

[9] Gonzales, E., Matz-Costa, C. and Morrow-Howell, N. "Increasing Opportunities for the Productive Engagement of Older Adults: A Response to Population Aging," *The Gerontologist*, 55, 2015, 252–261.

[10] Moody, H. "Productive Aging and the Ideology of Old Age," in N. Morrow-Howell, J. Hinterlong and M. Sherraden (eds.), *Productive Aging: Concepts and Challenges*, (Baltimore: Johns Hopkins University Press, 2001), pp. 175–196; Cook, J. R. "Strategies for Building Social Capital," in A. G. Greenberg, T. P. Gullotta and M. Bloom (eds.), *Social Capital and Community Well-being: The Serve Here Initiative*, (Switzerland: Springer International Publishing, 2016); Lane, A. P., Wong, C. H., Mocnik, S., Song, S. and Yuen, B. "Association of Neighbourhood Social Capital with Quality of Life Among Older People," *Journal of Aging and Health*, 32(7–8), 2020, 841–850.

will happen when Singapore cannot generate sufficient resources? What hard social policy decisions would have to be made on the allocations of resources? The answers are already often fraught with trade-offs and contentions? These are important questions that need to be addressed and there are no easy solutions to the complex issues facing Singapore ageing. Unless more capital and skilled labour resources are available and all social and community groups can work within societal means, it will indeed be difficult to improve the standard of living of our ageing workforce and population.

With Singaporean aged living longer, one can expect older persons needing continued employment. The surplus older workforce compounded by the reduction of the younger labour force will be a scenario of the future. Such an older social labour force landscape is inescapable.[11] Therefore, Singapore society must plan for productive ageing where every older person is valued and can be engaged in meaningful jobs for which they have been trained or retrained to adapt to the workplaces in which they have worked for most of their lives.[12] The issue of engaging silver seniors must be seriously reviewed as the matter has been brushed over as a surreal problem that can be postponed to the next time.[13] The seniors need to be trained and made digitally literate so that they can become more employable in the working world, which is digitally driven.[14]

As most seniors depend on their retirement savings in the Central Provident Fund and other Saving Accounts, these funds must be managed prudently and safeguarded. There have been reports of mismanagement of

---

[11] Transitions in Health, Employment, Social Engagement, and Intergenerational Transfers in Singapore study, 2017.
[12] Morrow-Howell, N. and Mui, A. C. "Introduction," in N. Morrow-Howell and A. C. Mui (eds.), *Productive Engagement in Later Life: A Global Perspective*, (Routledge, 2012).
[13] Prime Minister's Office Singapore (2019).
[14] Tan, T. K. "Humanising Technology for Older Adults," *Ethos*, Issue 20, 28 January 2019, Civil Service College Singapore. https://www.csc.gov.sg/articles/humanising-technology-for-older-adults; Tan, T. K. "How to Help Seniors be More Digitally Connected," *Today*, 8 December 2020, https://www.todayonline.com/commentary/how-help-seniors-be-more-digitally-connected; Pan, Z. J. "Information Technology's Role in Aging and Community Service," in *Singapore Ageing: Issues and Challenges Ahead*, (Singapore: World Scientific Publishers, 2023).

retirement funds and savings in some places in the world.[15] Singaporeans must ensure that people of integrity and impeccable responsibility are elected into government to look after the institutions which manage their assets. Otherwise, seniors and their families will be depleted of their hard-earned retirement savings and funds. All will end up losers if we do not have good and honest people to run our social institutions such as government bodies and private sectors. If we do not have quality people to manage them, then retirees will not be able to have a fruitful retirement but one full of misery. Retirees' lives will become worse and they will suffer impoverishment in the end. It is therefore crucial that our Singaporean society has in place succeeding groups of people who are committed to doing the best for people through to their senior year. Many elderly will have long years to live after their mandatory retirement.

In fact, the whole aspect of retirement has to be reviewed, as the elderly of tomorrow will have much knowledge and expertise, which can still be tapped to contribute socio-economically to our society. Indeed, it will be demeaning to let ageism dictate the working shelf life of the seniors. With declining population, retirement issues deserve a relook and lifelong working could be planned.[16] Our society must be graceful in valuing the seniors and find various ways to engage them in productive and meaningful activities.[17]

Singapore and the Asian region will face obvious changes in the demographic landscape. As one views the community in 2040, there will be about one in four persons who will be 60 years or above.[18] Various societies will be confronted with the silver tsunami, which will pose many challenges to cope with, and some will succeed in managing well and

---

[15] Central Provident Fund Reports, Singapore, 2020.

[16] Yap, M. T. and Gee, C. *Population Outcomes 2050.* (Singapore: Institute of Policy Studies, 2014); Chia, K. S. and Chong, S. A. "Most Singaporean Are Living Longer — But Are They Ready for Old Age." 2017.

[17] Morrow-Howell, N., Hinterlong, J. and Sherraden, M. (eds.), *Productive Aging: Concepts and Challenges*, (Baltimore: Johns Hopkins University Press, 2001); Matz, C., Sabbath, E. and James, J. "An Integrative Conceptual Framework of Engagement in Socially-Productive Activity in Later Life: Implications for Clinical and Mezzo Social Work Practice," *Clinical Social Work Journal* (Special Issue on Productive Aging), 48, 2020, 156–168.

[18] *Singapore Population 2021*, (Department of Statistics, and Population Census, 2020).

others may face real human miseries of a kind which can lead to family breakdowns and societal meltdowns,[19] which will be less likely to abate, leading to cumulative social burdens. Many observers tend to see social ageing as a resource to society but this perspective is a rather romantic picture about life as we age. Such a rosy notion becomes not so rosy when resources in various societies are limited and shrinking. The social situation becomes rather bleak and gloomy when people whether young or old contend for their share of community resources, especially when there is not much to spare or redistribute. Inevitably, the ability to get access to the limited community resources will vary directly in response to those who have power to influence and control the available resources.

As societies transform from being young and vibrant to decrepit and sluggish with older members, the aged will be seen as less useful and worse still useless because they can be relegated to consumptive status, in short an economic liability in most economically centric societies, which we are likely to witness in the next 50 years. This social scenario is plausible as people are likely to be more egocentric and engage in self-centred transactions without taking into consideration the social ecology and the social needs of others.

We will witness silver neighbourhoods by the end 2035, where more families will face increasing burdens in caring for their less mobile elderly parents. This social burden will be more pronounced among dual-career young families and more so if they have terminally sick elderly parents. Besides social and economic costs, families may have to find more accessible social and day-care service.[20] Along with this need for supportive care services, families will also face grief and loss of their elderly parents. More social care services to help family members cope with grief and loss will have to be set up.[21]

---

[19] Mehta, K. "Stress Among Family Caregivers of Older Persons in Singapore," *Journal of Cross-cultural Gerontology* Special Issue, 20, 2006, (Special on Aging in Asia) 319–334.
[20] *Agency for Integrated Care*, (Singapore: Ministry of Health, 2018).
[21] Mehta, K. and Vasoo, S. "Community Programmes and Services for Long-Term Care of Elderly in Singapore: Challenges for Policy Makers," *Asian Journal of Political Science*, 8(1), 2000, 125–140.

The social, psychosocial and health consequences facing the greying elderly population require attention too. Personnel working in health and family service settings can play a role in helping promote community care cooperatives, hospice care services and grief services that will be required to support families with elderly needing types of different social care and support.[22]

The rise in the many elderly needing healthcare and social service support will lead to debates on issues related to the end of life and the allocation of healthcare resources.[23] Human service professionals will have to face such debates in Singapore society and prepare families with elderly persons to have plans before life ends.[24] This is to ensure that one will have less traumatic trouble in living through the tertiary period of one's life. Therefore, it will be helpful if social agencies involved in elderly care can engage families at the appropriate time in making end-of-life plans for elderly relatives in their frail years.[25] Such preparations are critical as families will be better prepared to deal with issues of death and dying.[26]

Another pressing elderly issue that will be faced is loneliness among the seniors. As many seniors are likely to outlive their spouses and friends,

---

[22] Mehta, K. and Thang, L. L. "Experiences of Formal and Informal Caregivers of Older Persons in Singapore," *Journal of Cross-cultural Gerontology*, 32(3), 2017, 373–385.

[23] Aw, T. C. and Low, L. "Health Care Provisions in Singapore," in T. M. Tan and S. B. Chew (eds.), *Affordable Health Care*, (Singapore: Prentice Hall, 1997), pp. 50–71; Lim, J. "Health Care Reform in Singapore: The Medisave Scheme," in T. M. Tan and S. B. Chew (eds.), *Affordable Health Care*, (Singapore: Prentice Hall, 1997), pp. 277–285; Chia, K. S. and Lim, M. K. "Healthcare Reforms in Singapore," in K. Okma and T. Tenbensel (eds.), *Health Reforms Across the World*, (World Scientific Press, 2018).

[24] Howe, J. L. and Daratsos, L. "Roles of Social Workers in Palliative and End-of-life Care," in B. Berman (ed.), *Handbook of Social Work in Health and Aging*, (Oxford University Press, 2006), pp. 315–323; Lai, L. "IPS Report Urges Better End-of-life Planning," *The Straits Times*, 13 July 2019. https://www.straitstimes.com/singapore/report-urges-better-end-of-life-planning.

[25] Lai, L. "IPS Report Urges Better End-of-life Planning," *The Straits Times*, 13 July 2019. https://www.straitstimes.com/singapore/report-urges-better-end-of-life-planning.

[26] Malhotra, C., Chan, A., Do, Y. K., Malhotra, R. and Goh, C. "Good End-of-life Care: Perspectives of Middle-aged and Older Singaporeans," *Journal of Pain and Symptom Management*, 44, 2012, 252–263.

their social network will shrink and they have limited support to draw on.[27] Lives for these lonely seniors can be miserable and they will have less and less persons to rely on if they need social care and assistance.[28] For some time, it has been known that some seniors die in their flats without notice by neighbours or friends. Such episodes will become common when the ageing community is depleted of human resources to extend care and monitoring for the welfare of single seniors who have to fend on their own. However, the problems of lonely seniors are likely to become more acute, especially in ageing housing estates where rejuvenation or renewal of these neighbourhoods is slow or delayed inadvertently. It will be evident that in the next two decades we will see a number of silver neighbourhoods. If attempts by the public housing authority to renew and rejuvenate these neighbourhoods are slower than population ageing in these places, then these ageing neighbourhoods will become listless and socially run down.[29] In order to revitalise these silver neighbourhoods, the seniors living in bigger flats can be given attractive offers to resize their flats so that they would be able to realise some funds for their assets and at the same time enable estate renewal to take place at a quicker space in the future as more older housing flats will be held by the seniors. The public housing market can also become more vibrant. Otherwise, these housing assets will be frozen and the public housing market can be less active because seniors will hold a sizeable proportion of flats.[30] Besides this social silver situation, the social and economic activities will also slow down and younger people will not want to live in these ageing neighbourhoods; as seniors will dominate ultimately, one will see more families facing the need for care of lonely elderly parents or relatives. As many of

[27]Teo, P., Mehta, K., Thang, L. L. and Chan, A. "The Journey After Widowhood," in P. Teo, K. Mehta, L. L. Thang and A. Chan (eds.), *Ageing in Singapore: Service Needs and the State*, (London: Routledge, 2006), pp. 134–146.

[28]Thang, L. L. and Mehta, K. K. "Teach Me to be Filial: Intergenerational Care in Singapore Families," in J. Shea, K. Moore and H. Zhang (eds.), *Beyond Filial Piety: Rethinking Aging and Caregiving in East Asian Societies*, (Berghahn Books. Life Course, Culture and Aging: Global Transformations, 2020), pp. 142–165.

[29]*Institute of Public Health Metrics and Evaluation*, 2019.

[30]Hongbao, J. and Vasoo, S. "Housing as Asset Building in Singapore," in S. Vasoo and B. Singh (eds.), *Critical Issues in Asset Building in Singapore's Development*, (Singapore: World Scientific Publishers, 2018).

these families have working family members, they will face the burden of care. Social breakdowns are likely to surface if there is limited access to social support and community care services delivered at the neighbour-hood levels. Therefore, there will be high demand for more community-based programmes to cater to the needs of families who have frail lonely seniors and those affected by dementia. The number of such families is expected to increase in the next decade. In light of the greying of neigh-bourhoods, more community groups, voluntary welfare organisations and healthcare groups, together with the participation of residents as well in different settings, will have to work closely and be inclusive[31] in the provi-sion of community care services such as home help, meals service, day care, integrated housing and community nursing.[32] Here, community care cooperatives could be established to offer services, which will be more convenient and accessible to the families with lonely, frail and demented elderly needing care and attention. With the ageing population, we will likely see an increase in the number of seniors afflicted by cognitive decline leading to dementia, namely, Alzheimer's disease. Singapore like many societies will not escape this dementia route facing some of our seniors. To prepare for and face this reality, we can encourage more inno-vative community efforts with funding support from public and private sources, which can lead to the formation of various social and healthcare enterprises with the involvement of the families who are interested and in need of support services.[33]

[31] Mehta, K. K. "Social Integration and Creating an Age-inclusive Community in Singapore," *SUSS — Researchers @ Work, Issue 3*, 2021. https://www.suss.edu.sg/about-suss/centres/centre-for-applied-research/researchers-at-work/issue-3/social-integration-and-creating-an-age-inclusive-community-in-singapore.

[32] Mehta, K. and Vasoo, S. "Organisation and Delivery of Long Term Care in Singapore: Present Issues and Future Challenges," *Journal of Aging & Social Policy*, 13(2/3), 2001, 187–201; Ngoh, C. and Sim, A. "Building Social Support Networks for Older Adults: A Nation-wide Initiative by the Singapore Silver Generation Office," *Singapore Ageing: Issues and Challenges Ahead*, (Singapore: World Scientific Publishers, 2023).

[33] Ministry of Health, Government Health Expenditure and Healthcare Financing, 2020. https://www.moh.gov.sg/resources-statistics/singapore-health-facts/government-health-expenditure-and-healthcare-financing; Ministry of Health, Frequently Asked Questions on Medifund, 2020. https://va.ecitizen.gov.sg/CFP/CustomerPages/MOH/explorefaq.aspx?category=12667.

Another emerging area facing the seniors will be mental health issues. As we are aware, ageing does affect our physical, social and psychological well-being. In senior years, our health can deteriorate and one can be pre-occupied by worrying over it. Consequently, mental health issues such as anxiety, depression and psychosomatic problems can surface, and those unable to resolve them will face psychiatric breakdowns. The mental health issues facing seniors require more attention because this aspect is often given less priority by healthcare policy makers as there is no return on investment. However, in recent years, there has been a shift in orientation as ageing concerns have added pressure on policy makers to provide more resources to tackle mental health issues not only for the seniors but also for the young. This move has prompted more social service and voluntary organisations to implement mental healthcare programmes. With growing mental health breakdowns among the seniors, both outpatient and inpatient treatment services will have to be arranged by healthcare providers from the public and as well as the non-profit sectors. More importantly, because of the long-term nature of their mental illnesses, the cost for care has to remain affordable and accessible.[34] Otherwise, the seniors with serious mental breakdowns will become more depressed because they will see themselves as a burden to their families and in some cases, they can take their lives by committing suicide.[35] Such episodes have emerged in many advanced urban societies such as South Korea, Japan, Hong Kong and Europe.[36]

The last but crucial matter that will be confronting Singapore ageing more transparently will be in the arena of death and dying. The aspects dealing with the preparation for death have already been discussed in some depth. The end of life matters to all of us and in particular family members who survive us.[37] They have to be primed early in life to learn

---

[34] Clare, H. *Heavy Light: A Journey Through Madness, Mania and Healing*, (London: Chatto Windus, 2021).

[35] Registry of Births and Deaths, *Report on Registration of Births and Deaths 2019*, (Singapore, Immigration and Checkpoints Authority, 2020).

[36] Pesut, B., Greig, M., Throne, S. *et al.* "Nursing and Euthanasia: A Narrative Review of the Nursing Ethics Literature," *Nursing Ethics*, 27(1), 2020, 152–167.

[37] Earlie, S., Komaromy, C. and Bartholomew, C. (eds.) *Making Sense of Death, Dying and Bereavement — An Anthology*, (Open University, 2008).

how to cope with family members who are dying, some of whom because of terminal illnesses.[38] In this case, there is time at hand for family members to cope with the grief and loss processes. Such an anticipated death can be less traumatic as the immediate family members are better prepared to handle the grief and loss stages without serious setbacks to their lives.[39] As for families that face sudden death of loved ones, such a crisis can be very traumatic and the grief and loss can be prolonged, especially for those who are closely bonded to the departed. In some cases, serious depression can occur and they will have to seek therapeutic help. However, as the population becomes more enlightened, different thoughts and ideas about the right to die will surface and there will be moral, ethical and legal tussles over the question over the decision on one's choice to die.[40] With a steep increase of seniors in the near future, Singapore will inadvertently see a higher number of elderly sick with terminal illness. These well-informed elderly are likely to advocate for termination of their lives, as they do not want to suffer further and be a burden to their families and society.[41] Our society like many other places will be drawn into a protracted controversy between those pro-choice and pro-life advocates.[42] These divisions can lead to the formation of different interest groups, each lobbying for their views to be heard and decisions in their favour to change policy measures. In any case, some seniors who vehemently strive for pro-choice will seek solutions to end their lives by going to places where merciful death is practised. In the future, one will see an increase

---

[38] Ministry of Health, *Advanced Medical Directive.* (n.d.). https://www.moh.gov.sg/policies-and-legislation/advance-medical-directive.

[39] Vidal, M., Rodriguez-Nunez, A., Hui, D., Allo, J., Williams, J. L., Park, M., Liu, D. and Bruera, E. "Place-of-death Preferences Among Patients with Cancer and Family Caregivers in Inpatient and Outpatient Palliative Care," *BMJ Supportive and Palliative Care*, 2020.

[40] Allen, J., Chavez, J., DeSimone, S. S., Howard, D. D. *et al.*, "'Americans' Attitudes Towards Euthanasia and Physician-assisted Suicide, 1936–2002," *Journal of Sociology and Social Welfare*, 33(2), 2006, 5–23.

[41] Byock, I. R. "Measuring Quality of Life for Patients with Terminal Illness: The Missoula–VITAS® Quality of Life Index," *Palliative Medicine*, 12, 1998, 231–244.

[42] Golingher, E. C., Ely, E. W., Sulmasy, D. P., Bakkar, J. *et al.* "Physician-assisted Suicide and Euthanasia in the ICU: A Dialogue on Core Ethical Issues," *Critical Care Medicine*, 45(2), 2017, 149–155.

in the number of countries having merciful death services. The debate between pro-life and pro-choice advocates is unlikely to simmer down but might instead be fired up by more seniors who believe in having the right to die when they are faced with incurable health conditions that cause unbearable pain and are burdensome to immediate family members. This intractable health and human controversy will eat into the moral and ethical fibre of our Singapore society and the controversial issue will be soul wrenching,[43] going as far as to tear the social and religious fabric of Singapore.[44] The best way to resolve such a controversy is to have an independent tribunal of medico-legal experts to give their recommendation to the healthcare setting. Singapore's policy makers and the Singaporean community will be confronted by controversial dilemmas as the general population becomes more well-informed and especially where seniors will face the choice of the right to live or die in dignity.[45] This matter will not elude our ageing Singapore; in particular, doctors, families and patients must be better prepared to handle painful matters when they surface in the near future when the silver tsunami comes our way without fail.[46]

[43] Mason, C. M. S. E. "Ethical Issues and Attitudes Towards Euthanasia," *Modern Psychological Studies*, 22(2), 2017, 149–155.
[44] Cambell, A., Gilbert, G. and Jones, G. *Medical Ethics* (4e), (South Melbourne, Australia: Oxford University Press, 2005).
[45] Onwuteaka-Philisen, B. D., Muller, M. T. *et al.* "Euthanasia and Old Age," *Age and Ageing*, 26(6), 1997, 487–492; Gawande, A. *Being Mortal: Medicine and What Matters in the End*, (United Kingdom, Large Print Press, 2017).
[46] Volandes, A. *The Conversations*, (London: Bloomsbury Publications, 2015).

Chapter 1

Social and Healthcare Issues of Singapore Ageing: Some Implications and Challenges

S. Vasoo

Abstract

This chapter will discuss some of the major social and healthcare issues facing the elderly population in Singapore and examine some of implications and challenges. The development of key social policy measures and constraints will be touched upon. The various concerns about social consequences of ageing and affordability of healthcare will be addressed. Some suggestions to strengthen the service delivery will be presented. The future challenges of Singapore ageing will be discussed, taking into consideration the lessons learned about the consequences of ageing and ways to reduce the impacts on the vulnerable elderly. There is an urgency to consider in the setting up of a national body to plan and formulate various policies and coordinate services in preparation to meet the challenges of ageing Singapore.

Introduction

Singapore and the Asian region will face changes in the demographic landscape. If one walks around the community in 2030, there will be about one in four persons who will be 65 years and above.[1] Various socie-ties will be confronted with the silver tsunami, which will pose many challenges to cope with. Some will succeed in managing well and others may face misery of a kind that can lead to family breakdown and societal meltdown, which will be less likely to abate, leading to them becoming cumulative social burdens. Many observers tend to see social ageing as a resource, but this perspective is a romantic picture about life as we age. Such a rosy notion becomes not so rosy when resources in various socie-ties are limited and shrinking even though there are good plans to deal with ageing and make it successful.[2]

The recent COVID-19 pandemic has demonstrated the serious adverse impact on social life not only for the young but also on the elderly who have suffered some casualties and loss of life. The pandemic has taught us all not to take life for granted but to take preventive steps to avoid disas-trous consequences on the way we manage our livelihood and take steps to be inoculated with antigens to deal with the vagaries of life.

The social situation becomes rather bleak and gloomy when people whether young or old contend for their share of community resources, especially when there is not much to spare or redistribute. Inevitably, the ability to get access to the limited community resources will vary in direct relation to those who have powers to influence and control the available resources.

As societies transform from young and vibrant to one that becomes decrepit and sluggish with older members, the aged will be seen as less useful, worse still useless because they will be relegated to a consumptive status. In short, they will be considered an economic liability in most eco-nomically centric societies, which we are likely to witness in the next 50 years.[3] This social scenario is plausible as people are likely to be more

---

[1] Teo, Z. W. and Zainal, K. "Successful Aging: Progressive Governance and Collaborative Communities." *Ethos*, Issue 19 (8 July 2018), Singapore: Civil Service College. https://www.csc.gov.sg/articles/successful-ageing-progressive-governance-and-collaborative-communities, (Singapore: Population Census, 2020, Department of Statistics, Singapore).
[2] *Action for Successful Aging* (2018), (Singapore: Ministry of Health).
[3] Yap, M. T. and Gee, C. *Population Outcomes 2050*, (Singapore: Institute of Policy Studies, 2014).

egocentric and engage in self-centred transactions without taking into consideration the social ecology and the social needs of others.[4]

In Singapore, the ageing population will impose more burdens on healthcare provisions. The elderly who are better educated and endowed will be more vocal and lobby for higher concessions for using health services. The establishment of pressure groups among the elderly is likely to increase the competition for health resources. Such a situation has to be mediated by policy makers.[5] Besides future pressure on healthcare issues that will be explored in detail, there are other social and political issues which are likely to surface as Singapore ages. These are societal life course trends, which cannot be avoided. Every society will encounter these issues and the questions are how these social and political topics compounded by healthcare issues are appreciated and tackled. In some cases, societies failed to face and address them satisfactorily, leading to increasing protracted societal breakdowns and complex societal fractures. Some aspects of this chapter will touch on key concerns that are likely to surface as Singapore's population ages. Only significant social issues that have political implications will be touched upon as one can keep painting many pictures, which may be too pontificating and overwhelming to present. To start, those social issues which have critical bearing will be covered in the following discussion and some solutions, which are relevant, will be proposed, as these may not fully deal with the social issues touched upon.

Contention for Resources

For small countries like Singapore and others, human capital, land and natural resources are limited. As such, when resources become limited and there is finite growth in these resources, people are likely to contend

---

[4]Thang, L. L. and Mehta, K. K. "Teach Me to be Filial: Intergenerational Care in Singapore Families", in J. Shea, K. Moore and H. Zhang (eds.), *Beyond Filial Piety: Rethinking Aging and Caregiving in East Asian Societies*, (New York: Berghahn Books, 2020), pp. 142–165.

[5]*Inter-Ministerial Committee (IMC) Report on The Ageing Population*, (Singapore: Ministry of Social and Family Development, 1999); and Yap, M. T. and Gee, C. *Population Outcomes* 2050, (Singapore: Institute of Policy Studies, 2014).

for resources, namely, for food and space. Food will be a primary contention; the world's population has increased significantly in the last 20 years,[6] and there are more mouths to feed but less food is being produced because of increasing desertification of various regions.[7] With the serious state of desertification of arable land, less food will be produced for the growing population and countries without adequate land like Singapore will face food shortages even though they have funds to purchase food. The aged citizens will have to vie for their quota of food, but with their lack of productive contribution and depleting financial resources, they are likely to be relegated to the end of the food chain as world communities become more contentious for food and other related resources to meet basic human needs. This competition for food resources will affect the ageing population; besides, the young and the elderly will inevitably get fewer resources allocated, with the young having a longer life journey to go through.

Besides desertification, sea resources will be depleted because countries with marine and technical skills are likely to exploit it without maintaining an ecological balance. They will acquire whatever marine resources are available, more than what they need. Without prolonged mining of marine and other seabed resources, the ocean will be slowly destroyed and will be too toxic to support future marine life. In this case, the seniors, who tend to be the less exposed generation in acquiring technical skills, will be displaced from accessing marine resources, which can help sustain their livelihood. No matter how compassionate societies are, they can turn ugly. When compassion fatigue sets in, the old person's needs will be given less priority than those of the young. Indeed, this human dilemma is likely to be faced in societies driven by materialistic values. It will be a dog-eat-dog world and the elderly will be given little attention. A mediatory approach can be taken to have all the key groups, young, middle-aged and the old, form a think-tank to propose allocation of resources in an equitable manner. There is also a necessity for all policy-making sectors to have both the young and elderly be involved in

[6] UN Population Report (2019).

[7] Arnalds, O. and Archer, S. (eds.) *Rangeland Desertification*, (Switzerland: Springer Nature, 2000).

policy formulation in resource allocation to the respective population groups.

The fight for housing is likely to become more exaggerated between the young and the old. The situation will be precipitated by the fact that as the old were in the queue earlier, they will occupy prime space leaving behind limited space for the younger generation.[8] In many urban cities, there is overcrowding due to rural-to-urban migration. People live in crammed spaces and the old who are at the top of the space chain will become an object of envy of the young, who will land up living in cubicles at prices which are very exorbitant and at times beyond their financial means. Living space and environment will indeed become a critical resource for which the young and old will compete, especially in societies where land resources are limited.

We must use land well, plan space for housing well and calibrate its tenure properly to enable the succeeding generation to have an opportunity to enjoy the living space. This can avert the competition for living space between the old and young. In the longer term, for affordable housing, land must be set aside for the old to have a decent living space. This will prevent them from being edged out due to future private market demands for housing spaces. It would be a pity for the Singapore society, with a good historical record of housing 85% of our population in public housing, to witness more elderly being de-housed and becoming homeless because of poverty. One can see this happening in many advanced economies. In Singapore, policy makers will need to ensure that the elderly, who have limited savings in spite of having sold their assets to downsize to smaller living units during the tertiary period of life, have support for living space.[9]

Employment and Employability Issues in Ageing

There will be increasing focus on employment and employability of the elderly.

---

[8] Martin, D. and Miller, B. "Space and Contentious Politics", *Mobilization: An International Journal*, 8(2), 2003, 143–156.

[9] Hongbao, J. and Vasoo, S. "Housing as Asset Building in Singapore", in S. Vasoo and B. Singh (eds.), *Asset Building in Singapore*, (Singapore: World Scientific Publishers, 2018).

Table 1.   Median CPF Savings Range by Age Group

Age Group	Median CPF Savings Range
>60 to 65	$140,000 to $160,000
>65 to 70	$100,000 to $120,000
>70 to 75	$60,000 to $80,000
>75 to 80	$20,000 to $40,000

One cannot take it for granted that the elderly will have financial resources to see them through their old age.[10] Some will face lean years in their old age. Savings will run dry because many of the Pioneer Generation will have low CPF savings and will find it trying to cope with life. The CPF balances for older age groups are listed in Table 1.[11]

As can be seen, the older the age groups, the lower the amount of savings, and one can deduce that this will mean that they have to continue to be employed so that they can continue to meet their basic needs. The employability for the Pioneer and *Merdeka* generations will be tougher as they are not only past the retirement age for work at 67 years but they also have less marketable work skills that will be required by the digitised workplace. Both older PMETs and non-PMETs have seen a higher unemployment rate of about 3.1 and 5.0, respectively, between 2015 and 2020.[12] This increasing rate, though small, can rise in the future because of major changes in the various industries and the push into a digital economy.

As more young persons will join the workforce, the elderly will face greater competition with the young for jobs. Ultimately, given the changing employment landscape towards automation, robotics and digitalisation, the elderly will be outpaced and even displaced from the working world. Such will be the dictates of the digital world requiring specialised skills at all levels of manufacturing and production of goods and services. The elderly will be sidelined and their earning capacity will be very low without appropriate skills. Consequently, the number of poor old will

---

[10] Chia, K. S. and Chong, S. A. "Most Singaporean are Living Longer — but Are They Ready for Old Age", *The Straits Times*, (30 June 2017). See https://www.straitstimes.com/opinion/a-lifetime-of-health-and-wealth-makes-for-good-retirement.
[11] CPF: Sg.data 2019.
[12] Labour Force Report (2020). Singapore: Ministry of Manpower.

increase if they run out of savings and have less opportunity for work to earn an income, and hence they will also become more reliant on financial aid.[13]

It will be prudent for policy makers to take steps to implement policy measures to increase the retirement age to 75 years and higher when needed as this will ensure protection for the elderly workers from being disengaged from the workplace where they have spent a large proportion of their working years. More retraining schemes are needed to prepare the elderly to have the necessary skills for them to adapt to the changing employment landscape. Unless there are legislations in place, some mercenary companies will want to replace the older workforce with cheaper and younger workers given the globalised world. Due to the shortage of workers in the face of the declining birth rate, corporations whether private or public will have to review their plans for retention of elderly workers who will be still rather active despite their age.

Loneliness and Mental Health Issues in Ageing

It is noted from population data that there will be more elderly widows in the future[14] as many survive their spouse and more prefer to remain unmarried.[15] Many of these elderly live in high-rise public housing flats. With poor mobility and an enclosed environment, these elderly will face isolation and loneliness. Loneliness will take a toll on their mental health because their social network will become depleted due to the loss of their spouse, relatives and friends. Many studies have found that loneliness has adverse effects on mental health and psychiatric problems increase. Consequently, there are higher suicide rates among lonely elderly and in 2020 the number of suicides increased steeply[16] and this could also be due

---

[13]Tong, T. and Wong, C. "More Families Depending on Long-term Financial Aid from Government to Get By: MSF", (2017). See https://www.straitstimes.com/singapore/more-families-depending-on-long-term-financial-aid-from-government-to-get-by.

[14]Department of Statistics Singapore Census (2020).

[15]Teo, P., Mehta, K., Thang, L. L. and Chan, A. "The Journey After Widowhood", in P. Teo, K. Mehta, L. L. Thang and A. Chan (eds.), *Ageing in Singapore: Service Needs and the State*, (London: Routledge, 2006), pp. 134–146; Population Census (2020).

[16]SOS Report (2020).

to prolonged isolation as a result of the COVID-19 pandemic. As Singapore's population ages in the next three decades, the number of less mobile and lonely old people will triple. A recent study indicated that there are about 100,000 elderly who are immobile.[17] This number will increase in time. It is thus important for the social profiles of this group of elderly to be analysed by social service agencies and social policy makers so that more effective service delivery programmes can be implemented.

For a longer-term strategy, there will be a need for social service and healthcare agencies to develop a social care network to reach out to the lonely and vulnerable elderly. Preventive healthcare programmes can be organised for those diagnosed early to have potential for chronic illness so that steps can be taken to prevent their health from deteriorating and perhaps to maintain their healthiness. Otherwise, many family caregivers and informal caregivers will be stretched and face tremendous stress.[18]

More community health interventions and education programmes could be implemented as these efforts are worthwhile and can minimise healthcare cost in the longer term as those who have vulnerable health can have reduced prevalence for hospital admissions. As one will note, the frequency of hospitalisations is likely to increase with age and chronic health conditions. In the end, our society will have to incur a heavy budget for healthcare in the future unless more efforts are taken to inspire people, particularly the ageing population, to adopt healthy lifestyles. The revolving door in hospitalisations can be minimised.

Death and Dying Matters in Ageing

In all societies, like Singapore, one cannot avoid the issues related to end of life.

Increasingly, we will be confronted with matters like death and dying. Families will encounter a member of their household dying due to old age. Dying in varying conditions in old age, such as in dignity, despair,

---

[17] *The Straits Times*, (June 2021); Singapore Population Census (2020), Department of Statistics.

[18] Mehta, K. and Thang, L. L. "Experiences of Formal and Informal Caregivers of Older Persons in Singapore", *Journal of Cross-cultural Gerontology*, 32(3), 2017, 373–385.

loneliness, tragedy, ill health and suicide, will surface commonly as the population ages.[19]

In the future, controversies will be apparent when the number of people who opt for pro-choice about end-of-life issues increases. Family members, social and healthcare institutions can be fractured, as those affected may want to assert their choice on their own to terminate their lives whilst others opt to keep them alive. This is a rather stark picture. Our society may have to grapple with this issue and there will be no easy answer to the grief and pending loss.[20] The answer to grief and loss, tied up with death and dying, is not only a personal and familial agenda but also a societal matter.[21]

Healthcare Cost in Ageing Singapore

This section will dwell on the healthcare cost in ageing Singapore and the various measures taken to provide affordable healthcare programmes. Healthcare policies and provisions are indeed socially and politically contentious. Many governments have yet to find competent and satisfying solutions for health consumers such as older residents. This is because healthcare issues are very complex and at times not predictable. In most developing economies like Singapore, healthcare cost is an attractive socio-political agenda for various aspiring political parties. Promises of cheap healthcare services continue to be made as it has good voter appeal, particularly in ageing societies. However, many of the governing parties fail to keep their promises, as the tide of rising health cost is not stoppable, except for when it could be absorbed by increasing government subsidy and charges. However, giving higher and higher subsidy for healthcare is not an effective long-term solution, as government expenditure has to be met by introducing more direct and indirect taxes. On the other hand,

---

[19] Howe, J. L. and Daratsos, L. "Roles of Social Workers in Palliative and End-of-life Care", in B. Berman (ed.), *Handbook of Social Work in Health and Aging*, (London: Oxford University Press, 2006), pp. 315–323.

[20] Malhotra, C., Chan, A., Do, Y. K., Malhotra, R. and Goh, C. "Good End-of-life Care: Perspectives of Middle-aged and Older Singaporeans", *Journal of Pain and Symptom Management*, 44, 2012, 252–263.

[21] Singhealth Academy (2009).

making end users bear the whole cost of medical treatment can make it more burdensome for families with dependent elderly. This is not a realistic solution either. Policy makers must moderate the increasing demand for healthcare. This is because runaway demands and public pressure for increase in subsidy for healthcare for the elderly can dislocate governments facing inadequate financial resources.

Healthcare reforms for the ageing population

Different policy strategies have to be adopted by the government to tamper the demand and contain the healthcare cost. Policy measures based on the principles of personal responsibility for health and tripartite partnerships comprising individuals, government and employers have been formulated. This is evident under the various plans, the first which began in 1983,[22] then in 1993 under the MOH White Paper, which was followed by the IMC Report in 1999. Following these policy recommendations there were other healthcare reforms mooted to improve the health service delivery.[23]

The thrusts of the healthcare service delivery take into consideration issues such as co-payment of healthcare cost and the rationing medical care, besides the restructuring of the hospitals, which are held accountable for the government funds allocated. The policy measures are beginning to produce respectable results and have so far received positive feedback from the public and patients.

Healthcare delivery in Singapore has undergone major reforms in the last 40 years. This is because of the increasing government expenditure in the provision of health services in the light of the population ageing. Most policy makers have been confronted by two dilemmas, namely, the need to maintain affordability of health services for the general population and containing the escalating healthcare cost for the growing vulnerable ageing population. In short, health cost has to be seen and felt to be reasonable for families with aged sick. Healthcare, whether needed or not, has

[22] *Ministry of Health, White Papers on Affordable Health Care*, (Singapore, 1993).
[23] Ong, S. E., Tyagi, S., Lim, J. M., Chia, K. S. and Legido-Quigley, H. "Health Systems Reform in Singapore: A Qualitative Study," *Health Policy*, 122, April 2018, 431–443.

become a matter of concern for families with ageing members, as at any given time, some family members who are old and vulnerable have been or will be the end users of the health services. The demand for healthcare services for the elderly will rise and this is inevitable as one becomes prone to ill health in the tertiary years.

Reforms in healthcare were initiated in 1982 to find solutions to improve the health services and contain the long-term increase in cost and government subsidies in the provisions of healthcare for the population as well as the increasing needs of the elderly. The National Health Plan (NHP) was developed and released in 1983.[24] This was the start of a comprehensive proposal to restructure the healthcare system and to tackle several underlying concerns in the healthcare scene in anticipation of Singapore ageing. There was recent coverage on healthcare reforms[25] and the comments are useful for those interested in following the issue.

The very highly subsidised healthcare services provided across the board without weighing the economic circumstances of the consumers generated wastage and an increased health burden. The buffet syndrome effect was prevalent and consumers of healthcare helped themselves to a mixture of health menus, which were at times not directly relevant to their medical conditions and treatment. Unless such a buffet syndrome is treated quickly, the healthcare system would succumb due to excessive demand and eventually buckle under the added healthcare needs of the elderly.

The healthcare professionals face competing demands from various quarters within and outside the hospitals and cope with a heavy patient load of sick and vulnerable elderly people. Their quality of care suffers and, in the end, neither the professional nor the patient will be satisfied with services rendered. With the private sector hospitals providing better support facilities and remuneration, the turnover of healthcare

---

[24] Phua, K. H. *Privatization and Restructuring of Health Services in Singapore*, Occasional Paper No. 5, (Singapore: Institute of Policy Studies, Times Academic Press, 1991).

[25] Chia, K. S. and Lim, M. K. "Healthcare Reforms in Singapore", in K. Okma and T. Tenbensel (eds.), *Health Reforms Across the World*, (Singapore: World Scientific Press, 2020), pp. 275–297.

professionals will worsen. Although this situation is not stoppable, the high leakage of staff needs to be plugged as Singapore's demography shifts to the ageing range.

The earlier plan to centralise specialised medical services in one premier hospital, namely, the Singapore General Hospital, created serious medical bottlenecks. This was not a sound solution to meet the medical needs of the growing older population. Hence, concrete action was initiated to reorganise the delivery of medical services.[26]

As in Hong Kong, Singapore took a pragmatic decision to establish more general hospitals to cater to large population centres. Along with these developments, specialist services like geriatric care have been instituted. This change in medical service delivery helped to redirect and disperse the consumers, especially the elderly, to the various public sector hospitals in Singapore.[27] To maintain good-quality medical services, the medical workforce has also increased significantly since 2016 and there are close to 60,000 or more professional and allied healthcare personnel delivering medical services.[28]

The main emphasis in healthcare has been primarily geared towards the provision of tertiary medical treatment and in this case the hospitalisation of many vulnerable elderly. The hospitalisation and treatment of the elderly have been the focus. Preventive healthcare of the general population and the elderly, although considered important, did not get much attention. In 2018, the government spent only 12% of its operating budget on public health services as compared to 80% in public hospitals.[29] The budget spent on preventive health has indeed been small and such an emphasis could have prevented longer periods of hospitalisation of the elderly if the general public had been exposed to early health education and intervention programmes. Such an outcome is highly debatable, as a randomised control study has not been conducted.

Since the implementation of the Primary Health Care Plan of 2011, efforts have been made to direct more resources to improve primary

[26] Aw, T. C. and Low, L. (1997). "Health Care Provisions in Singapore", in T. M. Tan and S. B. Chew (eds.), *Affordable Health Care*, (Singapore: Prentice Hall, 1997), pp. 50–71.
[27] MOH Annual Report (1999), p. 98.
[28] Ministry of Health Singapore (2016).
[29] MOH Annual Report (2018).

healthcare for the community and for the health issues facing the elderly.[30] This is a good direction to take. I hope more attention will be paid by health policy makers to strengthen preventive healthcare services.

The number of elderly needing medical care has increased over the years. In 2018, the admission rate of elderly between 60 and 64 years of age was 160.4 per 1,000 resident population and for those between 65 and 69 years of age, it was 205.3 per 1,000 resident population.[31] A sizable proportion of inpatient care was for elderly patients, and they are likely to occupy increased beds in the future.

The elderly may not be discharged quickly because of chronic illness and this situation has become more evident in the hospitals today. The danger that modern hospitals are likely to face is that more healthcare resources would have to be deployed for chronic care than acute medical treatment. Hospitals can become homes for the aged if not carefully managed and even with the establishment of Community Hospitals, the General Hospitals will see a long beeline of older patients who require prolonged periods of medical treatment. Healthcare professionals are now facing this dilemma in discharging the elderly patients who have limited caregivers to follow up the care at home.

Healthcare policy measures to meet the ageing population

The healthcare policy measures are driven by a few fundamental principles, which centre primarily on curbing overconsumption of healthcare and the induced demand for health services, and this could be contributed by the ageing population. Unless overconsumption of healthcare is tackled effectively, the problems of increasing healthcare cost will not be effectively contained as this is related to life course demands. In this case, the ageing population trend has changed where the average median age

---

[30] Chia, K. S. and Lim, M. K. "Healthcare Reforms in Singapore", in K. Okma and T. Tenbensel (eds.), *Health Reforms Across the World*, (Singapore: World Scientific Press, 2020), pp. 275–297.

[31] Ministry of Health. *Hospital Admission Rates by Age and Sex 2018*, (Singapore: 2020). https://www.moh.gov.sg/resources-statistics/healthcare-institution-statistics/hospital-admission-rates-by-age-and-sex/hospital-admission-rates-by-age-and-sex-2018.

has gone from 29.8 years in 1990 to 41.1 years in 2019 and therefore the need for a healthcare setup has increased.[32]

Generally, most ageing consumers are required to make co-payment for the usage of the healthcare services. Such payments are based on the class of medical care the patients opt for. The better the class, the higher the medical charges. The emphasis on co-payment for medical care has not only created awareness of the medical cost but also made these consumers more cautious about their demands for various medical treatments.

Ageing individuals are encouraged to be responsible for looking after their own health and they have to save for their healthcare needs.[33] Individual responsibility is a motivating factor for maintaining good health behaviour. The more one keeps himself healthy, the less he would spend from his savings in the Central Provident Fund (CPF). This will also prevent overreliance on state welfare and medical insurance.

There is a basic medical provision, which is an affordable package of health service for any citizen, including the elderly who require medical care. Such a basic medical package will be met by various financial mechanisms organised by the state to settle the unsubsidised part of the hospitalisation cost.[34] The basic medical package is a respectable medical service, which is within the reach of even the poorest in the community. However, with the rise of chronic illnesses and more hospitalisation of the elderly, the cost burden for the elderly and their families as well as the state will increase dramatically.

The premise that the provision of healthcare for the citizens inclusive of seniors should be subjected to competition between the public and private sectors may not be workable because the former is a public goods issue, whereas the latter is more or less a private goods matter. Market forces can influence the delivery of healthcare, but the outcome may not necessarily be that more efficient and better services will be provided to the consumers. Where necessary, the government should intervene to ensure that public healthcare cost is kept within the reach of the ordinary

[32] Population Trend, Department of Statistics (2019).
[33] Lim, J. "Health Care Reform in Singapore: The Medisave Scheme." In T. M. Tan and S. B. Chew (eds.), *Affordable Health Care*, (Singapore: Prentice Hall, 1997), p. 278.
[34] *Ibid.*

consumers, especially the elderly, and any anticipated runaway increases in medical cost are tackled quickly by government provision of medical workforce, medical supplies, facilities, and funding. In view of ageing Singapore, there will be more calls by families with ageing parents and relatives for affordable healthcare provisions.

In response to making healthcare more accessible, both state and health consumers must bear the financial burden. Four specific policy measures have been implemented to cater to citizens and the elderly who are prone to require medical care and treatment. At the same time, no cumbersome administrative structure or bureaucracy has been established to implement these policy measures, namely, the Medisave, Medishield and Medishield Life, Medifund, and Eldershield. All these financial pooling approaches require the participation of both state and consumers to fund the healthcare cost which can be very explosive as Singaporean society ages.

Medisave scheme

Medisave has become an innovative scheme to meet medical and hospitalisation expenses and this scheme is indeed beneficial to meet the health expenses of retirees and the elderly.[35] This scheme was implemented in 1984 under the CPF, which is a compulsory national savings account for meeting the retirement needs of workers. Currently, the total monthly CPF contribution is 37% for employees aged 55 and below. This amount is derived from the 17% contributions from employees and 20% from employers.[36] Both employees and employers are required by law to make the CPF contributions. Actions are taken against employers for failing to meet their obligations.

Medisave covers all workers including the self-employed persons who earn a yearly net trade income of more than S$6,000 a year.[37] The

[35] Ministry of Health, Medisave Pamphlet, (Singapore, 2000).

[36] Central Provident Fund. *CPF Contribution and Allocation Rates*, (Singapore, 2020). https://www.cpf.gov.sg/employers/employerguides/employer-guides/paying-cpf-contributions/cpf-contribution-and-allocation-rates.

[37] Central Provident Fund. *Self-employed Matters*, (Singapore, 2020). https://www.cpf.gov.sg/members/FAQ/schemes/Self-Employed-Scheme/Self-Employed-Matters/FAQDetails?category=Self-Employed%20Scheme&group=Self-Employed%20Matters&folderid=12405&ajfaqid=2188316.

coverage appears broad and inclusive of workers who have low income. Such a wide coverage ensures that most individuals are encouraged to save and set aside some funds for their medical needs, especially in their old age. The administration of Medisave has not posed any difficulty as it is managed under the purview of CPF, and the contributions are deducted at source from the workers' wages. The employees contribute between 8% and 10.5% of their monthly wages to their Medisave accounts. Those who are 35 years and below contribute 8% of their salary. Those between 35 and 45 years of age contribute 9% of their salary. Those from 45 to 50 years of age contribute 10% of their salary. Employees above 55 years have to make 10.5% contribution of their monthly salary. As medical needs increase with age, older employees are required to increase their Medisave contribution. This is to ensure that they do not become dependent on the state to pay for their entire hospitalisation charges and a shared burden is encouraged. The co-payment system does empower the employees to decide on the class of ward they prefer during hospital admission.

The unique feature about Medisave is that inter-generation transfers are allowed, and this is useful for families with dependent elderly. Besides usage by the individual account holders, it can be used to cover hospitalisation expenses and other medical treatments of family members, including relatives who have either no or low Medisave funds. Such an extended coverage of Medisave for the kin group strengthens mutual support, strengthens familial bonds and enables the elderly to receive medical treatment. Medisave could support even distant relatives if it is established that they have no means to pay for their portion of hospitalisation cost.

There are about 3.6 million Medisave accounts as of 2019 and the total Medisave balance stands at about S$102.0 billion. This is indeed a healthy saving balance to meet future medical expenses. The current total Medisave withdrawal is expected to be in the region of S$1,089 million in 2019. It is also estimated that the ratio of contribution to withdrawal is positive now. This reasonable utilisation rate is due to the relatively lower ageing rate of the Singapore population, but this scenario will change to a silver tsunami by 2030. However, it is noted that the average Medisave balance in the year 2020 for those 70 years and above will be less than S$80,000 and this amount will be depleted in due course, particularly for those in the Pioneer and senior generation groups who are granted healthcare subsidies as special seniors who have contributed to Singapore in their pioneering years.[38] Without this subsidy, some would not be able to shoulder a heavier medical bill. It is envisaged that with the falling old age support ratio per person aged 65 years standing at 1:9 in year 2000 and 1:4.5 in 2019, the public and familial burden for healthcare situation will worsen by 2030.[39]

The Medisave policy measure encourages the elderly individual to exercise responsibility for his immediate and future healthcare needs. Elderly individuals will have to be cautious about splurging away their funds, as they must pay their medical expenses on the point of consumption. Unlike other social security policies for healthcare in developed western nations, which are based on common pooling funds, the Medisave fund is different in the sense that it is a personal healthcare saving and can only be tapped by the specific contributor. The cumulative public burden for healthcare is not passed from one generation to another under the Medisave scheme.

When each generation looks after its healthcare needs, then the succeeding generation of a smaller population base of younger adults will not be placed under a heavy financial burden.[40] On the contrary, this intergenerational ecological chain can be disrupted when the population stagnates and does not regenerate itself. In short, there will be more elderly persons surviving as there will be less newborns to succeed. In Singapore, the fertility rate has reduced from 1.6 in year 2000 to 1.14 in year 2018. The difference between the crude birth rate (8.8 per thousand persons) and the death rate (5.0 per thousand persons) will be narrowing too without an increase in fertility.[41]

Medishield and Medishield Life scheme

It has been realised that elderly individuals who are affected by chronic and catastrophic illnesses can be financially burdened in meeting their

[38] MOH 2020. Ministry of Health. *Medisave Pamphlet*, (Singapore, 2000).

[39] Population Trend, (Department of Statistics Singapore, 2019).

[40] Lim, J. "Health Care Reform in Singapore: The Medisave Scheme." In T. M. Tan, and S. B. Chew (eds.), *Affordable Health Care*, (Singapore: Prentice Hall, 1997), p. 281.

[41] Population Trend. (Department of Statistics Singapore, 2019).

expenses for medical treatment. As chronic illnesses are inescapable and can befall on some elderly individuals, a more comprehensive insurance coverage was thought to be necessary and the Medishield scheme was implemented in 1990 and later replaced in 2015 by Medishield Life that is designed as a health insurance scheme. This compulsory scheme is affordable even to low-income wage earners and it complements the Medisave scheme. The elderly are protected under such a scheme as their savings would not be wiped out by medical cost for treatment of catastrophic illnesses. The yearly premium for the Medishield Life scheme is based on the contributor's age and the premium payment is subsidised based on income levels. Table 2 shows the range of premiums payable, and these seem to be reasonable and affordable as Medisave could be tapped.

Eldercare and Eldershield/Careshield Life

Because of the growing concern for the care of the elderly, the Eldercare Fund was established in the year 2000 by voluntary organisations. This was inadequate and a more sustainable Eldershield scheme was initiated in 2002 to help meet the cost for severe disability and long-term care. The beneficiaries of the scheme will get a financial grant of around S$300–S$400 per month for a period of about 72 months.[42] Such a financial grant helps to provide relief from the financial burden on families having to care for the severely disabled and those elderly requiring long-term care. The premium for the said scheme could be paid out from Medisave.

To provide better coverage for the care of disabled elderly, Careshield Life was recently introduced. The take-up rate of Careshield Life for Pioneer and *Merdeka* Generation groups needs to be monitored so that steps can be taken to cover more of them.[43]

---

[42] Chia, K. S. and Lim, M. K. "Healthcare Reforms in Singapore", in K. Okma and T. Tenbensel (eds.), *Health Reforms Across the World*, (Singapore: World Scientific Press, 2020), pp. 275–297.

[43] Careshield Life. About Careshield Life, (Singapore, 2022). https://www.careshieldlife. gov.sg/careshield-life/about-careshield-life.html.

Table 2. Medishield and Medishield Life Premiums (Non-pioneer Generation) in 2019/2020

Age Next Birthday	Current Annual Medishield Premiums (I\$)	Annual Medishield Life Premiums Before Subsidy (\$)	2019 Medishield Life Premiums After Subsidy							
			Lower-income		Lower-middle-income		Upper-middle-income		High Income	
			Annual (\$)	Monthly (\$)	Annual (\$)	Monthly (\$)	Annual (\$)	Monthly (\$)	Annual (\$)	Monthly (\$)
1–20	50	130	98	8	104	9	111	9	130	11
21–30	66	195	146	12	156	13	166	14	195	16
31–40	105	310	233	19	248	21	264	22	310	26
41–50	220	435	305	25	326	27	348	29	435	36
51–60	345	630	441	37	473	39	504	42	630	53
61–65	455	755	491	41	529	44	566	47	755	63
66–70	540	815	530	44	571	48	611	51	815	68
71–73	560	885	575	48	620	52	664	55	885	74
74–75	646	975	634	53	683	57	731	61	975	81
76–78	775	1,130	678	57	735	61	791	66	1,130	94
79–80	865	1,175	705	59	764	64	823	69	1,175	98
81–83	1,123	1,250	750	63	813	68	875	73	1,250	104
84–85	1,150	1,430	858	72	930	77	1,001	83	1,430	119
86–88	1,190	1,500	825	69	900	75	975	81	1,500	125
89–90	1,190	1,500	825	69	900	75	975	81	1,500	125
>90	—	1,530	765	64	842	70	918	77	1,530	128

Source: MOH website, https://www.moh.gov.sg/cost-financing/healthcare-schemes-subsidies/medishield-life/medishieldlife-premiums-and-subsidies/premium-subsidy-tables.

Medifund scheme

This scheme is indeed very helpful to elderly persons who have a low income. It was recognised that some individuals have very small CPF or Medisave accounts and some are poor. The Medifund scheme was implemented in 1993 to help these people pay for medical care. In addition, those individuals who, despite the subsidies and payments from the Medisave and Medishield schemes, are unable to settle their medical bills can apply for assistance under the Medifund scheme. It is noted that many low-income elderly have been assisted under the scheme.

The Medifund is a government endowment fund that has been set up from government surplus funds each year. An initial capital of S\$200 million was set aside and with subsequent contributions over the years, the Medifund has grown. As of fiscal year 2017, the capital sum for Medifund was S\$4.5 billion and only the interest income earned could be used to assist individuals who face financial hardship in paying their medical bills; many elderly have benefited from this.[44]

The medical social work service undertakes the assessment of cases which require Medifund help and quite a number of them are elderly patients. These cases are then recommended to a Hospital Medifund Committee for consideration and approval of funding. The members of the Committee are drawn from professional groups and grassroots organisations, and they give an objective decision on the cases applying for Medifund. It has been observed that most of the applications do get approval for financial assistance and it accounts for about 98% of the cases. In FY2018, about 12,40,000 applications were approved for Medifund assistance, amounting to a total of S\$156.5 million.[45]

The Medifund Scheme provides a safety net for the poor who have little to no personal savings to pay their medical care. Most of them are elderly persons who did not have the benefit of the CPF Scheme during their employment. The various Medifund Committees comprising local

---

[44] Ministry of Health, Frequently Asked Questions on Medifund, (Singapore, 2020). https://va.ecitizen.gov.sg/CFP/CustomerPages/MOH/explorefaq.aspx?category=12667.
[45] Ministry of Health, Government Health Expenditure and Healthcare Financing, (Singapore, 2020). https://www.moh.gov.sg/resources-statistics/singapore-health-facts/government-health-expenditure-and-healthcare-financing.

community leaders have the responsibility to ensure that the applicants are not denied the medical care they require.

Some Key Challenges and Concerns in Meeting Singapore's Ageing Needs

The Singaporean population is ageing fast and between year 1990 and 2019, the average median age has sharply increased from 29.8 years to 41.1 years.[46] The silver picture is becoming more obvious and in 10 years' time, one in four will be 65 years and above. With such a substantial proportion of the population being elderly, it is envisaged that there will be higher aspirations for better social support and healthcare, and this is likely to be taken advantage of by political groups. Because of the size of the elderly population, there is a likelihood of them forming their own advocacy groups to lobby for such needs as employability, social support, financial security and healthcare. As the future scenarios can be more contentious, Singapore must have people-centric, politically capable and socially righteous individuals in the government to implement effective solutions for more complex human, socio-ecological and economic problems facing Singaporean society.

The healthcare needs of the Singapore ageing population are addressed by the implementation of four significant policy measures, which discourage excessive consumption and enhance individual responsibility for good health, especially in old age. Although the policy measures are directed at self-reliance and prevention of state dependency, one cannot deny that there are some policy gaps, which have to be dealt with, especially in the context of Singapore's elderly. The ageing trend has been moving steeply, as in year 2000 the people aged 65 years and above accounted for 7.2% of the population and in 2019 they comprised 14.4 %.[47] This ageing picture will be glaringly silver by 2040.[48]

The elderly population must be further enlightened about the frugal use of Medisave, which is commonly perceived as funds locked up by

---

[46] Population Trend, (Department of Statistics Singapore, 2019).

[47] *Ibid.*

[48] Yap, M. T. and Gee, C. *Population Outcomes* 2050, (Singapore: Institute of Policy Studies, 2014).

government during the individual's lifetime. It cannot be used for any other purpose except for medical care expenses. As this is the case, there is always a high temptation among the elderly to empty their Medisave coffers by opting for a better class of wards and better medical attention by specialists. The human desire for better facilities appears to be the trend as elderly Singaporeans become more affluent and have higher aspirations. The spendthrift desire of elderly patients is compounded by their ignorance and inability to make informed decisions about medical outcomes even with the information available. More elderly patients are not able to make a good evaluation of medical information and the chances are that Medisave can be indiscriminately used.[49] In order that Medisave funds are not exhausted too quickly, it is important that elderly patients are counselled and guided by healthcare professionals to select the appropriate ward class and types of medical treatment. In this way, elderly patients do not spend beyond their Medisave means. However, patients are sometimes helpless, and they must depend on healthcare professionals for recommendations. These patients may at times be tempted to consume higher frill types of medical treatment than required.

The restructuring of all public sector hospitals in Singapore has given rise to autonomous management of the hospitals, and given that more patients that are elderly are likely to be admitted, there will be a need for hospital administration to exercise more cost control measures in health-care consumption. All restructured hospitals are given government sub-vention and they are expected to manage and account for their operations, including employment and remuneration of their personnel. They have to maintain a balanced budget, but because the bottom line is watched care-fully, there is a desire for these hospitals to not show that they are in the red. As competition in terms of service and for patients, especially for the elderly, becomes acute in the near future, there will be a tendency for the hospitals to recoup their expenses through an increase of the hospital charges on their patients as well as the ordering of more medical tests and treatments than necessary. Consequently, medical treatment cost can

---

[49] Lim, J. "Health Care Reform in Singapore: The Medisave Scheme", in T. M. Tan and S. B. Chew (eds.), *Affordable Health Care*, (Singapore: Prentice Hall, 1997), p. 283.

increase beyond the means of ordinary patients and in this case the elderly who are more prone to hospitalisation and follow-up healthcare. In this case, the government has to put in place a proactive hospital audit system to monitor the cost and service delivery of hospitals. To ensure that the hospital charges for medical treatment are reasonable, the hospital revenue caps are adjusted annually to cater for inflation, medical advances and productivity gains.

Another policy gap of the Medisave scheme is that it does not fully cover the increasing cost of treating people, especially the afflicted elderly, with chronic and catastrophic illnesses such as diabetes, kidney failure, stroke, cancer and HIV AIDs. Most of these illnesses affect the older population. Even with the complement of the Medishield or Medishield Life scheme, those requiring long-term treatment for medical conditions may be financially stretched if they must be treated with expensive drugs for a prolonged period. To deal with this policy gap, it would be helpful to revise upwards the claimable limits for chronic illnesses, especially for the elderly as well as those who now have some financial relief for disability under the Eldershield scheme.

Primary healthcare for the ageing population has received less attention until recently. Such a mindset among health policy makers emphasising more on residual rather than preventive healthcare does have some long-term ramifications. One may argue that ill health is genetically programmed and there is nothing one can do except to remedy the medical condition through hospitalisation. This view that preventive healthcare is unimportant and not cost effective has however been demolished. There is increasing advocacy that more attention should be paid to primary healthcare for the ageing sector starting when people are young. Health screening, follow-up and health education could be stepped up so that the vulnerable elderly could be treated earlier, and this could delay or prevent them for consuming more health services and avoid hospitals being crowded with increasing chronic sick elderly.[50]

Singapore is one of the fastest ageing societies in the Asia-Pacific region after Japan. At least one in four persons will be 65 years and above

---

[50] Ministry of Health, (Singapore: Institute for Health Metrics and Evaluation, 2019).

in the year 2030.[51] This significant demographic transition will have serious implications on provisions of healthcare for the elderly who will occupy most of the hospital beds with a low turnover. It is estimated that about more than 5% of the elderly population will require long-term geriatric care. However, this provision will not be an effective solution in the longer term as the number of elderly requiring geriatric care and assistance will be increasing, and the building of more geriatric facilities will not be a realistic solution to cope with the demands, which cannot be curtailed. It is therefore important for policy makers and service providers to think of other innovative services to help the elderly to remain healthy if possible. They should be socially integrated into the family and community. The cost issues will be the main concern to policy makers and therefore they should review the need to provide continual care in the form of institutional provisions such as community hospitals, nursing homes and hospice centres, which are going to be costly to run.

At the same time, more elderly should be not dislocated from their community to be placed in these institutions. This will also be a social cost to the elderly persons. In the provision of health-related services for the elderly, we must examine how preventive health and community-based programmes can be organised and delivered to them in their neighbourhood. Such an emphasis will make programmes accessible and enable the elderly to remain within their community and it will encourage the community to mobilise and participate in promoting long-term care programmes. This approach will make the programmes more cost effective and help the elderly to be independent. An innovative community care cooperative could be established to meet the long-term care and health needs of the elderly. Social workers can help to promote community care cooperatives in various neighbourhoods, and it can be a good long-term solution to cater to the frail or sick elderly. The cooperatives with the involvement of the concerned elderly, retirees and residents can provide a

---

[51] Inter-Ministerial Committee Report, (1999); Yap, M. T. and Gee, C. *Population Outcomes 2050*, (Singapore: Institute of Policy Studies, 2014); and Teo, Z. W. and Zainal, K. "Successful Aging: Progressive Governance and Collaborative Communities", *Ethos*, Issue 19, 8 July 2018, (Singapore: Civil Service College, 2018). https://www.csc.gov.sg/articles/successful-ageing-progressive-governance-and-collaborative-communities.

range of services such as home care, transport service, health screening and follow-up, health education, wellness programmes and day care service.[52] These services can be charged at affordable rates and members of the cooperatives will be granted rebates for use of the services. As more voluntary and public agencies will be providing services for the elderly, there should be more concerted effort by a central coordinating body to gather all those engaged in elderly care to come together periodically to share ideas and plan directions for the care of the elderly. Though Agency for Integrated Care (AIC) is attempting to do this in a modest way, it needs more teeth and resources to help shape the development of well-integrated and seamless services for the ageing population.[53] AIC could have more power and influence to manage the future critical issues of ageing in Singapore.

The globalisation process is being accelerated by information technology revolution and affluent Singaporeans will seek out excellent medical treatment through the Internet. It is also forecasted that when medical treatment becomes too expensive in Singapore and other developed countries, there will be an outflow of middle-income patients seeking the best medical treatment at a cheap cost in developing countries. This will leave elderly patients in need of more subsidised healthcare behind. Therefore, more voluntary sector hospitals are expected to be set up to ameliorate this problem to an extent.

To reduce future demand for healthcare for ageing Singapore and other countries with similar historical development in health services, more attention must be paid to preventive healthcare. Allocation of resources to this area has to be increased. Incentives in the form of insurance and higher tax rebates could be granted to individuals who keep themselves healthy. Health wellness programmes could be promoted at workplaces. Public health education programmes could be expanded to reach out to more people so that the elderly will engage in healthy lifestyle activities.

---

[52] Mehta, K. and Vasoo, S. "Community Programmes and Services for Long-term Care of Elderly in Singapore: Challenges for Policy Makers", *Asian Journal of Political Science*, 8(1), 2000, 125–140; and Vasoo, S. "Investments for the Social Sector to Tackle Some Key Social Issues", in S. Vasoo (ed.), *Collected Readings on Community Development in Singapore*, (World Scientific Publishers, 2019), pp. 601–617.

[53] *Agency for Integrated Care*, (Singapore: Ministry of Health. Singapore, 2018).

The issues of pro-life or pro-choice will be confronting healthcare policy makers more frequently in the future as the Singapore population ages. The healthcare professionals will be facing ethical dilemmas in their decision as to when life-support systems would have to be terminated. It is therefore important to revisit the legislation on Advanced Medical Directive (AMD) and redefine the legal issues related to brain death. The AMD legislation has already laid the foundation to tackle some of the prospective issues related to death and dying under medical care. However, Singaporean society can be polarised and fractured if the strident contentions between the pro-life and pro-choice sides are not carefully handled. Both moral and ethical issues are involved and mediatory groups under inter-religious persuasions can be mobilised to resolve protracted and difficult cases.

Conclusion

The COVID-19 pandemic has had a serious impact on Singaporeans' livelihood and mental health especially in how to cope challenges in their daily lives. It is therefore critical for policy makers to think and plan to manage another unanticipated pandemic which may be looming on the horizon with various ecological changes that Singapore and the other world communities will be facing.

There is an urgent need for policy makers to embark on more in-depth socio-environmental, economic and life course analyses of Singaporean multicultural communities as well as our demographic trends, which are ageing quickly. Through such analyses, it will be possible to have a more robust picture of various life roots, trunk and branches of Singapore and to see how we can respond to the challenges of Singapore ageing, as well as the country's growth and development.

In order to meet the social and healthcare issues of ageing Singapore, a tripartite system is needed, which requires the individual elderly together with his family, State and employer to share the burdens of care. The transitions to this type of tripartite partnership have not caused any social and personal disruptions, such as denial of access to healthcare for the elderly. The tripartite partnership, translated in the form of healthcare policy measures, namely, Medisave, Medishield and Medishield Life, Medifund, and Eldershield has worked well so far and has helped to meet the social and healthcare needs of the ageing population. However, these measures are effective only so long as Singaporeans enjoy full employment. A prolonged economic recession can destabilise the tripartite partnership. However, with sound deployment of accumulated surplus funds in Singapore and with a prudent government, the policy measures can be sustained to see through many successful Singaporeans ageing.

The accelerated population ageing, longer life at 84.8 years,[54] increasing aspiration of consumers for health services, changing disease patterns, competing demands for medical talents and globalisation through the Internet will all have implications on the delivery of healthcare service and care for the elderly in Singapore. There will be an increase in telemedicine and virtual medical consultations soon. The COVID-19 pandemic has had an impact on the way we deliver healthcare to the population and to the elderly in the community. Social and healthcare policy measures must be proactive and address the social changes anticipated, especially with the impending increase in elderly in our population. In this way, social and healthcare provisions will continue to remain affordable to most people growing old in the population.

The future will see a more visible silver population. This will precipitate more social and political challenges and problems, which must be dealt with by policy makers. If they fail, it will cause more restlessness in the silver community. Unless the silver generation feels that they are cared for with dignity, they will lobby policy makers for their betterment. Therefore, policy makers must be proactive by taking steps to consider establishing a statutory body to plan comprehensively to tackle the up-and-coming issues of ageing Singapore. In resolving all these future pressing challenges in the socio-economic, financial and healthcare realms, Singapore must have a good government that is able to garner relevant resources to enhance the livelihood of the silver generation and its younger population. Without growing and developing resources, life will be abysmal.

---

[54] Khalik, S. Singapore tops in life expectancy at 84.8 years. *The Straits Times*, 20 June 2019. See https://www.straitstimes.com/singapore/health/singapore-tops-in-life-expectancy-at-848-years; Singapore Census 2020.

Chapter 2

Singapore and the Politics of Ageing: An Overview

Bilveer Singh

Abstract

Ageing in any society is a highly political and politicised event. This is especially true when the number of aged is increasing incrementally and would be in a position to influence the electoral outcome of a country. According to the traditional definition of aged, it refers to those who are 65 years and above; in 2020, Singapore had an aged population of 614,400 out of a total population of 5,685,000. This constituted 15.19% of the total population, a relatively high percentage, with serious all-round implications, including in the arena of politics. In 2018, the Deputy Secretary (Development), Ministry of Health, Teoh Zsin Woon, highlighted this challenge by observing that Singapore's population was ageing fast: there was one aged out of 14 in 2000; in 2015, the figure stood out one in eight and in 2030 this will be one in four [Teoh, Z. W. and Zainal, K. "Successful Ageing: Progressive Governance and Collaborative Communities." *Ethos*, Issue 19, 8 July 2018, (Singapore: Singapore Civil Service College, 2018). See https://www.csc.gov.sg/articles/successful-ageing-progressive-governance-and-collaborative-communities.]. In view of this serious development, with possible dire political consequences, this chapter discusses the politics of ageing in Singapore and what is involved in this broad rubric of the issue.

Table 1.   Age Structure of Singapore's Population in 2020

Age Structure	Total Number	Percentage of Total
Below 20 years	803,400	19.87
26–64 years	2,626,400	64.94
65 years and over	614,400	15.19

Source: Population of Singapore 2020, (Singapore: Department of Statistics, 2021).

What is the Politics of Ageing?

In a broad sense, it encompasses how issues of the aged impact upon national politics. This can involve a number of facets. First, it involves the discussion as to how the issues of the aged are portrayed in the national discourse and the extent to which they are given credence or ignored. Are they discussed publicly and in key national foras or placed on the back-burner and the back pages of the national media and news? In short, what is the narrative on the aged in Singapore? Second, it involves the manner in which the issues involving the aged are addressed, especially their hardships, lack of financial and non-financial support, especially medical care. In other words, how are problems related to the aged addressed in Singapore? Third, it principally involves not just the discourse on the aged but also putting money where one's mouth is — how much resources are expended on the aged and which are expected outlay to grow year by year. All said and done, all the talk about who the aged are and what needs to be done, what is actually done in terms of resource allocation in Singapore and who in society is asked to bear the brunt of what is inevitable as everyone will eventually age, it is not whether or if, but when. In the end, it is political decisions that will determine the "politics of ageing" in any society — if the society and government respond positively, one can expect a more effective management of the political fallout of ageing in a society, just as a failure to do so will lead to an increase of political costs, not just for the government but society at large, especially the aged.

In this regard, according to Dr. Antonio Rappa,

> A politics of ageing is about how all individuals, society and the state reconcile the physiological, emotional, sexual and cultural needs,

expectations, functions and status of the elderly. A politics of ageing exists because the state and society are faced with a question of governance for this cohort of citizens: (1) Who are the elderly? (2) What policies and resources from state and society should be devoted to their needs? (3) Where will these resources be derived from? (4) When should such policies be implemented and resources delivered? (5) How will they be implemented? How will we know that the policies scheduled for implementation are effective? (6) Why should any policy or resource be devoted to the elderly? A politics of ageing also exists because they continue to play an active role as amplified in various forms of intergenerational social support exchanges and extended living arrangements.[1]

It will thus be useful to bear in mind these imperatives when discussing the issue of ageing and politics in Singapore. Probably more important, when analysing the politics of ageing in Singapore, what is also clear is that the importance of politics is evident in the government's intervention in providing resources and addressing the rising concerns of the aged. Hence, it is not just simply due to rising opposition or criticism from the aged but the government's deployment of resources to address the manifold issues of the aged. If politics is who gets what, when and how, then in Singapore, over the last few decades, the politics of ageing has been about the government increasingly identifying the aged and their concerns, and providing resources to meet their needs and challenges. It has largely been top-down politics with increasingly some pressure building up from below due to various factors that will be discussed in the chapter.

In this regard, the politics of ageing in Singapore is about many things: Who is an aged in today's contextual term when people are working and living longer? How do the government, society and the aged self-perceive themselves as far as their role and contributions to society are concerned? How are the issues related to the aged reported, narrativised and addressed? Is there a conflict of interest between promoting the interests of the aged and the rest of society? How are national resources channelled to the interests and concerns of the aged? Who are the champions of issues related to the aged? Is enough being done to address the concerns

---

[1] Rappa, A. L. "The Politics of Ageing: Perspectives from State and Society in Singapore", *Southeast Asian Journal of Social Science*, 27(2), 1999, 127–128.

of the aged? What are the achievements and failures as far as the aged in Singapore are concerned? Politically, what has been the impact of the aged on national politics and what can be expected in the future as the number of the aged and issues related to them will increase? These will be some of the questions that will be worth bearing in mind when analysing the politics of the aged in Singapore

This discussion takes on a special importance as there is a dearth of literature on the politics of ageing in Singapore. Whatever is the cause of this, be it the small number of the aged in Singapore in the past or the general belief that aged Singaporeans are not a liability politically, economically or socially, very little attention has been given by writers and researchers to this issue. Yet, a deeper analysis will show that as in any society, more so a developed one, and where the size and issues related to the aged will increase, there is definitely a need for more research on not just the aged per se but equally important, on the politics of the aged. This is especially if the aged, say in the next 10 to 15 years, become a powerful political constituency in view of the power of the ballot that this group of aged Singaporeans will lobby to assert their interests. Will the issue of the aged be politicised in coming general elections and what will be the impact of this in marginal seats where the aged may be in a position to sway the outcome in one way or another, as has happened in many developed societies, including in Asia, say in Japan and South Korea.

The Rise of the Aged in Singapore

Table 2 clearly shows that Singapore's aged population has been rising incrementally since 1970. Constituting only 2.5% in 1970, it grew to 7.2% in 2000 and since then has been on an upward trend, hitting 11.8% in 2015 and 15.2 in 2020. According to projections, this number would increase to 22.5% in 2030 and 33.3% in 2050.

The big question is a simple one — What will the rising aged population in Singapore mean for the state and society in the coming years, especially for a society that is not on a welfare-centric mode, as in the West, or say, in Asia, such as Japan and South Korea? The trend of ageing cannot be resisted, especially for developed states such as Singapore. Due to

Table 2.   Residents Aged 65
Years and Older as Share of
the Resident Population in
Singapore from 1970 to 2020

Year	% of Aged in Total Population
1970	3.4
1980	4.9
1990	6.0
2000	7.2
2010	9.0
2011	9.3
2012	9.9
2013	10.5
2014	11.2
2015	11.8
2016	12.4
2017	13.0
2018	13.7
2019	14.4
2020	15.2

Source: R. Hirschmann, "Elderly
population as share of resident
population Singapore 1970–2020,"
Statista, 11 February 2021. See
https://www.statista.com/statistics/
1112943/singapore-elderly-share-
of-resident-population/.

declining fertility, declining death rates, and longer life expectancy leading to the expansion of old age cohorts or generations, their share of the total population has been steadily increasing. This has led researchers to talk of population ageing as the dominant demographic phenomenon of the 21st century. While this is unprecedented in human history, it is the consequences of this phenomenon that matter most as this has ramifications for jobs, savings, consumption, national economic growth and expenditure.

How Has the Singapore Government Responded to the Aged and Their Issues?

In any state, the nature and structure of political system plays a cornerstone role in determining its policies towards the aged. Not only is Singapore a relatively young society, as seen in the overall population of almost 85% being below 65 years of age in 2020, but it is also a relatively new state, having gained its independence in August 1965. As such, being almost totally resourceless and located in a highly vulnerable region, the focus of state policies was on nation and state building, especially in terms of economic development and national security. Even more critical is the fact that Singapore is a one-party dominant state with the ruling People's Action Party (PAP) having been in power, with no challenge in sight, since 1959. This has given the ruling political elites immense leeway in determining its priorities and developing appropriate narratives and discourses to justify its policies as well as undertake long-term planning.

In this regard, partly due to the relatively youthful population and the need to address critical national political, economic and social issues, little or no attention was paid to the issue of its "silver or grey" population. Historically, Singapore's mindset towards welfare, in general, and the issue of the aged, in particular, was one of minimalism. However, by the beginning of the early 1980s, this changed with attention being paid to issues relating to the aged as its consequences came to be seen in grave terms, as had happened elsewhere in the developed states such as Japan and South Korea.

In Singapore, the turning point about doing more for the aged took place in 1982. It is not to say that nothing was done for the aged before that; it was just that the issue was not on the forefront of national issues or politics. However, after 1982, this changed with the authorities realising that there was a trend towards declining population, people living longer due to better standards of living and healthcare, and consequently the greying of the national demography and a clear rise in the "silver" generation. As was stated by an analyst, "Two main reasons exist for the year 1982 being crucial for the politics of ageing in Singapore: (1) there was no immediate need to devote state resources to a relatively young population before 1982; (2) from 1965 to the early 1980s, state resources were primarily channeled towards policies and programmes in economic development, housing, education and defence."[2]

Since then, as in most things in Singapore, which are largely "top-down" in nature, the prioritisation of the aged became an important part of the national discourse and agenda, especially since the 1980s. The challenge of the "Third Age" was to be met through a broad range of policies and approaches. Still, in a time-honoured fashion of being an "Asian society", the family remained the primary caregiver with the state and the private sector supplementing, not supplanting the centrality of the family as the centre of gravity for eldercare. Policies involving affordable housing and medicare as well as leading to successful ageing and ageing with dignity became the new mantras of Singapore's aged care with the state playing a critical role of ensuring that its Silver Generation was cared for. Fundamental in this regard, especially since the 1980s, has been the drive to ensure a mindset change in society about the aged and ageing in the hope of reshaping values, attitudes and perceptions towards the society's fast-rising Silver Generation.

Since the 1980s, there have been manifold interventions by the state to assist the aged in terms of policy making, financial assistance and affordability, among others, through the Central Provident Fund (CPF), employment and retirement policies, provision of healthcare, aged-linked legislations, housing policies, elderly integration into society and provision of accessibility in public spaces.

Policy Making and Commitments to the Aged

Since 1982, the Singapore government started talking about the importance of the aged and the need to address their concerns. However, due to the 1985 economic recession, little was implemented. In this regard, a number of high-level committees have been established to effect a balanced and effective aged policy and programme in Singapore. In 1982, the Committee on the Problems of the Aged under the Ministry of Health was established. In its report, it called for improved societal attitudes towards

---

[2] Rappa, A. L. "The Politics of Ageing: Perspectives from State and Society in Singapore," *Southeast Asian Journal of Social Science*, 27(2), 1999, 129.

ageing and the elderly. As part of the then existing belief of the family being the centre of gravity of eldercare, it called for the fostering of greater filial piety and responsibility among children and relatives for their parents and elders as the core of social and old age support. The committee also called for the greater integration of the elderly in families and society but warned against the "extreme measure" of institutionalisation as the key to eldercare. The report talked of keeping seniors healthy and leading a normal life, of increasing their role in society and economy, of the need to raise retirement age and age for retirement fund withdrawal in stages, and of the need for alternative employment such as part-time, flexi-time and work-from-home.

The 1985 recession badly hit Singapore. Partly to cater to societal needs, in 1988, in the Agenda for Action Programme, six advisory councils were rolled out that related to "issues concerning the disabled, the aged, sports and recreation, youth, culture and the arts, and family and community life".[3] In 1989, the National Advisory Council on the Family and the aged was formed with the Committee on the Aged tasked to look into four aspects of the aged, namely, involuntary neglect, upgrading skills of caregiver, changing society's perceptions and new programmes that would be needed for the aged.

In 1995, the National Survey of Senior Citizens in Singapore had important consequences for the Singapore aged. This survey led to the establishment in 1999 of the Inter-Ministerial Committee on the Ageing Population. This committee focused on various dimensions relating to the aged: housing and land use, accessibility, healthcare, eldercare, financial security, employability, lifestyle and elderly well-being. It also called for a four-tier involvement, namely, individual, family, community and state as the framework to deal with elderly issues. However, the committee still emphasised the family as being the primary caregiver, with the state and community playing supplementary roles. Still, the committee discussed ways and means of constructing elder-friendly homes, various housing options, integrated community planning and

---

[3]Goh, C. T. *Singapore: The Next Lap*, (Singapore: Government of Singapore, 1991), p. 13.

provision of healthcare and social services for the elderly by Voluntary Welfare Organisations.

In 2001, the Ministry of Community Development and Sports published the Eldercare Masterplan (AY2001–2005) Report. In 2004, the Committee on Ageing looked at the various issues that affected the elderly in Singapore with the need to maintain a high quality of life for the seniors as its priority. In the 2006 report, four proposals were put forward: housing for seniors with the need for elder friendly housing; accessibility for seniors through a barrier-free society; caring for seniors through a holistic and integrated affordable healthcare and eldercare system; and opportunities for seniors to live an active lifestyle. In the State of the Elderly in Singapore in 2008–2009, the concept of active and successful ageing was promoted. In 2015, the Ministerial Committee on Ageing launched the Action Plan for Successful Ageing.

Pensions and CPF

A key plank of helping the aged in Singapore is to enhance their financial independence and well-being. In this regard, for those on pension service, especially former civil servants, the government has tried to increase their allowances where possible. More importantly as most Singaporeans, especially the elderly, are on CPF, the aim has been to ensure that their basic living expenses, medical and housing needs are met in old age. It is also to increase the Special Account contribution rates when CPF contribution rates were restored to 40%.

Employment and Retirement

An important element has been to change the mindsets of the elderly as well as Singaporeans as far as employment and retirement are concerned. Part of the aim was to allow the elderly to keep jobs as long as possible, keep them healthy, provide financial security and integrate them into the society at large. In this regard, it is also to tap older workers to meet manpower needs, among others, through extending retirement and retraining older workers.

Medical Care

For the aged, the most critical aspect of assistance is the provision of adequate medical care. This has led to an array of measures to enhance and meet the medical needs of the aged in society. The authorities have established new and technologically advanced polyclinics and community hospitals to supplement outpatient, clinical and caregiving, in addition to traditional sites like general hospitals and homes for the aged. The new mantra has been holistic and affordable healthcare through the promotion of health promotion, disease prevention, personal responsibility and remaining active and healthy. Promoting healthy lifestyles and regular health screening has become a key element in this regard.

This has seen various healthcare and eldercare policies to respond to the basic needs of the less privileged and aged. The Medisave saving scheme was introduced in April 1984 to help individuals put aside part of their income in personal accounts to meet future medical needs for themselves and their immediate family. In 1990, Medishield was introduced, being a co-paid, low-cost insurance scheme, to help meet medical expenses from major or prolonged illness if Medisave balances were insufficient to cover the expenses. In April 1993, Medifund, an endowment fund, was set up by government to help the needy who are unable to pay for their medical expenses. The government has also provided for subsidies for Class B2 and Class C restructured wards in government hospitals. In 2001, the Eldercare Fund was established to subsidise healthcare services for needy seniors. In 2002, Eldershield, an insurance scheme to cover severe disabilities at old age, was introduced. The insurance scheme is managed by Aviva, Great Eastern and NTUC Income to provide cash payouts if one becomes disabled. At the same time, for less-off Singaporeans, their Medisave accounts have been topped up when national budgets permitted.

To facilitate the medical needs and assistance of the aged, a special Foreign Domestic Worker Grant of $120 monthly cash payment was provided for those who need a helper to care for someone with disabilities. Additionally, a Foreign Domestic Worker Levy Concession was introduced. This is a cheaper monthly levy if one hires a foreign domestic worker to care for an elderly person with disabilities or a child or grandchild. The regular monthly levy is $265 and the concession rate is $60. Additionally, a Pioneer Generation Disability Assistance Scheme was provided with a $100 monthly cash payment for seniors who are disabled as part of the Pioneer Generation package.

In 2018, Minister Indranee Rajah noted the following:

> Previously, the Ministry of Health (MOH) said it is aiming to build 10 Active Ageing Hubs in new public housing developments by 2020 to provide integrated health and social care services for the elderly. It also piloted the Community Networks for Seniors in 2016, spanning areas like Choa Chu Kang, Marine Parade and Tampines, where seniors are linked with befrienders or volunteers and attend weekly active ageing programmes.
>
> At last year's Committee of Supply debates, Minister for Health, Mr Gan Kim Yong said that since 2012, it has opened Ng Teng Fong General Hospital, Changi General Hospital Integrated Building, Jurong Community Hospital and Yishun Community Hospital. This resulted in an additional 2,500 hospital beds, on top of the expansion of existing facilities.
>
> Sengkang General and Community Hospitals are expected to open by the end of 2018, and construction is underway for Outram Community Hospital, which is scheduled to open by 2020.
>
> From 2011 to 2017, MOH also increased the aged care capacity, more than doubling home care places from 3,800 to 8,000, and day care places from 2,100 to 5,000.[4]

In general, between 2015 and 2019, the government has invested $3 billion with an additional $14.1 billion for Pioneer and *Merdeka* Generation seniors. This includes Medisave top-ups, Medishield Life Premium subsidies, outpatient care subsidies at polyclinics, public specialist outpatient clinics and Community Health Assist Scheme clinics. The authorities have also expanded Community Network for Seniors nation-wide, including adding 3,600 day-care places, 2,600 home-care places and 3,700 nursing home beds since 2015.

---

[4]Toh, E. M. "Healthcare Expenditure on Seniors One of 'Big Items' in Budget 2018: Indranee," *Today*, Singapore, 25 January 2018.

Aged-linked Legislations

An important role of the government has been through legislations such as the Maintenance of Parents Act in 1995 where parents could seek assistance from children legally.

Facilitation of Access in Public Spaces and Facilities

As part of the effort to provide respect, accessibility and integration of Singapore seniors into society, various measures have been implemented, especially with regard to ease of mobility. In 2001, the Lift Upgrading Programme was introduced to allow lifts to be provided at every level of high-rise Housing and Development Board (HDB) blocks where feasible. Where possible, traffic lights have been slowed down to allow the elderly to cross with ease. Ensuring access to public facilities, especially for the aged and handicapped, has been a key plank so as to permit the elders' integration into society. In this regard, in 2000, the Land Transport Authority began retrofitting existing Mass Rapid Transit (MRT) subway stations to ensure elder accessibility. Low-floor, step-free and wheelchair accessible buses have been introduced. The government has introduced a Seniors' Mobility and Enabling Fund to offset costs for those who need equipment to stay independent, such as walking sticks, electric wheelchairs, spectacles and hearing aids. Specialised transport to government-funded eldercare, dialysis or day hospice services as well as subsidies for medical supplies such as adult diapers or wound dressing have also been introduced. Additionally, to promote and facilitate aged travel in public transport services, various discounts have been made available.

Housing for the Aged

A roof over the head is a key sense of aged security, and making this affordable and sustainable, especially in view of rising costs and changing family attitudes, is key to welfare of the seniors. In this regard, over the last three decades or so, despite family being promoted as the anchor caregiver for the elderly, the government has made numerous policy changes to assist the elderly. There have emerged notions of Granny HDB flats and extended family housing in HDB estates. The government has provided grants for working Singaporeans who choose to live within a specific distance from their parents' HDB flats. In 1990, the Code on Barrier Free Accessibility in Buildings was aimed at assisting the elderly to move with ease in the HDB estates so that their quality of life can be enhanced. Since 1998, the HDB has constructed studio apartments equipped with elder friendly fittings and features.

Under the Action Plan for Successful Ageing, tailor-made housing such as the Kampong Admiralty project was created. This was a new public housing system designed for residents of all ages with facilities for the aged and children as part of the goal of promoting cohesion. For example, elsewhere, since 2017, the St Joseph's Home, which in the past was used for nursing and hospice services, was provided with infant and childcare facilities in the same location, partly in an effort to sensitise and socialise on the needs of the elder as part of the "whole-of-community" effort in successful ageing. The government has also been promoting senior-friendly homes by, among others, providing subsidies of up to 95% to install non-slippery flooring and grab bars in their toilets and ramps to make it easier for wheelchair users to get around as part of the Home Improvement Programme (HIP). In a more comprehensive scheme, there have been various schemes as far as aged housing or promoting family members to live closer to elderly family members. The schemes include Silver Housing Bonus, provision of a 1-room rental unit, studio apartments, 2-room flexi scheme, tri-generational flats, married child priority and multi-generation priority scheme. The Silver Age Housing scheme provides for monetisation options to unlock the value of their home depending on whether they chose to stay or move out of the current flat. There are also new flat typologies with housing and care facilities as part of the senior-friendly features under Enhancement for Active Seniors Programme. This provides housing, accessibility, integrated healthcare and eldercare, opportunities and space for active lifestyle and well-being.

Assistance to Public and Private Institutions Caring for the Aged

While the family is seen as the anchor caregiver and the government has stepped up its efforts to assist the elderly, especially since the 1980s, leveraging on the private sector and volunteers in the society has also been another key plank in the manifold programmes to assist the seniors in the country. An important part of this is the assistance that is provided to public and private institutions caring for the aged. The Senior Group Homes provide low-income elderly who are eligible for HDB rental flats and have little or no family support with an assisted living model where elderly can live independently with co-tenants supported by community-based services including Senior Activity Centre and SAC Cluster Support. A Sheltered Home is where the elderly with little or no family support and needing long-term accommodation can stay at the Ministry of Social and Family Development-licensed Sheltered Homes. The Ministry of Health also assists in providing befriending and counselling services, senior activity centres and SAC cluster support.

The Ministry of Community Development has also provided assistance to Voluntary Welfare Organisations that have programmes for the aged. The Ministry of Health runs five community and chronic sick hospitals, 22 voluntary nursing homes, 19 rehabilitation centres, 21 home-care centres and geriatric departments in three public hospitals. There are plans for more community hospitals, chronically sick hospitals, 10 nursing homes and 10 rehabilitation centres to cater to the growing elderly in the nation. The government has also provided caregiver training grants where a subsidy of $200 per year is given to train caregivers, including foreign domestic helpers, for courses in managing patients with dementia, strokes, and tube feeding, among others. The National Council for Social Services has provided more resources for civil society-run institutions such as Little Sisters of the Poor and Assisi Home, among others.

Politics and the Art of Deployment of Public Funds for the Aged

The big question then is why the government is spending so much of its hard-earned resources on the aged, a cohort that is not primarily economically active and worse, a growing burden for the family, community and the nation as a whole. First, two inter-related imperatives are at play: The authorities encourages the families and the society by and large to look after its aged and the governmental assistance where needed. As an Asian society, caring for one's elders is part of the Asian cultural ballast and hence, the government's response is almost a knee-jerk reaction that its seniors must be looked after and helped wherever possible. In view of the government has been in power since 1959 and where it is almost part of its DNA to respond and demonstrate it cares and will take the lead in solving whatever problems the nation faces, this helps one to view how the government responds to the issues related to the aged. Second, the declining population, declining childbirth and late marriages have produced a population crunch. The total fertility rate (TFR) is in a crisis and without immigrants, Singapore's population would be in a decline.

Third, the total costs — political, economic and social-cultural — of a fast greying population are immense. The warning bells were already rung long ago, including in 1999. That is to say, in 1990, eight workers supported one elderly person; in 2020, six persons supported one elderly person; in 2030, only 2.2 workers would support one elder person.[5] Hence, dealing with this elderly time bomb is an important part of the government's response to issues related to the aged. Fourth, it was also the government and society's way to pay back the aged as they were the backbone of Singapore's progress and success, especially from the Second World War onwards. Writing in 1999, Antonio Rappa argued the following:

> The proper treatment and accordance of respect to elderly Singaporeans is of ethical importance and reflects social compensation for their contribution to Singapore over the last three decades. Rather than a romantization of the elderly, the state and society have taken a moral position to demonstrate their care for the people who have made and continue to make known and unknown sacrifices.[6]

---

[5] Goh, C. T. *Singapore: The Next Lap*, (Singapore: Government of Singapore, 1991), p. 22.
[6] Rappa, A. L. "The Politics of Ageing: Perspectives from State and Society in Singapore," *Southeast Asian Journal of Social Science*, 27(2), 1999, 131.

There was the need for a somewhat "extreme" institutional response as the crisis was fast expanding and social attitudes and families were under stress due to the rising aged population and the associated costs. While the family remains the core of society, all-round changes were affecting the society as a whole, including the women workforce due to higher education, being career oriented and marrying late or remaining single. Hence, the government intervened in terms of the following: raising the age of retirement, increasing productivity of workers, grooming foreign talent to create more job opportunities for Singaporeans, a culture of wellness, improving healthcare financing, modifying public pension and CPF plans and increasing retirement-based products from the private sector. The raison d'être was to address the challenges thrown up by the growing numbers of elders in Singapore, where they would form a sizeable proportion of the population in the coming years.

Political Implications of the Aged in Singapore

From the generic point of view, the political implications of ageing stem from a number of factors. In some societies, the "Silver or Senior Vote" has been highly politicised, in part, due to the fact that the elderly constitute a substantially influential proportion of the electorate and where voting is optional, the elderly are more likely to vote than younger voters, thus affecting the electoral outcome. Hence, political parties and interest groups that are able to effectively "mine" the Silver or Senior votes would find the rise of the aged in a society as a big political blessing. In this regard, as far as politics is concerned, the issue of ageing in matured democracies has focussed its attention on two areas: the political behaviour of the elderly and the impact that the elderly and aged-based advocacy organisations have on public policy. This has led to a focus on issues such as elders' voting patterns and forms of political participation, the power and influence of older people as perceived by politicians and the effectiveness of pressure and interest groups for the elderly.[7]

[7] Wong, Y.-C. and Borowski, A. "The Politics of Aging Under a Hybrid Regime: The Case of Democratization in Hong Kong," *Journal of Aging & Social Change*, 33(1), 2019, 1–2.

The political concerns arising from the growing aged population have much to do with the negative impact it will have on society as a whole, especially on the economy and various social arenas. Living longer but not in terms of quality of life can have serious societal effects. As Singapore has developed, it has also undermined the traditional family structure, especially the nuclear family. Moving away from the traditional extended family, as the children grow up and have their own families and homes, the "birds have flown out of the nest", leaving the elderly parents to fend for themselves. This in turn can lead to various issues related to care and helplessness of the aged. This can be related to basic living costs, especially in view of the rising cost of living, access to basic public facilities such as travel, all the more if one has certain disabilities, and finally, issues relating to access to medical care.

While Singapore has done well, in general, the state can be credited for having undertaken effective intervention through leadership in looking after its aged cohort. This partly stems from Singapore as a paternalistic state where the government is highly proactive in addressing and antici- pating issues that can afflict its society. Still, concerns are continuously raised, partly due to the rising educated and vocal population with unhap- piness raised by the aged and younger Singaporeans due to the heavy burden of looking after the elderly. Over the last decade or so, there is also the increasing importance of aged issues being raised by civil society and opposition political parties, in turn, becoming part of mainstream political discourse that has also compelled the government to do more for the aged. The social media has also become an increasingly important tool to high- light and weaponise issues of the aged, leading to its politicisation and acting as a pressure group on the government.

The impact of rising aged could also have serious implications for political recruitment. While Singapore is known for and prides itself for recruiting younger leaders, in the future, to represent and articulate the interests of the aged, there may be the need to retain senior politicians who can champion elderly causes and interests more effectively than younger political leaders. Hence, the greying of the population may lead also to the greying of the political elites and representatives in parliament. Here, the key question and issue would be whether there would be a need to recruit "silver and senior politicians" to represent the interests of a sizeable proportion of the population and voters in any general elections and whether there would be a knock-on effect on Singapore politics of the rising aged population in the country.

A major political issue would be to balance the expenditure of the nation in terms of what is expended on the elderly and others in society. As the elderly cohort increases in size and in a paradigm of demands on healthcare, housing, transportation and basic needs, the politics of resource allocation would be one that needs to be watched. In short, how much to spend on the young and old can cause political tensions in the coming years. This is also related to the median age of Singapore's population. Singapore's future demographic trajectory and eventually the confidence in Singapore's future would also be determined by what has been called the "demographic time bomb". Even based on the present data, in Southeast Asia, on average, Singapore has the oldest population. While the median age of Singapore's resident population is 40.5 years old, in Southeast Asia, this is 29.8 years. What this means in reality is that "not only will the increase in spending widen the budget deficit, the slowdown in economic contribution as more of the population drops out of the labour force will also reduce tax revenue for the government, resulting in a double whammy".[8]

In this regard, the politics of the aged is also driven by the increasingly important "Silver Votes". What has not been publicly discussed in a big way is the impact of the aged voters on general elections. While in 2020 the aged constituted 15.19% of the population, in the 2020 general elections, of the 2,540,359 who voted, hypothetically, the 614,400 would constitute 24.18%, almost a quarter, indicating how important the aged have emerged politically in Singapore and are likely to become in the coming years. This would imply that there is a rising electoral power of the aged where it can have the ability to impact on political decisions, especially in various marginal seats in matured housing estates where most of the elderly reside. In short, it is not just issues of the aged being politicised, including through resources being expended on them, in the

---

[8] Shiao, V. "Singapore's Ageing Population a Ticking 'Time Bomb'", *The Business Times*, 7 December 2017.

coming years, the voting power of the aged is likely to rise and can be crucial in certain wards during elections.

Conclusion

Clearly, there is the politics of ageing in Singapore. Singapore's demographic playbook has arisen from low fertility, rising life expectancy and rising ageing population. The changing demography can have serious implications for the country's economic growth and force the government to increase immigration and import more foreign workers to keep the economy and society at large functioning effectively. At the same time, failing to address issues relating to the elderly can lead to the politicisation of the elderly, especially if the various political forces, including the opposition parties, decide to exploit issues of the aged. As this is a zero-sum game and the number of the aged is expected to increase, this is an important area of rising politicisation that needs to be watched.

https://doi.org/10.1142/9789811265198_0004

Chapter 3

Family Policies, Family Relationships and Older Adults

Kalyani K. Mehta

Abstract

This chapter focuses on seniors in Singapore, using a strengths perspective, and examines the family policies relating to seniors from a critical gerontology framework. The current cohort of seniors, 65 years and above, consists of the baby-boomer generation, alongside seniors 80 years and above who belong to the pre-baby-boomer generation. The latter are often referred to as the pioneer generation. Policies regarding family support, vulnerable seniors, caregiving and grandparenting will be analysed for their social impact as well as influence on positive ageing. Legislation enacted with the intention of protecting vulnerable seniors will be critically analysed. Using a macro perspective, the chapter will conclude with identification of social trends in family structures, and how future policies could be shaped by keeping these in mind.

Introduction

Singapore is the fastest ageing society in Southeast Asia, and it has the highest life expectancy in the world (as of 2017, the average life expectancy at birth was 84.8 years according to the Burden of Disease in

Singapore 1990–2017 report).[1] However, quality of life is of concern as the same report mentioned that 10.6 years, out of the 84.8 years' life span, would be spent in poor health. Quality of life is impacted by several factors, that is, physical and mental health, availability of family support, accessibility to healthcare, financial adequacy and personal resources such as positive attitude towards ageing.

In keeping with the general approach of this book, the present chapter will adopt a macro perspective towards the issues and challenges of an ageing population and a time perspective spanning the last 20 years. Trends in family structure, Singapore's multiracial, multi-religious composition which has a salient effect on policies, the dependence on foreign manpower, globalisation, digitisation and disruption caused by the COVID-19 pandemic on Singapore residents will be discussed.

The analysis of family trends will be done by reviewing the population demographics, anchored by recent research on ageing societal challenges by applying the strengths perspective.[2] The author examines family policies and legislation that have been introduced and implemented to tackle some of these ageing societal challenges, with the aim of identifying gaps and shortcomings so that suggestions for improvement of the well-being of ageing families can be drawn from an informed analysis. The critical gerontology approach is applied to tease out the shortcoming of policies, either in their formulation or implementation, and in some instances unintended consequences.

An Asian Context

Singapore is a cosmopolitan city-state with land as a scarce resource and human potential its greatest asset. It is a multi-ethnic, multi-lingual, multi-religious society with about almost two-fifths of its population comprising non-citizens. One of the key concerns of policy makers is the low fertility rate that is propelling the ageing demographic profile. Immigration and globalisation have helped Singapore tackle its manpower shortage in the short term, but in the long term depending on foreign manpower is risky.

---

[1] See *Burden of Disease Report in Singapore 1990–2017* (2019).
[2] Saleebey, D. *The Strength's Perspective in Social Work Practice*, (3rd ed.), (Boston: Allyn and Bacon, 2002).

A majority of the population are of Asian descent, and therefore Asian values and norms are prevalent, as recent studies on family attitudes and values have indicated.[3] Scholars have warned that Asian values of family-centredness, or familism, may not continue into the future due to globalisation as well as physical distances between family members when migration for economic prospects attracts the younger generation to settle abroad. The reduction of multi-generational households in Singapore with a parallel increase in seniors living alone or living as a couple (without adult children) is a demographic statistic that reflects some of the current social trends.[4]

Other trends that may spell some concerns are the increase in numbers of singles in the age range 35–49 years, a trend that portends higher numbers of seniors in future that may not have family support in their fourth age as they are very likely not to have adult children support.[5] The divorce rates have also increased since the year 2000, which helps to explain in part the rise of seniors living alone.[6] This means that they would probably have to rely on community-based care when they are dependent, and at a frail stage they may need admission to Nursing Homes.

On the more positive side, as long as the single elderly are healthy and capable of self-care, they may be able to age-in-place, with some community and neighbourly assistance. This depends on the affordability of community-based care and accessibility to day care. The various schemes such as Befriender Groups, Community Network of Seniors, Silver Ambassadors and grassroots informal support, e.g., Neighbourhood Community Committees (for private housing) and Residents' Committees (for public housing), have expanded over the last few decades and have enhanced the social environment.

---

[3] Quah, S. *Study on the Singapore Family*, (Singapore: Ministry of Community Development, 1999); and Thang, L. L. and Mehta, K. K. "Teach Me to be Filial: Intergenerational Care in Singapore Families," in J. Shea, K. Moore and H. Zhang (eds.), *Beyond Filial Piety: Rethinking Aging and Caregiving in East Asian Societies*, (New York: Berghahn Books, 2020), pp. 142–165.

[4] Singapore Department of Statistics, *Census of Population 2020*, (Singapore: Singapore Department of Statistics, 2021), p. 21.

[5] *Ibid.*

[6] Statistics Singapore, Singapore Department of Statistics, *Statistics on Marriages and Divorces*, (Singapore: Ministry of Trade and Industry, 2019), p. 13.

On the negative side, despite all these community-based efforts, there are older people and families that fall between the cracks. They are unable to tap the formal safety nets due to their inability to meet the criteria, e.g., for community financial assistance or for rental housing. Hence, the issue of homelessness has been identified as an important concern in Singapore, with a local study estimating about 1,000 homeless people at any one time (National Volunteer and Philanthropy Centre, 2021).[7] Since the General Elections in 2015, the Ministry of Health announced the ramping up of Nursing Home beds, day-care centre places and hospices.[8] However, the waiting list is still long, and it is estimated that applications to Nursing Homes should be prepared for a six-month wait.

There is another group that requires greater attention, which is the family caregiver segment. There are no conclusive statistics on the number of family caregivers for vulnerable populations, such as children with special needs, dependent elders and those who are terminally ill or non-ambulant. However, a population-based national survey on informal caregiving documented that 60% of informal caregivers are female and nearly half of the families that were surveyed hired a migrant domestic worker (MDW) to care for the senior(s) in the family. The popular strategy adopted by Singaporean households to provide eldercare is to deploy a MDW to carry out elder caregiving tasks alongside household chores.

The caregiving paradigm in Singapore is a combination of self-reliance, family support and community care/dependence on foreign domestic care. State support is usually tapped as a last resort. This is the manifestation of the "many helping hands approach" that is implemented in Singapore as it involves all stakeholders and does not overly burden the government. The analogy of a "trampoline" was used by then Deputy Prime Minister Tharman in 2019 to illustrate that while Singapore has adopted a non-welfare state approach due to its very limited resources, it has a safety net that allows its vulnerable to "bounce back" and not be reliant on government or community help in the long term.[9]

---

[7] National Volunteer and Philanthropy Centre, *Report of Survey on Homelessness*, (Singapore: National Volunteer and Philanthropy, 2021).

[8] www.moh.gov.sg.

[9] Centre for Liveable Cities, *Towards Ageing Well: Planning a Future-ready Singapore. Urban Systems Studies Series*, (Singapore: Centre for Liveable Cities, Ministry for National Development, 2021), p. 16.

Family Policies Relating to Caregiving, Grandparenting and Inter-generational Transfers

Table 1 summarises the main ageing-related policies on the topics of car-egiving, grandparenting and inter-generational transfers. Schemes and policies that may have a direct impact on family members are included, while symbolic national recognition such as Caregivers Week, Grandparents Day, Caregiver Awards and other types of family awards have been excluded. Grants or funds available for certain categories of seniors such as Seniors Mobility and Enabling Fund for seniors with mobility difficul-ties, or Seniors Go Digital Programme for the less IT savvy seniors have also been excluded. Family-related policies may be a wide spectrum of

Table 1.   Summary of the National-level Family Policies in Singapore

Target Group	Caregiving	Grandparenting	Inter-generational Transfers
Family members and MDW	Caregiver Training Grant		
Family member caring for elders and children with special needs	Home Caregiving Grant		
Adult children		Grandparent Caregiver Relief	Tax relief for providing care to parents (Parent Care Relief)
Parents of children below 12			Tax relief for children below 12
All family members			Central Provident Fund (Medisave top-up);* Housing and Development Board ** (inheritance) (Housing Proximity Grant)

Notes: MDW = migrant domestic worker.
* See website of Central Provident Fund (CPF) www.cpf.gov.sg.
** See website of Housing and Development Board (HDB) www.hdb.gov.sg.

Table 2.   Singapore Legislations Related to Older People

Target Group	Legislation	Links
Adult family members	Maintenance of Parents Act (1995)	https://sso.agc.gov.sg/Act/ MPA1995
Seniors and persons aged 18 years and above with physical and mental disabilities	Mental Capacity Act (2008)	https://sso.agc.gov.sg/Act/ MCA2008
Vulnerable seniors and persons with disabilities	Vulnerable Adults Act (2018)	https://sso.agc.gov.sg/Act/ VAA2018
Older family members who have suffered abuse	Women's Charter (1961)	https://sso.agc.gov.sg/Act/ WC1961

policies such as relating to adoption, custody of children, divorce and so on. For the purpose of this chapter, only policies and schemes that deal with families and older adults, as well as inter-generational issues, are focussed upon. Table 2 summarises the legislations that are relevant. For readers who wish to understand the legislative tools better, they could read the various legislations to protect elderly as well as access the links provided in Table 2.[10]

From the macro perspective, Singapore seems to have advanced in terms of its network of schemes and programmes to support ageing families. The Agency for Integrated Care (AIC) is a centralised body that has been commissioned to oversee the entire spectrum of needs of not only seniors but also the caregivers. It also strategises the approach towards people with mental health problems and needs. Family caregivers have been supported mainly through the digital platform as well as CARE LINKS that perform the role of navigators to bridge the gap between the demand and supply of resources to family caregivers. AIC also manages the Caregiver Training Grant which is a subsidised training programme for family caregivers as well as migrant domestic workers from overseas. The roles and portfolios entrusted to AIC by the government are

---

[10] Centre for Liveable Cities, *Towards Ageing Well: Planning a Future-ready Singapore. Urban Systems Studies Series*, (Singapore: Centre for Liveable Cities, Ministry for National Development, 2021), p. 17.

multiplying and this has slowed down its efficiency in responding to the residents' needs, a result that was to be expected. For an organisation to be nimble, it should not be overburdened. In addition, the bureaucracy or "red tape" involved in applications and meeting criteria for various schemes is a deterrent to people who wish to tap the subsidised workshops/training seminars.

The longevity of Singaporeans is a boon which comes with a downside, that is, poorer quality of life, especially for women, a longer period of loneliness and frailty culminating in dependency, financial insecurity and fear of burdening the family members. Healthcare costs are a financial burden, and although the government has increased subsides to seniors through the Pioneer Generation Package and the *Merdeka* Package, the principle of co-payment translates to mandatory payments by all income groups. The lower-income groups have higher levels of subsides in acute hospitals and community hospitals (known as "step-down care" or a transition facility before the patient is able to return home). It is often the middle-class ageing families that feel the greatest pressure both financially as well as emotionally, as they may not meet the criteria for "means testing" in order to tap the full subsidy. With smaller family sizes, the bulk of the healthcare burden tends to fall on one or two children, unlike the past when family sizes were much larger. With daughters and daughters-in-law being stretched with employment responsibilities, childcare duties and household chores, the major caregiving tasks tend to be performed by the spouses, who are ageing themselves. This brings us to the crux of the family issue. Family caregiving is a heavy burden on small families, particularly dual-income middle-generation families. While the Asian norm of family care first is revered, and the Singapore government reinforces the mantra of "family is the first line of defence", the reality is that the family members can only stretch themselves to a limit, before they themselves burnout.[11]

Table 1 illustrates the policies that are targeted at family caregivers, including those caring for children with disabilities and seniors, the latest being the Home Caregiving Grant, consisting of $200/- per month for a

---

[11] Mehta, K. "Stress Among Family Caregivers of Older Persons in Singapore," *Journal of Cross-cultural Gerontology*, Special Issue on Aging in Asia, 20, 2006, 319–334.

family caregiver looking after a care recipient with a minimum of three Activities of Daily Living (ADL). Unfortunately, it is silent on the family caregiver caring for seniors with cognitive disorder and dementia. From the author's viewpoint, Singapore could have taken a leaf from South Korea's approach wherein family caregivers of a relative with dementia are eligible for the caregiver grants. It is well established that medication for dementia, Parkinson's disease and similar mental health issues is expensive. Above that, the stress of caring for a person suffering from dementia is higher than most other chronic conditions.[12] Physical and mental exhaustion, loneliness and social isolation, emotional burden and a feeling of being "trapped" are some of the poignant experiences that the caregivers face.

Universally, a majority of family caregivers are women. The caregiving experience is both positive and negative. However, if it drags over the years, it becomes a heavy burden with the negative stressors being compounded such as behavioural and psychological projections of frustration by the care recipient on caregiver. The feminisation of ageing, another global phenomenon, translates to poor quality of life experienced by elderly women as they outlive their spouses.[13] Many elderly women are dependent on their adult children after their entry into widowhood; after caring for their spouses, these women eventually feel unwanted and financially inadequate. Due to a lack of financial planning for old age, lack of financial literacy skills and education, women in the current older

---

[12] Mehta, K. "Stress Among Family Caregivers of Older Persons in Singapore," *Journal of Cross-cultural Gerontology*, Special Issue on Aging in Asia, 20, 2006, 319–334; Tuomola, J., Soon, J., Fisher, P. and Yap, P. "Lived Experience of Caregivers of People with Dementia and the Impact on Their Sense of Self: A Qualitative Study in Singapore," *Journal of Cross Cultural Gerontology*, 31(2), June 2016, 157–172; and Tew, C. W., Tan, L. F., Luo, N., Ng, W. Y. and Yap, P. "Why Family Caregivers Choose to Institutionalize a Loved One with Dementia: A Singapore Perspective," *Dementia and Geriatric Cognitive Disorders*, 30(6), 2010, 509–516.

[13] Gubhaju, B., Malhotra, R., Chan, A. and Ostbye, T. *Deteriorating Health but Still Working Very Long Hours — A Profile of Singapore's Older Family Caregivers*, (Singapore: Centre for Ageing and Research, 2017); and Teo, P., Mehta, K., Thang, L. L. and Chan, A. "The Journey after Widowhood," in P. Teo, K. Mehta, L. L. Thang and A. Chan (eds.), *Ageing in Singapore: Service Needs and the State*, (London: Routledge, 2006), pp. 134–146.

cohorts in Singapore lack financial security. The life course perspective has been applied by gerontologists to explain the cumulative disadvantage faced by Asian women in their old age.[14] In Singapore, the government has identified the year 2021 to focus on the Development of Singapore Women, and many of these issues have been highlighted in the Singapore Conversations held with focus groups, a majority of whom are females. It is clear that policies are currently inadequate in addressing the dilemmas and pressures on women in their mid-life stage (usually family caregivers tend to be between 45 and 60 years) culminating in negative outcomes when they are in their old age.[15] Areas that demand greater attention are as follows:

(1) Lack of universal parent care leave.
(2) Lack of affordable and accessible respite care.
(3) Stringent criteria for accessing Home Caregiving grant.
(4) Inadequate options for non-working caregivers who wish to return to the workforce after their loved one passes on.

While it is also true that many male caregivers are also stressed, and their marriages are sometimes negatively affected in the process, in terms of numbers, male caregivers are relatively fewer than female caregivers.[16]

COVID-19 Pandemic

Policy makers face the perennial issue of limited resources and trade-offs, and in the field of ageing policies this is applicable. However, in the

---

[14] For discussion on the interactive effects of low savings, low salaries, and checkered work career due to caregiving and other family responsibilities on old age conditions of older Asian women, see Wee, V., Harding, S. C., Geronimo, M. A. B. and Bezbaruah, S. "Singapore", in V. Wee, S. C. Harding, M. A. B. Geronimo and S. Bezbaruah (eds.), *Financial Security of Older Women: Perspectives from Southeast Asia*, (Singapore: Tsao Foundation, 2018).

[15] Chin, C. W. W. and Phua, K. H. "Long-term Care Policy: Singapore's Experience," *Journal of Aging and Social Policy*, 28(2), 2016, 113–129.

[16] Survey on Informal Caregiving (2013).

context of a fast ageing society, the national priority has to be on ageing families. In the years 2020 and 2021, Singapore has been grappling with the unprecedented public health and economic challenges of the COVID-19 pandemic, with the rest of the world. Many livelihoods have collapsed, with the lower-income groups affected most by the pandemic. It is to the government's credit that the country's national reserves have been available to help the needy and vulnerable in Singapore. The fault lines in most societies have been exposed, and Singapore is no exception. The surge in infections in its migrant worker dormitories had to be grappled with in mid-2020, and the positive result is that in a short time these migrant workers stay in better accommodation and receive treatment to the virus when infected. Singapore is fortunate that its fatalities have been relatively low, and currently the vaccination drive is in full swing. However, family ties have been tested with employees having to work from home, students adapting to online learning and older family members adjusting to a "full house" which has its upside as well as downside. Senior care facilities were closed during a large part of 2020, and this affected the seniors who had been enrolled, for example, in adult day-care centres and social activity centres. Anecdotal observations reflect that seniors have been feeling lonely and bored, socially disengaged due to the stringent safe management measures imposed for their own safety, and some have slipped into poorer health. Families that have survived successfully are the ones that have a unified base and similar values. Families that lost a loved one due to COVID-19 were not allowed to hold customary rites and funerals, and this left them feeling deprived of a dignified farewell.

Overall, family relationships have been challenged, but we have also learnt to be resilient and cooperative. This is the only way to survive. The gerontological lens of biopsychosocial and spiritual analysis of the family during unusual times inform this discussion in a unique way. From the author's viewpoint, Singapore's historical legacy of adversity and survival, together with the wisdom of its current senior population, permeates its people and the leaders. Being small and nimble, this "red dot" has emerged even stronger in the past after adversity was overcome, and there is a strong chance this will be repeated.

Discussion and Critique

This section will take a critical stance, similar to the critical gerontology approach towards policy analysis adopted by scholars such as was argued by Moody (1988) and Luborsky and Sankar (1993).[17] Going beyond the biomedical model assumptions, it is imperative that the exercise of examining age-related policies studies salient ageist stereotypes, assumptions that older people are recipients of care (while in reality they are both providers and recipients) and the influence of cultural norms on policies. One example of the latter is the enactment of the Maintenance of Parents Act (MPA) in 1995 as a tool to deter adult children from shrugging off their filial responsibilities. The maintenance orders have not risen since 2010, but this may be due to the fact that a majority of applications are resolved through reconciliation. In 2011, the number of cases seen by the Commissioner for the Maintenance of Parents was 286, as compared to 98 in 2020.[18]

In the Asian context, it is shameful for parents to sue their adult children in court; therefore, the option of reconciliation has reduced the cases heard at the Tribunal. Let us look at the legislations relating to protection of vulnerable seniors. The Ministry of Social and Family Development set up an APS in 2015 to help vulnerable adults, families experiencing violence, and women and girls below 21 years who have suffered ill treatment or are in mortal danger. In 2019, it was reported that the number of elder abuse cases had risen from 77 in 2017 to 127 in 2019.[19] Elder abuse statistics can be derived from the Women Charter as well as the Adult Protective Services. During the COVID-19 pandemic (2020 and first half of 2021), family violence cases have risen in Singapore, as in other parts of the world, due to financial as well as emotional stress on the family. While the latest statistics are unavailable, it would not be wrong to assume

---

[17] Moody, H. "Toward a Critical Gerontology," in J. Birren and V. Bengston (eds.), *Emergent Theories of Aging*, (New York: Springer, 1988); and Luborsky, M. and Sankar, A. "Extending the Critical Gerontology Perspective: Cultural Dimensions," *The Gerontologist*, 33(4), 1988, 440–444.

[18] *The Straits Times*, 14 June 2021.

[19] *Ibid.*, 15 June 2020.

that older adults may have suffered neglect and physical/emotional abuse. One indicator is that the APS received 1,196 enquiries in 2020 compared to 607 in 2019. The Vulnerable Adults Act (VAA) (2018) helps to protect seniors who may suffer from physical or mental disability, neglect or self-neglect, as well as adults 18 years and above who have a disability and are unable to protect themselves.

However, there are two gaps in the VAA. Firstly, it is not compulsory to report, although outsiders who report such cases in the community are assured of anonymity; secondly, financial abuse is not included in the definition. Regarding the protection of seniors who are of "unsound mind", e.g., suffer from dementia, the Mental Capacity Act (MCA) was introduced in 2008. The process has been made easier with online applications, and since 2019, the $50/- fee has been waived. In 2013, there were 2,594 Lasting Power of Attorney (LPA) applications, which rose to 4,096 in 2014.[20] However, many are deterred from applying due to lack of a suitable or willing donor (guardian), and others may be afraid that the family may take advantage of the LPA. When a donor cannot be found, the applicant can request the state to appoint a Deputy (a trusted professional). A critique levelled at the MCA is that many have faced hurdles in obtaining a witness (who has to be a lawyer/doctor chosen from the Panel appointed by the Ministry of Social and Family Development) due to their busy schedule. Although the process has been streamlined after receiving public feedback, if the senior is unwell or fearful of being exposed to coronavirus, the LPA cannot be done until the witness is able to assess the mental capacity of the senior.

The strengths perspective encourages us to seek the strengths and assets of seniors, but generally societal attitudes tend to focus on the deficits. There are no laws in Singapore to protect the senior worker from being unfairly dismissed as Singapore does not have an Age Discrimination law, although there is a channel for recourse by applying to the Tripartite Alliance for Fair and Progressive employment practices (TAFEP). For a senior to take his/her case to TAFEP, it would require him/her to have sufficient evidence to prove the case of wrongful dismissal and this is often difficult to do. While the Retirement and Re-employment Act (2012) is

---

[20] MSF Statistics in Brief 2015.

revised regularly and employers are encouraged to retain older workers, due to the economic challenges posed by the pandemic, many businesses have been forced to close. In many cases, the older workers are the first to be fired. In a recent research on well-being of older workers that the author was involved in, many of the respondents cited examples of unfair treatment by their bosses such as being forced to take unpaid leave, being denied wage increments and health benefits, as well as having to endure poor work conditions.

In the earlier section, the situation of older women was discussed, as well as the financial retirement inadequacy of female seniors due to a lack of financial planning, financial literacy and insufficient Central Provident Fund (CPF) savings. Many female seniors have grandparenting responsibilities and so they are keen to take up part-time or flexible work rather than full-time work. However, these opportunities are not common. This is another gap in the workplace, signalling that there is a policy lag between the reality on the ground and the human resource policies.

Conclusion

Policies have to keep up with changing circumstances, demographics and social forces in the nation. Trends in the increase of singles in their 30s and 40s (discussed earlier), in the increase of couple-based households (in 1990 it was 8.4% and in 2010 it was 14%) and seniors living alone (in 1990 it was 5.2% and in 2010 it was 12%) are important social choices and lifestyles that hold implications for housing, financial security, as well as health and social care. The Singapore Census of Population 2020 released in June 2021 has revealed that the percentage of residents above 65 years increased to 15.2%. The increase in seniors living alone doubled over the last 10 years, from 4.6% in 2010 to 9.3% in 2020.[21] In terms of gender, more than 12% of females 65 and above were unable to perform or had difficulty performing at least one ADL.[22] In the same report, 100,000 seniors living in the community were estimated to have difficulty with basic daily activities. While it cannot be assumed that all seniors who

---

[21] Census of Population 2020.

[22] *The Straits Times*, 19 June 2021.

live alone or as couples (without children) will need community and state help, to some extent they would be vulnerable at the frail stage. These statistics have implications for policies and programmes in future. Greater attention will need to be given to developing an affordable suite of services for the frail and vulnerable seniors in the community, and a larger proportion of them are likely to be singles and/or women. The homeless population is made up of a majority of men, and their issues are complex. Their problems are not only related to family issues but also housing policies that have stringent criteria for rental flats. Hence, the case management approach would be recommended so that the strengths of this population can be tapped.

The idea of *Time Banking* was proposed at the recent Gender Conference organised by the Institute of Policy Studies on 3 June 2021. This may be a "good bartering" scheme that Singapore can adopt, as it has proven its value in 34 countries across the globe. Singapore can learn from other nations the idea of a sharing economic infrastructure that does not depend on a cash economy. The key principle is that people "pay forward" and this incentivises social and civic engagement. Singles as well as "young old" seniors are capable of "paying forward" so that in their later age when they need assistance, they would be reassured that assistance (physical, emotional as well as spiritual) would be available.

Policy makers have to take a whole-of-government approach towards reducing gender inequality in the life course journeys as well as caregiving roles and responsibilities within families to create a better gender balance. The long-term outcome would be that female and male seniors would have a greater likelihood of work–life balance and retirement adequacy. Over time, it is possible that Singapore's below-replacement total fertility rate (TFR) may be raised. Singapore has advanced in its economic progress, but in terms of social and ethnic cohesion, it has to continuously devise policies and schemes that would be relevant in the ageing societal context, as well as cater to the needs of the different cohorts of seniors.

https://doi.org/10.1142/9789811265198_0005

Chapter 4

Organization and Delivery of Long-term Care in Singapore: Present Issues and Future Challenges*

Kalyani K. Mehta[†] and S. Vasoo[‡]

---

*From Mehta, K. K., & Vasoo, S. (2001). Organization and delivery of long-term care in Singapore: Present issues and future challenges. *Journal of Aging & Social Policy, 13*(2/3), 185–201. Reprinted by permission of the publisher (Taylor & Francis Ltd, http://www. tandfonline.com).

The article provides an overview of the long-term care services available for the elderly followed by a discussion of the policy issues put forward by the Inter-Ministerial Committee (IMC) on Ageing Population.

[†]Dr. Kalyani K. Mehta is former Associate Professor, Department of Social Work and Psychology, National University of Singapore. She has done research on elderly services and policies for the past 10 years, has published articles in international and regional journals, and presented conference papers in the United States, China, Australia, and South East Asia. As a member of the National Committee on the Aged as well as a consultant to the United Nations Economic and Social Commission for Asia and the Pacific (ESCAP), Dr. Mehta has recommended policies and services for the improved quality of life of older persons. Her edited volume, *Untapped Resources: Women in Aging Societies Across Asia* (1997), added greatly to the literature on the status and roles of older women in aging societies. Her research interests include family caregiving, religion and aging, widowhood, remarriage, and cross-cultural patterns of aging.

Summary

This paper focuses on the Singaporean model of long-term care for older people. With only about 2% of the older population living in institutions, the mainstay of long-term care is community care. The reader is provided an overview of the Singaporean services, including case management, followed by a discussion of the current issues and future challenges. In keeping with the prospect of a rapidly aging population profile, the Singapore government plays a leading role in framing policy and planning for future needs of this sector of the population. [Article copies available for a fee from The Haworth Document Delivery Service: 1-800-HAWORTH. E-mail address: <getinfo@haworthpressinc.com> Website: <http://www.HaworthPress.com> © 2001 by The Haworth Press, Inc. All rights reserved.]

Keywords: Aging policy, long-term care, Singapore

The Need for Care

The demographic revolution of population aging that was well advanced in most developed countries by the end of the 20th century is evident in Asia, too. After Japan, Singapore is the fastest aging nation in the Asia Pacific region, and in recognition of the significance of this development,

‡Dr. S. Vasoo is Associate Professor, Department of Social Work and Psychology, National University of Singapore. He is actively involved as an advisor to many social and community organizations, including NGOs of senior citizens. He is a member of the Inter-Ministerial Committee on Ageing and has chaired its Committee on Social Integration of the Elderly. He studies voluntary action of the elderly.

Both authors can be contacted at the National University of Singapore, 10 Kent Ridge Crescent, Singapore 119260 (Dr. Kalyani Mehta's E-mail: swkkkm@nus.edu.sg; Dr. S. Vasoo's E-mail: swkvasoo@nus.edu.sg).

[Haworth co-indexing entry note]: "Organization and Delivery of Long-Term Care in Singapore: Present Issues and Future Challenges." Mehta, Kalyani K., and S. Vasoo. Co-published simultaneously in *Journal of Aging & Social Policy* (The Haworth Press, Inc.) Vol. 13, No. 2/3, 2001, pp. 185–201; and: *Long-Term Care in the 21st Century: Perspectives from Around the Asia-Pacific Rim* (ed: Iris Chi, Kalyani K. Mehta, and Anna L. Howe) The Haworth Press, Inc., 2001, pp. 185–201. Single or multiple copies of this article are available for a fee from The Haworth Document Delivery Service [1-800-HAWORTH, 9:00 a.m.–5:00 p.m. (EST). E-mail address: getinfo@haworthpressinc.com].

an Inter-Ministerial Committee (IMC) on Health Care and another on the Aging Population were convened by the Singapore Government in 1997 and 1998, respectively. The IMCs released two reports on their deliberations in 1999, and these reports both review the need for care and preview the challenges that are likely to be forthcoming in the early years of the 21st century.

As an island state with a total resident population of just over 3.5 million in 2000, the impact of the demographic processes of population aging is highly visible in Singapore. Life expectancy at birth is already high, at 75 years for males and nearly 80 years for females, and these figures are expected to rise further. The demographic data given in Table 1 show that the proportion of the population aged 65 and over will almost double from 7.3% in 1999 to 13.1% in 2020, and by 2030, close to one in every five Singaporeans will be aged 65 and over. Within this rapidly aging demographic profile, the increase of those in late life, above 75 years, is even more conspicuous.

The doubling of the proportion aged 65 and over in Singapore will occur in a far shorter time, less than 25 years, compared to up to 150 years in the already older countries of western Europe, and around 80 years in the developed Pacific Rim countries of North America, Australia, and New Zealand, which are now reaching the 14% mark (ESCAP, 1996). The speed of this demographic transition has major implications not only for health and social services but for other sectors of society as well, and the planning of long-term care for the elderly population requires consideration of both the development of formal services and the changing roles of families in informal care.

Table 1. Characteristics of Aged Population, Singapore, 1999–2030

Characteristic	1999	2000	2020	2030
Aged 65+ (,000)	235	312	529	796
Proportion of total population aged 65 and over	7.3	8.4	13.1	18.9
Median Age (Yrs)	33.4	36.9	39.3	41.2
Dependency Ratio Total	42.0	38.7	44.9	56.4
Young (0–14 years)	31.7	27.1	25.9	26.9
Old (65+ years)	10.4	11.6	19.0	29.5

Source: Singapore Department of Statistics, cited in the Inter-Ministerial Report, 1999: 29.

Changing family structures and roles

The IMC has noted that one key concern is that the sheer rise in the numbers and proportion of older persons could potentially put stress on families and eldercare services (IMC Report, 1999b). As in other Asian countries, the family in Singapore has been providing the major part of care and support for elderly family members (Knodel & Debavalya, 1997). Although there are no strong data to show that families are shirking their filial responsibilities, several social and demographic changes mitigate against the continuity of family care as the primary form of eldercare in Singapore.

These trends take on added importance in the context of the present paradigm of eldercare in Singapore, which is a partnership among the government, the community, and the family (Mehta, 2000). In tandem with the "Many Helping Hands" policy of the Ministry of Community Development, the community and the government are expected to lend a hand to aging families in order to reduce the stress of caregiving for older members. Reiterating the government's long-standing position at the opening of a conference on choices in financing health care and old age security, convened under the auspices of the World Bank in Singapore in 1997, the Minister for Health noted that "the family setting is still the best approach; it provides the elderly with the warmth and companionship of family members and a level of emotional support which cannot be found elsewhere" (Prescott, 1998).

In line with this partnership approach, the government encourages voluntary welfare organizations (VWOs) in their efforts to offer quality long-term care in the community through provision of financial and other forms of support. These services and programs are discussed in detail below, but it is becoming apparent to many in government, in VWOs, and in the community at large that with rising numbers of older Singaporeans, non-family partners will be required to play bigger roles over the next few decades.

Declining mortality and low fertility rates mean that the aged are being recognized as a more integral part of Singaporean society. As in Japan, the Singapore government recognizes that a large proportion of citizens is fast approaching the age of retirement, and acknowledges the implications of aging for policy-making and government expenditures. There is a concern to maintain the health and vitality of the elderly as their life spans increase, so that the older population does not become an unduly heavy financial and social burden on the society. Perhaps even more so than in Japan, the Singapore government sees a viable family structure that is able to provide love, care, and support for its elderly members as crucial, and indeed the ideal, if the formal support system for the elderly is to be kept to a minimum.

At the same time, and notwithstanding a continuing Confucian value system, the traditional caregivers of the family, and more specifically female relatives, are coming under increasing pressures from modernization and urbanization. These changes include a shift to dual-income nuclear families, living apart from older generations, increasing levels of education and high rates of participation in the formal workforce for women, more young Singaporeans working and living abroad, more single elderly among the generation for whom family formation was interrupted by World War II, and changing social values. Two demographic indicators point to the extent of these intergenerational changes.

First, age-specific sex ratios provide an indicator of need for health care services arising from the interaction of advancing age, gender differences in chronic diseases, and social support from spouses. In the 1990 census, men constituted 47% of the aged population, but the sex ratio dropped from 97 males per 100 females at age 60 to 69 years, to 80 in the 70–79 age group, and only 60 at 80 years and above. Since women generally outlive men and mortality rates are falling faster among females than males, the net result is a growing sex imbalance, especially with increasing age (Shantakumar 1994, 1995). The health problems of the elderly consequently reflect the conditions and needs of a larger proportion of older women, and as women generally use health services more often than men, differential demand will be increasingly pronounced in future. The lower sex ratio with increasing age does not of itself necessarily lead to a higher demand for social services, as family structure and marital status come into play. Again in the 1990 census, 29% of the aged population were widowed, but the figure was 54% for aged women compared to about 19% for aged men.

Second, the ratio of the elderly to the working-age population, the old age dependency ratio, is projected to increase from around 10 currently to 30 by 2030. The need for more old people to be supported by a proportionately smaller working population has major implications for labor supply and financial security, and for the provision of social services, especially health care, as alternatives or adjuncts to family care (Teo, 1994). Population movements due to changes in living arrangements and employment patterns can exacerbate the need for external assistance (Ministry of Health, 1984).

Vulnerable groups

Given the differentials in aging patterns, not all older persons require continual care. However, those in the "old old" and "very old" categories are generally more likely to need constant supervision, social and emotional support as well as instrumental help. Focusing on these categories as the potential target groups for care services, population projections show that the 75-and-over age group will increase even faster than the 60–75 years age group (Cheung, 1993). This older group is at risk of needing care and attention, and as more family resources will have to be drawn into attending to the social and physical requirements of very old relatives, some families are likely to face considerable stress in providing care to the sick and disabled.

Another vulnerable category are aged couples living on their own, who have increased from 9% of households with persons aged 60 years and above in 1990 to 15% in 1997. Poor older people living alone are also identified as being at risk, and the aging process has become especially apparent in housing estates that were constructed in the 1960s. There are increasing numbers of older senior citizens living in these estates, and it is urgent that community groups and organizations begin to plan the establishment of more community-based programs such as day care, meals programs, home-help service and domiciliary nursing care, and crisis-response services. In taking a proactive approach to initiate a network of services in older housing estates, it will be possible to provide support for families with vulnerable aged relatives and minimize disruptions to the social and economic lives of the families.

Services Provided by the Social Welfare System

Those involved in developing community-based services in Singapore can draw on several decades of experience in the United Kingdom and in the United States and other countries that have sought to expand community care as an alternative to institutional care (Challis & Davies, 1986; Gordon & Donald, 1993). As well as recognising that the trend towards community-based long-term care is not only feasible but also the preferred choice of the elderly themselves, as in other countries, Singapore is starting from a very different position. With only some 2% of its elderly living in institutions at present, Singapore is well-placed to embark on the development of community care as the mainstay of long-term care rather than as an alternative to the kind of large, long-established, and costly institutional care sectors that most other countries are seeking to counter.

The paradigm of elder care in Singapore has been evolving for some time now and as with other areas of health and social services, a distinctive Singapore model has emerged. Three main features of this model are the interweaving of informal and formal care to suit the needs of individual clients and their families; the support of a diversity of VWOs to provide a range of services and develop innovative projects in service delivery, including case management; and the attention given to improving health and well-being among vulnerable groups with a view to reducing future needs for long-term care services. The range of services now available is summarized in Table 2, which shows the different levels of care provided by sub-systems of home-based, community-based, and residential services. The following account focuses on community care, detailing the non-institutional services delivered to the home and semi-institutional services based in the community.

Table 2.   Long-term Care Services and Programs in Singapore

Community Care		Institutional Care
Home-based (Non-institutional)	**Community-based (Semi-institutional)**	**Residential Services**
1. Socio-recreational	1. Day activity centres	1. Sheltered homes
2. Befriending/counselling	2. Social Centres	2. Hospices
3. "Doorstep" services delivered in the home	3. Day Care Centres and Rehabilitation Centres	3. Nursing Homes (private & VWOs)
		4. Community Hospitals

Who are the providers of community-based long-term care?

The main providers are voluntary welfare organisations (VWOs), with the private sector playing a role only in the delivery of nursing home care. As of January 2000, there were 24 private sector nursing homes compared to VWO provision of 23 nursing homes, three hospices, and one residential facility for dementia patients. In addition, there were four community hospitals and two hospitals for the chronically sick.

The Ministry of Community Development and Sports and the Ministry of Health support the efforts of VWOs and administer mechanisms for quality management. As well as mandatory guidelines for nursing homes, the Ministry of Community Development and Sports has issued a set of guidelines for community-based services for the elderly. The guidelines are strongly recommended but not mandatory (Ministry of Community Development, 1998). A third statutory body, the National Council of Social Service, plays a coordinating role among non-government welfare organizations and helps in representing their views to the government.

Day care and home modification services

In 1998, there were 20 day care and rehabilitation centers distributed across the island and operated by a variety of government and non-government organizations. Six are Senior Citizens' Health Care Centres that offer both social and health care programs especially for patients newly discharged from acute hospitals. These services play a crucial role in the smooth transition of elderly from acute care to home care. Family caregivers are given informal training at these centers. Three day care centers specialize in the care of elderly suffering from dementia.

Other day centers are operated by secular and religious organizations, for example, the Wan Qing Lodge and the Adventist Church. Some day centers are located within the premises of residential homes, thus providing a dual function for the latter as well as a source of income generation. Day care centers have been found to help relieve the stress of family caregivers by providing respite care and ensuring the safety of the elderly, especially if other family members are not at home during the day (Kua, 1987).

In planning to meet the projected increase in need for day care centers, there has been some experimentation in different forms of provision. One such experiment takes the form of 3-in-1 centers, where day care for three age groups is located within one vicinity. Bringing young children, school-age children, and elderly together in intergenerational programs such as the celebration of festivals, teaching of handicrafts, and community singing inculcates a greater sense of affiliation between the generations.

There are 11 social day centers that cater mainly to the relational and social needs of elderly citizens. These centers are neighborhood hubs characterized by informality and self-management by the senior citizens. Most are located within Family Service Centres and require minimal funds and manpower because volunteers, including robust young elderly, are the backbone of these programs.

Day activity centers are different again in that they meet the needs of low-income elderly who live alone in government flats. This vulnerable group has been identified as needing community support and companionship, and the day activity centers are linked to a joint project between the Ministry of Community Development and the Housing Development Board (HDB), the statutory body in charge of the government-housing program. A reputable voluntary welfare organization is selected by the Ministry to run the day activity centers with a lean staff and a large volunteer input. The day activity center provides an opportunity for social interaction for these poor and lonely elderly and a contact to depend on in times of crisis. Together, the day care and rehabilitation centers offer comprehensive services for the senior citizens living with their family members, while the day activity centers offer social and emergency services for the poor elderly living alone.

A further function of the HDB is the upgrading of the low-rent, one-room flats at no cost to tenants. Installation of elderly-friendly amenities, such as non-slip tiles in the bathroom, handle bars, and pedestal toilets, and an alarm system that alerts neighbors and the day activity center nearby of an emergency, are the main features of this Congregate Housing project that in the last seven years has been expanded to 25 blocks, each housing approximately 150 elder tenants.

Home care services

Care services delivered in the home, or "door-step" programs as they are known in Singapore, provide a wide range of services for vulnerable and frail older people, including home help and household chores, meal delivery, escort to polyclinics and hospitals, home nursing and home medical care, and befriending services. The organizations concerned usually draw geographical boundaries for their services due to limited resources, both financial and manpower.

Other community-based services are located in the VWO rather than being delivered to the home. These include telephone hotlines for counseling, face-to-face casework and counseling, caregiver support groups, and weekly lunches prepared by volunteers. There are two key organizations, the Singapore Action Group of Elders (SAGE) and the Tsao Foundation, that specialize in the delivery of aged care services. The former not only provides direct services but also has a Centre for the Study of Ageing (CENSA) because research is seen to be of paramount importance in charting changing profiles and needs of successive cohorts of elderly in Singapore's fast-changing society. The Tsao Foundation, in contrast, focuses on the delivery of medical services to low-income elderly and the training of informal caregivers; it also runs an Acupuncture clinic. Other voluntary bodies provide free Chinese medical treatment, in one case via a mobile clinic staffed by volunteer doctors.

Socio-recreational services

Socio-recreational community-based programs form an integral part of the repertoire of elderly services and are directed to the "young old" who are usually active and desire to remain productive members of society. The Retired and Senior Volunteer Program (RSVP) provides an avenue for professional and educated retired senior citizens. For the wider majority, there are almost 400 Senior Citizens' Clubs (SCC) established by the People's Association scattered across the island. Most SCCs are located in Community Centres, which are multi-purpose, secular centers catering to the general Singaporean population, regardless of age, ethnicity, or religion. Programs organized by the SCCs include tours to Malaysia, dancing, singing, exercise classes such as Tai Chi and Qigong, and competitions between clubs. The SCCs play a very active part in the celebrations for Senior Citizens' Week held in November every year.

Some of the social programs have an emphasis on education. For example, SAGE offers a program of lifelong learning that includes Chinese calligraphy and traditional crafts, and other organizations conduct training in computer skills, training for family caregivers, and enrichment skills. As future cohorts of Singaporean elderly will be better educated and will have greater savings, there is likely to be a greater demand for these programs.

Case management

The introduction of case management in Singapore illustrates the way in which a distinctive Singaporean approach has been developed from the experience of other countries. Besides using case management to address the problems of duplication, fragmentation, and frustration for consumers as reported by Austin (1986) and Schneider *et al.* (2000) and to achieve added cost-effectiveness in comparison to institutionalization as argued by Greene *et al.* (1998), Singapore has embraced case management as a means to gaining wider benefits of community development (Atchley, 2000).

The National Council of Social Service (NCSS) launched a two-year pilot project in case management in May 1998 through the Tsao Foundation and SAGE. In this project, case management was defined as a new service that involves the assessment of an elderly person's health and psychological and social needs, and maximization of services to attain optimal and most cost-effective care of the elderly and their caregivers to prevent unnecessary institutionalization (SAGE, 1998). This strategy of service delivery is being examined to mitigate the problems of uneven distribution and fragmentation in service delivery, and aims to develop viable models of case management to suit the Singapore context.

Since public awareness of services is relatively low, as evident from the 1995 National Survey of Senior Citizens (Ministry of Health, 1996), and services are often dispersed and fragmented, the case management concept is attractive in Singapore's context. It is, however, a costly service, and the IMC has noted that case management needs to be closely targeted to those who need it most, namely the poorly-educated senior citizens without families or the frail senior citizens with multiple needs and problems (Ministry of Community Development, 1999b).

Eligibility criteria for the pilot project were frail elderly, 60 years and older, regardless of gender or ethnicity, who required three or more community-based services, and whose gross household income did not exceed S$2000 per month. The SAGE project covers applicants in the Central geographical region and the Tsao Foundation project covers the Western region. At present, the National Council of Social Service funded the project, including the salaries of the staff, but in time it may be expanded to higher income groups on a paid basis.

The SAGE Case Management Service offers more than 15 different types of services to a caseload of 76 clients, as of January 2000. The initial holistic assessment is very thorough, covering demographic, family, medical, financial, and psychosocial dimensions. Most referrals to date have come from a government hospital in the Central region, and other sources include family service centers and VWOs. The staff includes two professionals and one administrative support officer. A brokerage model is used, whereby no direct service is rendered but the case manager taps the community-based services and coordinates them for the client's benefit. During the two-year pilot period, the service has been provided free of charge to users.

The problems identified in this pilot project have been a shortage and lack of training of volunteers, pressure of time when services must be arranged prior to a client's discharge from hospital, monitoring of quality and efficiency of services, and lastly, difficulties in meeting ethnic preferences of diet of the clients, especially minority groups. Much time is spent building rapport with family members where they are involved since a family-oriented approach is applied.

While the case-management team at SAGE consists of social workers, the Tsao Foundation team consists of a psychologist and a retired nurse. This team is linked to a home medical team at the Tsao Foundation's Hua Mei Clinic, facilitating provision of immediate medical care and guidance where necessary. The SAGE team relies on doctors from the hospital of referral as well as nurses from the Home Nursing Foundation for medical support. At the end of the pilot project, the NCSS conducted an evaluation to determine the feasibility of continuation of the project. Positive outcomes were identified, thus leading to the expansion of the Case Management Service to three organizations altogether.

Current Issues–Future Challenges

In the Singapore context, the mechanism of IMCs has proved to be highly effective. The Committee consists of high-level representatives from the ministries concerned, as well as other relevant statutory boards and selected voluntary welfare organizations. At the initial stage, the IMC is assigned the task of collating data as well as feedback from the public with regard to the matter at hand. At the later stage, when the report of the IMC is released, the status of the Committee can change into a standing Committee. The standing IMC is a national-level, policymaking and decision-taking tool established by the state to integrate policies and services in a particular sector or for a particular population. The IMC on Ageing Population currently oversees the implementation of the recommendations of the Report. Needed resources, such as funding and staff, are also channeled to the respective sector to ensure that the process is smooth and efficient. In multidisciplinary areas such as aging, where several ministries are involved, such a strategy is highly apt and effective. With the state's backing, the recommendations tend to be translated into reality with minimum barriers.

Through 1999, six working groups convened by the Inter-Ministerial Committee on the Aging Population provided the means for assessing the present status of Singapore's long-term care services and identifying the issues that will have to be addressed to meet future needs. The working groups have been effective in generating feedback from various sectors of the population, and the IMC has initiated the crafting of a national strategy to deal with the challenges of an aging society in the coming decades. The scope of the IMC illustrates that long-term care is viewed in the wider context of aging in Singapore.

As a standing committee of the government, the IMC oversees the implementation of the resulting recommendations. It also serves as a coordinating body between the relevant Ministries, thus enhancing the prospects for a system of integrated service delivery. In its 1999 report, the IMC put forward proposals for two major service innovations and made six other suggestions for consideration by policymakers. It was clear from the outset that the IMC would be a standing committee, tasked to "Steer and guide the comprehensive, holistic and coordinated development of policies and programs for the elderly; review such policies and programs periodically..." (*Straits Times*, 15/11/98).

Service innovations

The first proposal for service innovation was the establishment of Multi-Service Centres across the island. These centers are conceptualized as centralized locations for the integration of health, social, and other community-based services. When implemented, they would contribute to boosting the array of services that are available but not easily accessible for the elderly and their families. The Multi-Service Centres would be at the core of the Five-Year Strategic Plan for an aging population. The government has announced its intention to allocate $(Singapore) 30 million towards setting up three centers to be ready by 2005.

The second proposal is for Golden Manpower Centres (GMCs), which would work with the Ministry of Manpower Career Centres and provide information, training, job placement, and access to voluntary work for older workers and retired people, particularly those with less education. Low-income elderly tend to form the majority of older workers who are least likely to find jobs due to their low levels of education and lack of skills. If these GMCs can provide training as well as job placement, poverty and health deterioration could be prevented. Retirement age in Singapore is currently 62, but the labor participation rate of those between the ages 55–62 years is relatively low. In 1997, the labor force participation rate for older persons 55–64 years was only 43%, while in Japan it was 67%, and the GMCs are seen as having a role in keeping more older workers in the workforce.

Policy issues

The first of the five policy issues identified by the IMC is how to contain the cost pressures associated with demands for setting up more and more institutional care programs. The pressures are largely coming from

Table 3.   Projected Need for Elderly Health Services, 2000 to 2030

Types of Services	Planning Ratio Per 1000 Aged 65 and Over	Projection Number of Places Needed				
		1997	2000	2010	2020	2030
Day Rehabilitation and Day Care Places*	3.5 places per 1,000	761 (701)	821 [820]	1,100	1,900	2,800
Home Medical Care	5 elderly needing 1 visit per month per 1,000	1,087 (750)	1,173 [825]	1,600	2,700	4,000
Home Nursing	15 elderly needing 2 visits per month per 1,000	6,522 (5,000)	7,035 [5,500]	9,400	15,900	24,000
Home Help	4 per 1000 needing daily visits	870 (255)	938 [300]	1,250	2,120	3,200
Acute Geriatric Beds	1 per 1000 elderly	217 (188)	235 [226]	310	530	800
Geriatric Specialist	1 per 10,000 elderly	22 (15)	25 [21]	30	55	80
Community Hospital Beds*	3.5 per 1000 elderly	761 (426)	820 [426]	1090	1855	2800
Chronic sick Beds*	1.5 per 1000 elderly	326 (218)	352 [218]	480	800	1200
Nursing Home Beds incl. for dementia patients*	28 beds per 1000	6087 (4703)	6566 [5635]	8800	14,900	22,400

Notes: ( ) availability in 1997
[ ] estimated availability in year 2000
*Estimated availability will improve by the year 2003: Community Hospital Beds to 940, Chronic Sick Hospital Beds to 400 and Nursing Home Beds to 7300

Source: Report of the Inter-Ministerial Committee on Health-Care for Elderly, 1999

families seeking alternative care arrangements, as well as from hospitals wanting to discharge patients who no longer require acute care. In seeking a balance between institutional and community-based services, projections of future needs have been made by the IMC, as set out in Table 3. It is evident that community services are already lagging behind the planning ratios, especially in home nursing and home help. Substantial additional resources are needed to reach the targets set for community care services in the future, but these resources are still fewer than those required for institutional care even within the target levels. Unless strictly controlled, expansion of institutional services will place an even greater burden on the government, which in turn would lead to higher taxation on the public, and at the same time, undermine the development of community care.

The path that Singapore intends to take is to examine how more preventive and community-based programs can be organized and delivered effectively in an integrated manner. This approach is consistent with the overall national policy of encouraging active and successful aging. The community emphasis will make services accessible and enable aging-in-place for the elderly, with concomitant community mobilization. It is believed that such a strategy will make the programs more cost-effective and help the elderly and their families to remain independent.

The second policy issue concerns manpower for long-term care. The combination of a well-educated, highly skilled labor force and a high demand for labor in Singapore means that, along with many areas of economic activity, long-term care faces a shortage of trained nurses, occupational therapists, and physiotherapists. A large proportion of staff aides in residential care institutions already consists of foreign workers, giving rise to cultural and communication problems. Residential care facilities and day care centers must train these staff members in the areas of dialects, attitudes, and skills in working with older people, in particular the frail and terminally ill. Another area that is likely to demand more attention in future is the training of family caregivers and volunteers to increase their effectiveness.

Third, in canvassing the need for more innovative elderly services suited to the local context to further the development of community-based long-term care, the promotion of community care cooperatives has been seriously discussed. The National Trade Union Congress (NTUC) has embarked on its first Eldercare Cooperative. As conceived, these cooperatives would provide a range of services at affordable rates, including home help, meal service, transport and escort service, employment placement, and day care. Members of the cooperatives would be eligible for rebates if they choose to use the services. Community mobilization of retirees, housewives, and even students looking for part-time employment could provide the much-needed manpower. For transport, voluntary organizations and residents could form a transport pool to meet the needs of elderly who require transport and companionship for the purpose of follow-up medical treatment. A well-managed database could match needs of residents in the vicinity with organizations and suppliers of skills or equipment. The cooperatives can be viable because volunteers and some paid staff will manage them on a not-for-profit basis. The notion of the common ownership of the cooperative *by* the members and *for* the members will be the key to the success of such cooperatives. Other innovative ideas have been proposed to expand services such as telephone contact, community kitchens manned by ethnic self-help community organizations, and caregiver support groups, as well as elderly self-help groups.

The growth of service provision through involving community organizations is highly consistent with the government policy of encouraging affordable and accessible community-based services. A further important corollary of this approach is that services provided by community organizations do not carry the stigma that is often attached to usage of "voluntary welfare" services. The emphasis on self-help organizations is also aimed at reducing the burden of expensive health and personal care of older relatives for their families, and these innovative programs are meant to provide more options for Singaporeans in addition to the ones that already exist.

The fourth policy issue concerns the need to nurture leaders and managers with vision and creativity. Problem solving in creative and cost-effective ways will be a major challenge to voluntary welfare bodies because demand for managerial staff exceeds the supply in many areas. Further, the spirit of voluntarism in Singapore is relatively low compared to many western countries. With less than 10% of the population involved in voluntary activities, it will be necessary to recruit more volunteers for community-based programs. One step toward this goal was the setting up of a National Volunteer Centre in 1998 to coordinate and promote the spirit of voluntarism. The healthy young old, those aged 55–65 years, are a potential target group to involve, bearing in mind their ability to empathize with problems of old age.

The fifth area for policy attention is the need for more research and data on the future needs of elderly cohorts. Both quantitative and qualitative data are needed to assist the process of planning of appropriate services and programs for future decades. Thus far, the emphasis has been on health and financial needs. However, social care must be factored in if a comprehensive plan is to be put in place for the future. This task is more challenging because social needs are more difficult to project.

Conclusion

The future of long-term care in Singapore will be shaped by the extent to which the recommendations of the IMC are implemented.

The announcement made by the Minister for Community Development and Sports at the opening of the Regional Gerontological Conference in January 2001, in which he outlined the Five-Year Masterplan of Elder Care Services, reflects the endorsement of a number of recommendations of the IMCs on Health Care and Ageing Population. In particular, the initiatives regarding Multi-Service Centres, community support for caregivers, and revamping of the funding formula for VWOs were emphasized.

The suggestions put forward in the IMC Reports first must be systematically examined by the government through its various ministries and, if feasible, implemented over the next five years as far as possible. The Singapore government has taken a different route from other countries, where policy challenges of preparing for an aging population are assigned to specific administrative bodies established for that purpose. Since Singapore is such a small country, geographically as well as population-wise, this path seems to be appropriate for its use, phased in over a specified time frame. The administrative functions of the IMC on Ageing Population are executed by the Elderly Development Division, which is located in the Ministry of Community Development and Sports.

Singapore has the advantage of a stable economic and political climate, a powerful factor in ensuring continuity of strategies and programs not only for economic development but also for social and health services.

Since the aging challenge affects almost every sector of Singaporean society, the government has decided on a holistic response involving several ministries, voluntary welfare organizations, the private sector, and even aging families. While Singapore is not a welfare state, the government takes a leading role in framing social policy. Thus, not only does the government promote the attitude that the public should look upon aging as a personal responsibility, shared with their immediate families; it also seeks to provide a social infrastructure in which these responsibilities can be realized. In so doing, the Asian cultural ethos of communal reciprocity as a public good is harnessed as a way of positive response to the societal challenge of an aging society.

References

Atchley, R. (2000). *Social Forces and Aging: An Introduction to Gerontology* (9th Ed.) Wadsworth: Singapore.

Austin, C. (1986). Case management in long-term care. In *C. Meyer's Social Work and Aging* (2nd Ed.). National Association of Social Workers. Silver Spring: MD.

Challis, D., & Davies, B. (1986). *Case Management in Community Care: An Evaluated Experiment in the Home Care of the Elderly*. Gower Publishing: Aldershot, UK.

Cheung, P.L. (1993). Population ageing in Singapore. *Asia Pacific Journal of Social Work*, *3*(2): 77–89.

Economic and Social Commission for Asia and the Pacific (1996*). Population Ageing in Asia and the Pacific*. ESCAP, Bangkok, with Japanese Organisation for International Cooperation in Family Planning, Inc., Tokyo. United Nations: New York.

Gordon, D., & and Donald, S. (1993). *Community Social Work, Older People and Informal Care: A Romantic Illusion?* Avebury: Aldershot, UK.

Greene, V.L., Ondrich, J., & Laditka, S. (1998). Can home care services achieve cost savings in long-term care for older people? *Journal of Gerontology*, *53B*(4): 228–328.

Knodel, J., & Debavalya, N. (1997). Living arrangements and support among the elderly in South-East Asia: An introduction. *Asia-Pacific Population Journal*, *12*(4): 5–16.

Kua, E.H. (1987). Psychological distress for families caring for frail elderly. *Singapore Medical Journal*, *3*: 42–44.

Mehta, K. (2000). Caring for the elderly in Singapore. In W. Liu & H. Kendig (Eds.). *Who Should Give Care to the Elderly? An East-West Social Value Divide*. Singapore University Press: Singapore.

Ministry of Community Development (1998). *Because We Care: Guidelines for Community-Based Services for Elderly*. Ministry of Community Development: Singapore.

Ministry of Community Development (1999b). *Report of the Inter-Ministerial Committee on the Ageing Population*. Ministry of Community Development: Singapore.

Ministry of Health (1984). *Report of the Committee on the Problems of the Aged*. Ministry of Health: Singapore.

Ministry of Health (1999a). *Report of the Inter-Ministerial Committee on Health Care for the Elderly*. Ministry of Health: Singapore.

Ministry of Health, Ministry of Community Development, Department of Statistics and National Council of Social Services (1996). *National Survey of Senior Citizens in Singapore*. National Press: Singapore.

Pelham, A., & Clark, W. (Eds.) (1986). *Managing Home Care for the Elderly*. Springer Publishing: New York.

Prescott, N. (Ed.) (1998). *Proceedings of a Conference on Choices in Financing Health Care and Old Age Security*. World Bank Discussion Paper No. 2. World Bank. Washington, DC: USA.

Richards, M. (1996). *Community Care for Older People: Rights, Remedies and Finances*. Jordans: Bristol, UK.

Schneider, R., Kropf, N., & Kisor, A. (2000). *Gerontological Social Work: Knowledge, Service Settings, and Special Populations*. Brooks/Cole: Australia.

Shantakumar, G. (1994). *The Aged Population of Singapore*. Census of Population 1990, Monograph No. 1, Singapore.

Shantakumar, G. (1995). Aging and social policy in Singapore. *Ageing International*, 22(2): 49–54.

Siegel, J.S., & Hoover, S.L. (1982). Demographic aspects of health of the elderly to the year 2000 and beyond. *World Health Statistics Quarterly*, 35(3/4): 140–141.

Singapore Action Group of Elders (SAGE) (1998). *Case Management Service*. SAGE: Singapore.

Straits Times (1998). *Committee's 21 Members Named*. Singapore, November 15.

Teo, P. (1994). The national policy on elderly people in Singapore. *Ageing and Society*, 14: 405–427.

World Health Organization (1995). *World Health Report, 1995. Bridging the Gaps*. WHO: Geneva.

Chapter 5

Building a Social Network for Older Adults: A Nation-wide Initiative by the Singapore Silver Generation Office*

Corinne Ghoh and Andrew Sim

Abstract

This chapter discusses the national initiative by the Singapore Silver Generation Office (SGO) in building a social network of support for older adults with the aim to enhance health and social outcomes in a rapidly ageing society. The discussions entail how the SGO seeks to build social capital at both the micro and macro levels to improve the social- and health-related outcomes of older adults in Singapore, and examine the issues involved in building a support network and the implications moving forward.

---

*The views expressed in this chapter are the authors and do not represent the views of the Agency for Integrated Care.

Introduction

Singapore is ageing rapidly. The census population[1] showed that in the year 2020, the resident population aged 65 years and above constituted 15.2%. This is an increase of 6.2% compared to the year 2010. This puts Singapore on the ranks of an aged society, which is defined by United Nations as one in which more than 14% of the population is 65 years and above. By 2030, Singapore will be classified as a super-aged society with more than 20% of its population aged 65 years and above. Singaporeans are also living longer with average life expectancy at birth at 83.9 years. Alongside the speed of ageing, there are structural changes to the demography of the family. The average household size has decreased from 3.5 people in 2010 to 3.2 people in 2020. The proportion of resident households with at least a member aged 65 years and over increased from 24.1% in 2010 to 34.5% in 2020. Households with all members aged 65 years and above had risen from 4.6% in 2010 to 9.3% in 2020. The resident total fertility rate remains below the replacement rate at 1.10. The implications of the changing demographic trends are that the smaller family households would need support with care of their older members and that older adults living on their own would need support to age well in the community.

At an older life stage, the functional decline could lead to lower quality of life as some individuals may find it harder to maintain their social networks given their declining capacities and changes in the life cycle such as changes in life events. Indeed, this is a major concern of countries as research has shown that social isolation and loneliness of older adults are detrimental to health outcomes and could lead to increased risk of mortality.[2] With longer life expectancy of Singaporeans, there is

---

[1] Department of Statistics, Singapore, https://www.singstat.gov.sg/find-data/search-by-theme/population/elderly-youth-and-gender-profile/latest-data.

[2] Holt-Lunstad, J., Smith, Mark Baker, T. B., Harris, T. and Stephenson, D. "Loneliness and Social Isolation as Risk Factors for Mortality: A Meta-Analytic Review," *Perspectives on Psychological Science*, 10(2), 2015, 227–237; Luo, Y., Hawkley, L. C., Waite, L. J. and Cacioppo, J. T. "Loneliness, Health, and Mortality in Old Age: A National Longitudinal Study," *Social Science & Medicine*, 74, 2012, 907–914; and Kaye, L. W. and Singer, C. M. "The Scourge of Social Isolation and Its Threat to Older Adult Health," in L. W. Kaye and

potential to capitalise on the strengths and assets of the older adults so that they continue to live well in an aged and soon-to-be super-aged society and contribute meaningfully to society. In the next decade, the building of a social network for older people is critical to enhance lives of older adults and in supporting families in caring for their older members.

This chapter discusses the development of a nationwide programme by the Singapore Silver Generation Office (SGO) in reaching out to older persons aged 65 years and above with the view of connecting them with government policies and schemes that would benefit them and in building a cohesive community that enables older adults to age actively without feeling isolated or lonely.[3] The discussions will entail how the SGO seeks to build social capital at both micro and macro levels in tackling the social- and health-related outcomes of older persons in Singapore and highlight implications on the way forward.

Building Social Capital for Productive Ageing

With longevity, it is opportune to focus attention on how older people can continue to live well and be productive citizens. The premise behind the concept of productive ageing is that the skills, expertise and experience of individuals in later life can be put to better use.[4] This is contrary to the traditional view of seeing ageing as an unproductive life stage where one leaves the workplace and reduces the contribution in the economic realm. It is critical that we see productivity beyond the labour market to the social realm where older adults are actively engaged in families, communities and society at large.[5] In the life course, older people have been contribut-ing members of society, caring for their families and loved ones,

C. M. Singer (eds.), *Social Isolation of Older Adults: Strategies to Bolster Health and Well-being*, (Springer Publishing Company, 2019).

[3] Ministerial Committee on Ageing, (Singapore: Ministry of Health).

[4] Morrow-Howell, N., Hinterlong, J. and Sherraden, M. *Productive Aging: Concepts and Challenges*, (Johns Hopkins University Press, 2001).

[5] Hinterlong, J., Morrow-Howell, N. and Sherraden, M. "Productive Aging: Principles and Perspectives," in N. Morrow-Howell, J. Hinterlong and M. Sherraden (eds.), *Productive Aging: Concepts and Challenges*, (Johns Hopkins University Press, 2001).

performing volunteering work and in supporting various causes in the community and society. We need to take an active interest to recognise the present and potential contributions of older adults, harness their strengths and enable them to continue to lead productive lives. In the context of Singapore, there is a wealth of resources that can be tapped on the expertise of older adults in various settings including the workplace, families, neighbourhood and community spaces. The building of social capital and a social network for older adults would provide opportunities for enabling active engagement of all citizens in an ageing society and, in particular, in the promotion of productive ageing.

Social capital is defined as a collective attribute of communities or societies and is operationalised by the norms of trustworthiness and reciprocity and the density of social networks.[6] Social capital focuses on resources embodied in social relations and social networks that bond families, friends and neighbours. The settings can be extended to workplaces and in communities including virtual communities which connect individuals via the Internet.[7] Social networks are critical to enable people to have access to others for social support. Social support can be broadly defined as support in the emotional, informational and instrumental areas.[8] This means that the characteristics of the social network matter on the type and amount of assistance that one can gain access to. Research has shown that social connections correlate with subjective social well-being of individuals, which is predicted by the breadth and depth of one's social connections.[9] The building of a social network is hence a powerful asset for both the individuals and the communities as support mechanisms to enhance quality of life. In the context of ageing, the building of social

[6] Putnam, R. D. "Tuning In, Tuning Out: The Strange Disappearance of Social Capital in America," *Political Science and Politics*, 28, 1995, 664–683.
[7] Lin, N. and Erickson, B. H. "Theory, Measurement, and the Research Enterprise on Social Capital," in *Social Capital: An International Research Program*, (Oxford University Press, 2008).
[8] Cook, J. R. "Strategies for Building Social Capital," in A. G. Greenberg, T. P. Gullotta and M. Bloom (eds.), *Social Capital and Community Well-being: The Serve Here Initiative*, (Springer International Publishing Switzerland, 2016).
[9] Helliwell, J. F. and Putnam, R. D. "The Social Context of Well-being," *The Royal Society*, 359, 2004, 1435–1446.

capital for older people will contribute to addressing issues of social isolation and loneliness as the social network formed could provide them with social support to better their quality of life.

A Singapore study by Lane *et al.* (2020)[10] which involved 981 older adults aged 55 years and above living in residential community dwelling showed that the social characteristics of neighbourhoods, which included neighbours, families and friends, played a key role in enhancing the quality of life of older adults and in addressing the risk of social isolation and loneliness. The findings showed that the cognitive aspect of social capital is key to enhancing the quality of life of older people. The study demonstrated the importance of promoting stronger links and interdependency amongst neighbours for better health outcomes. However, building community and neighbourliness takes time. The fast speed of ageing requires Singapore to take a quicker measure to reach out to older adults who are vulnerable and need support. What are other options to promote healthy ageing if the neighbourhood is not bonded or cohesive? Can we build a social network of support for older adults so that there remain opportunities for older adults to lead productive lives and that those who require some social support can gain easy access to them? The establishment of the SGO seeks to build bonds and bridge the social connections for the older adults in Singapore, especially those who are living on their own and are socially isolated from the rest of their communities.

The Establishment of the Silver Generation Office

Background

The establishment of the SGO in 2018 took an incremental approach through the integration of initiatives of the Pioneer Generation Office (PGO) and the Community Networks for Seniors (CNS) of which details will be provided below. The setup allows scaling of capabilities to reach out and connect with older adults and in mobilising the

---

[10] Lane, A. P., Wong, C. H., Mocnik, S., Song, S. and Yuen, B. "Association of Neighborhood Social Capital with Quality of Life Among Older People," *Journal of Aging and Health*, 2020, 32(7–8), 841–850.

community to be partners in providing support to those who are frail and vulnerable.

Pioneer Generation Office

In 2014, the Singapore government announced an S$8 billion Pioneer Generation Package (PGP) to meet the healthcare needs of the cohort of Pioneer Generation (PG), who were at least 16 years old in 1965 and includes those who became citizens before 1987.[11] An estimated 450,000 older citizens met the criteria to receive the benefits. The roll out of the PGP is to honour these pioneers for their early nation-building efforts for Singapore. The intent is to meet their healthcare needs as ground feedback showed that the long-term healthcare cost was the top worry of these citizens. The three key components to the PGP are (i) subsidies for outpatient care, (ii) Medisave Top-ups and (iii) MediShield Life (a public health insurance scheme) subsidies. The PGP enables the older citizens to enjoy generous subsidies for outpatient medical treatment, and for those with disabilities, they will receive an additional cash assistance of S$1,200 per year to support their caregiving needs under the Pioneer Generation Disability Assistance scheme. In addition, the older adults will receive annual Medisave top-ups of S$200 to S$800, and these are on top of other existing schemes enjoyed by older Singaporeans. MediShield Life insurance coverage is provided to this cohort of the PG including those with preexisting conditions, and special subsidies are given to ensure that the premiums are affordable. Those who are less well-off will benefit more from the PGP.

While the PGP benefits would go a long way to support the older adults, it was reported that PGs faced challenges gaining access to the information as the financial schemes were complex in design with multitiers of subsidies.[12] This made communication with PGs difficult given

---

[11] Ministry of Finance Singapore, Budget Speech 2014. Opportunities for the Future, Assurance for our Seniors. https://www.mof.gov.sg/docs/default-source/default-document-library/singapore-budget/budget-archives/2014/fy2014_budget_statement.pdf.

[12] Lai, S. H. "Communicating to Our Pioneer Generation. Institute of Governance and Public Policy," *Civil Service College.* Issue 15, 14 June 2016. See https://www.csc.gov.sg/articles/communicating-to-our-pioneer-generation; and Oei, C. "Going The Last Mile for Pioneers:

that many of them are above the age of 75 years and are of lower educational level, and they speak Chinese dialects or their mother tongues. Efforts are needed to reach out to them in a more personalised way so that there is good communication and connections with them. The Pioneer Generation Office (PGO) was set up by the government in 2014 with the strategy to reach out to the older citizens. The PGO deployed some 3,000 volunteers (called Pioneer Generation Ambassadors or PGAs) to make house visits to engage the older persons individually to directly explain the schemes and benefits.[13]

Community Networks for Seniors

In their outreach efforts, the PGAs uncovered the health and social needs of older adults which impacted their well-being and the need to refer and link them with support services.[14] To provide better coordination and support, the Community Networks for Seniors (CNS) pilot initiative was launched in 2016 by the Agency for Integrated Care (AIC)[15] with the aim to work alongside the PGO so that social support could be extended to the older adults in need through a systemic collaboration between government and community-based stakeholders with the aim to maximise resources in the helping process.[16] The CNS was set up to focus on three key areas:

Communicating the Pioneer Generation Package Differently," Challenge, Public Service Division, Singapore, 2016. See https://www.psd.gov.sg/challenge/ideas/feature/going-the-last-mile-for-pioneers-communicating-the-pioneer-generation-package-differently.

[13]Choo, C. "Govt to Expand, Consolidate Social and Health-Related Services for Seniors under Ministry of Health," *Today*, Singapore, 19 December 2018. See https://www.todayonline.com/singapore/govt-expand-consolidate-social-and-health-related-services-seniors-under-ministry-health.

[14]Mokhtar, I. A. "Engaging and Helping Seniors: The Case of the Pioneer Generation Ambassadors in Singapore," *International Journal of Academic Research in Business and Social Sciences*, 10(2), 2020, 439–451.

[15]Agency for Integrated Care is an independent corporate entity under the Ministry of Health Holdings Singapore. It is entrusted with the responsibilities to coordinate the delivery of aged care services across health and social domains and in enhancing service development and capability-building across the sectors. https://www.aic.sg/about-us.

[16]Ministry of Health Singapore website, 19 February 2018, https://www.moh.gov.sg/news-highlights/details/integration-of-health-and-social-services-to-support-seniors.

(i)   *Active ageing*

The intent is to introduce preventive health and active ageing activities and encourage older adults to keep well. Examples include providing health education, health screening and linkages with social interest groups.

(ii)   *Befriending social isolated older adults*

The aim is to work with the community to recruit, train and deploy volunteers to befriend older adults who face higher risk of social isolation.

(iii) *Care and support*

The aim is to assist the frail and vulnerable older adults in navigating and gaining access to systems of help so that they receive the necessary support.

With the above key focus areas, the CNS becomes a strategic entity to mobilise different stakeholders within the community setting to jointly engage and support older people within a locality. The stakeholders who are mobilised include social services agencies, grassroots organisations, regional health systems and government agencies. To illustrate, between the period from April 2016 to February 2018, CNS networked with more than 70 Residents' Committees (which are grassroots organisations) to provide active ageing programmes for some 70,000 older adults and referred more than 600 vulnerable older adults to befriending services. Another 800 older adults with more complex health and social needs were referred to support services for assistance. The successful implementation of the pilot CNS initiative and its abilities to network with community agencies led to the expansion of the CNS on a nationwide basis.[17] The development of the SGO helps integrate the outreach arm of the PGO and support services under the CNS so that there is a continuum of support for the vulnerable older adults.

---

[17] Ministry of Finance Singapore, Budget Speech 2018, "Together a Better Future," https://www.mof.gov.sg/docs/default-source/default-document-library/singapore-budget/budget-archives/2018/fy2018_budget_statement.pdf.

Formation of the Silver Generation Office

In 2018, the AIC being the lead agency in coordinating delivery of aged care services in Singapore, was given the task to integrate the services of the PGO (which is the outreach arm) and the CNS (which is the care and support arm) under the ambit of the SGO. The integration and consolidation of outreach and support services under a central body of the SGO enables a more client-centric approach to connecting with older adults and in the follow-up of support.

The structure and mechanism of SGO came in handy when the Singapore government decided to extend support to the younger cohort of older persons referred to as the *Merdeka* Generation (MG) who are age 60–69 years, though the provision of the *Merdeka* Generation Package (MGP) with funds amounting to S$6.1 billion. The aim is to recognise the MG for their contributions to nation building, particularly in areas of public services, modernisation of the economy and in supporting the forging of a multi-cultural, multi-racial Singapore society. The MGP benefits are largely healthcare related including Medisave top-ups, additional subsidies for outpatient care, Specialist Outpatient Clinics and Medishield Life premium for life. The SGO plays a key role in reaching out to the MG to explain the benefits and assist them to gain access to the schemes and to encourage them to stay active and healthy.[18] With the expansion of the MGP initiative, the SGO could potentially reach out to a network of more than half a million citizens aged 65 years and above.[19]

The SGO's network of outreach was further tapped during COVID-19 situation when the government strongly urged older persons to be vaccinated.[20] The SGO was able to engage more than 670,000 persons aged 60

---

[18] Ministry of Finance Singapore, Budget 2019, "Building a Strong United Singapore," https://www.mof.gov.sg/docs/default-source/default-document-library/singapore-budget/budget-archives/2019/fy2019_budget_statement.pdf.

[19] Choo, C. "Govt to Expand, Consolidate Social and Health-Related Services for Seniors Under Ministry of Health," *Today Newspaper*, 19 December 2018. See https://www.today-online.com/singapore/govt-expand-consolidate-social-and-health-related-services-seniors-under-ministry-health.

[20] Begum, S. "Nationwide Vaccinations Begin for Seniors Aged 70 and Above," *The Straits Times*, 23 February 2021, Singapore.

and above on the safety of COVID-19 vaccination and supported those who needed help in getting vaccinated.[21] For older persons with mobility issues or whose caregivers have difficulty taking them for their vaccine jabs, the SGO arranged for them to be escorted to nearby vaccination centres or arranged with the Ministry of Health (MOH) for them to be vaccinated at home. For older adults with underlying medical conditions, the SGO coordinated with the MOH to bring forward their medical appointments so they could consult their doctors on their suitability for vaccination. The older adults and their caregivers were provided with a SGO hotline number to call for advice and assistance.

The formation of the SGO at the AIC has strengthened the partnerships between the government and the community sector and in creating opportunities for further enhancements in aligning outreach, scheme applications and services referrals on the ground.[22] Within a short span of three years, the SGO's structure has been heavily tapped to reach out to vulnerable older persons.

Strategies in Building a Social Network for Older Adults

The building of social capital and social network in age-related outcomes in the context of the SGO can be viewed from both micro and macro system level perspectives. The micro strategies of building a trusting relationship with older adults and generating social support will be discussed. At the macro level, issues relating to volunteerism by old and young, and building social support through networking with external agencies will be elaborated.

Micro-level social capital perspective

Building trusting relationship with older adults

The building of social capital at the micro level can be seen in how the SGO officers and volunteers establish contact and build rapport with the

---

[21] Ang, S. "Over 670,000 Seniors Covered in Outreach Efforts on Vaccination," *The Straits Times*, 18 November 2021, Singapore.

[22] Ministry of Health Singapore, https://www.moh.gov.sg/news-highlights/details/integration-of-health-and-social-services-to-support-seniors.

older generations. The SGO has a staff strength of about 500 and it works through 20 satellite offices located in the heartland of Singapore. The decentralisation model enables the SGO to put a face of its existence at the community level where support and assistance are easily accessible to the older persons. Given that the government schemes involve multiple tiers of subsidy, it is not easy for the older generation to understand the intricacies and if they would benefit from the schemes. Personalising contact is key, and staff and volunteers went through series of training to enhance their communication skills and knowledge on the various schemes. Furthermore, as Singapore is a multi-racial society, it is critical that the messages are conveyed sensitively taking into consideration the cultural context.

To illustrate the personalised approach, in the process of outreach, a specially designed welcome package with an appreciation message penned by Singapore Prime Minister Lee Hsien Loong was presented at the house visits to affirm the message of how the government cares and would provide for welfare of the older citizens.[23] Findings from a survey conducted showed that the awareness of the PGP rose significantly from 65% to 95% from July to September 2014 and that a majority of older citizens felt assured and perceived that the government was sincere in its effort to honour them.[24] The personalised communication was reported to be well received by the PGs.

Besides educating the older adults on the various schemes that would benefit them, the SGO also provides assurance of support through practical actions like assisting the older persons to apply to the schemes and facilitating direct referrals to services for support. The various actions helped to reinforce a sense of trustworthiness of the SGO of being a reliable agent for support. At the community level, the face of the SGO became better known to the older adults and families, particularly during the COVID-19 situation with media reporting on how the SGO extended help for the vulnerable older adults.[25] The SGO is also on Facebook where

---

[23] Hao, L. S. "Communicating to Our Pioneer Generation," *Institute of Governance and Public Policy, Civil Service College*. Issue 15, 14 June 2016. https://www.csc.gov.sg/articles/communicating-to-our-pioneer-generation.

[24] Hao, L. S. "Communicating to Our Pioneer Generation. Institute of Governance and Public Policy," *Civil Service College*, Issue 15, 14 June 2016.

[25] Ang, S. "Over 670,000 Seniors Covered in Outreach Efforts on Vaccination," *The Straits Times*, 18 November 2021, Singapore.

there is direct showcase of its work and connections with volunteers, older adults and the community.[26] The building of relationship and trust between the state through the SGO and the older adults is critical as trust is a moral resource and if built on, will enhance cooperation of the participants.[27]

Generating social support with community partners

Research has shown that social relationships bring health benefits, and the bonds formed are protective against mortality risks.[28] As such, the building of social bonds at the micro level is critical, especially for older adults who are socially isolated from the community and are vulnerable due to unmet needs and other social circumstances. The SGO's outreach would help establish the social connections with these vulnerable older persons and identify those who may be at risk or in distress. In some situations, immediate assistance is extended at the frontline due to social or medical emergencies. For example, at a house visit, an SGO officer found an older adult staying alone with stroke symptoms and needing urgent assistance. The ambulance was called, and the older adult was admitted to the hospital for urgent medical attention. What is noteworthy is that the SGO officer stayed with the older adult and provided some comfort and emotional support till the ambulance arrived.

In situations where the older adults presented multiple needs and would benefit from more in-depth assessment, the SGO officers would do a referral to its CNS team to conduct further inquiry and to propose an action plan of support for the vulnerable older person. This may involve linkages with social services and community organisations. The social network of support for older adults built through the SGO generates ties of social support. According to House and Kahn (1985),[29] social support is *"the functional content of relationships such as the degree to which the*

[26] Silver Generation Office Facebook, https://www.facebook.com/silvergenerationoffice/.

[27] Putnam, R. D. "Making Democracy Work-Civic Traditions in Modern Italy," Princeton University Press, 1993, p. 167.

[28] Litwin, H. and Shiovitz-Ezra, S. "Network Type and Mortality Risk in Later Life," *Gerontologist*, 46, 2006, 735–743.

[29] House, J. S. and Kahn, R. L. "Measures and Concepts of Social Support," in S. Cohen and S. L. Synme (eds.), *Social Support and Health*, (Orlando, FL: Academic Press, Inc., 1985), pp. 83–105.

relationships involve flow of affect or emotional concern, instrumental or tangible aid, information and the like". The strengths of the social network of support were evident in the COVID-19 situation. During circuit breakers[30] where citizens had to stay home and all social activities were stopped, many older adults who lacked social support were negatively impacted. They needed help in their activities of daily living. The SGO through its volunteer network reached out to some 47,000 older adults and assisted them in various ways including delivering cooked meals, grocery shopping and simple household maintenance work. The SGO also used tele-engagements to reach out to some 20,000 vulnerable older adults to check in regularly on their overall well-being.[31] The human connections during the pandemic brought comfort to the older people who were homebound for prolonged periods. They were relieved that there was someone to talk to and knew that they were not alone. The SGO became their lifeline in case of need and is their social support.

Macro-level social capital

Promoting active ageing through networking with the community

In the respective communities, the SGO could tap on formal and informal resources to promote active ageing or initiate programmes to support older adults. For example, a programme called "Wellness Time" is a suite of regular active ageing and preventive health programmes including health screening, exercise classes, health talks and social activities introduced at community facilities island-wide to encourage older adults to keep active, healthy and socially engaged.[32] The intent is to promote preventive health by encouraging older persons to be more proactive in managing their own health and to age well. In linking older adults with community resources, it would enlarge the network of support for older

---

[30] Gov.sg portal. Singapore Ministry of Communication and Information. https://www.gov.sg/article/what-you-can-and-cannot-do-during-the-circuit-breaker-period.

[31] Agency for Integrated Care. "Apart But Not Alone — How SGO Helped Seniors During COVID-19," https://www.aic-blog.com/apart-not-alone-how-sgo-helped-seniors-during-covid-19.

[32] Ministry of Health Singapore, https://www.moh.gov.sg/ifeelyoungsg/how-can-we-build-stronger-ties/care-for-a-senior.

adults within respective community settings. This opens opportunities for the older adults to make new friends and be known to the community at large. In times of need, the social network of support can be mobilised, and help can be extended by the community. The reciprocal effect is that the community at large is educated on ageing issues, acquires knowledge on active ageing and can be mobilised to support older adults in their communities.

Senior volunteerism

Senior volunteerism in the context of the SGO contributes to building social capital of older people. Theoretical perspectives on senior volunteerism showed that volunteerism can prepare and empower older people to age well.[33] The activity theory, for example, suggests that activities are positively related to life satisfaction.[34] Volunteerism not only provides older people with opportunities to have meaningful activities but it is also an avenue for them to find substitutes for roles losses in their later life. Further, volunteerism is found to be an empowering process for older people as it can help enhance one's self esteem and image, and it can help in eliminating a sense of helplessness and powerlessness, and enhance self-efficacy.[35] A local study on volunteerism using data drawn from Singapore Longitudinal Ageing Studies, which involved 2,716 Singaporeans aged 55 or above at baseline and 1,754 at two-year follow-up, showed that older persons who volunteered had better cognitive performance scores, had fewer depressive symptoms and had better mental well-being and life satisfaction compared to the non-volunteering group.[36]

---

[33] Kam, P.-K. "Senior Volunteerism and Empowerment," *Pacific Journal of Social Work and Development*, 12(1), 2012, 112–133.

[34] Havighurst, R. J. and Albrecht, R. *Older People*, (New York: Longman, Green, 1953).

[35] Kam, P.-K. "Senior Volunteerism and Empowerment," *Pacific Journal of Social Work and Development*, 12(1), 2012, 112–133.

[36] Schwingel, A., Niti, M. M., Tang, C. and Ng, T. P. "Continued Work Employment and Volunteerism and Mental Well-being of Older Adults: Singapore Longitudinal Ageing Studies," *Age and Ageing*, 38, 2009, 531–537.

The SGO has the support of some 3,000 volunteers (called the Silver Generation Ambassadors) and slightly over 70% are aged 50 years and above. The proportion of older volunteers seems large compared to national statistics where senior volunteerism rate was only 26% in 2018 for those age 54–64 years and the percentage declined to 15% for those above the age of 65 years.[37] The older volunteers are much valued as many of them speak Chinese dialects or mother tongues, which are essential in communication and rapport building with the older adults who are in the older age category. Volunteering with the SGO offers the opportunities for older individuals to contribute to a meaningful cause, and at the same time enables them to build new friendships and relationships with others in the community. However, it is not easy to recruit and sustain older volunteers. A study by the National Volunteer and Philanthropy Centre in 2018 involving some 1,000 older adults aged 50 years and above showed that a majority placed priorities on leading a healthy life and having a relaxing time over contributions to society.[38] Furthermore, despite knowing societal needs, many older adults doubt their abilities to volunteer. As such, the SGO's recruitment strategies and volunteer management approach for older volunteers have to take into consideration the needs and preferences of older adults. More public education on the benefits and value of volunteering can be carried out to encourage older adults to volunteer and contribute to the work of the SGO.

Building social capital through inter-generational connections

The participation of the younger generation is critical to facilitate and support the development of social network for older adults. The SGO provides volunteering opportunities to the younger adults and allows them to be connected with the older generation. The inter-generational contacts of the young and older generations can have a positive impact of enabling both generations to understand the respective life experiences and create

---

[37] Individual Giving Study 2018 — Silver V Study. National Volunteer and Philanthropy Centre. https://cityofgood.sg/resources/individual-giving-study-2018-silver-v-study/.
[38] *Ibid.*

inter-generational solidarity and a sense of community.[39] With better understanding between generations, it helps to combat issues of ageism and foster a greater sense of empathy across generations. In their outreach home visits, the younger volunteers are exposed to the problems of ageing. Through interaction with the active older volunteers, they gain another perspective of how older people can continue to remain productive and active in society.

In promoting volunteerism, the SGO provides centralised structured training to volunteers, which includes knowledge and skills on engagement, information on programmes on active ageing, and health and social services. Volunteers are given an allowance to defray the costs of volunteering like transport or food, which is helpful for older persons who are retired, and without a stable source of income. On average, each volunteer conducts 85 engagements per year,[40] which translates to 255,000 visits a year or 191,250 hours of volunteering hours (assuming 3,000 volunteers and each visit takes 45 minutes to complete). The return on investment in the promotion of volunteerism cannot be underestimated.

Efforts are put in to recognise and retain volunteers. The introduction of the Silver Generation Ambassador Service Awards seeks to recognise volunteers who have contributed more than 500 hours of volunteering service and the Exemplary Silver Generation Ambassadors Awards recognise outstanding contributions.[41] One example cited was how volunteer Ms. Kalyanasundaram responded to an older adult staying alone who told her that he missed home-cooked Indian food. She found a friend who could cook Indian food and delivered the meals to him. Such human stories of kindness warmed the hearts of many people. The shared experiences and values will create deeper connections and build inter-generational solidarity.[42]

---

[39] Chung, S. and Park, N. S. "Editorial Comment: Intergenerational Issues in a Changing Society of South Korea," *Journal of Intergenerational Relationships*, 19(1), 2021, 1–4.

[40] Ministry of Health Singapore. Silver Generation Office — Home visits. https://www.moh.gov.sg/news-highlights/details/silver-generation-office-(sgo)---home-visits.

[41] Prime Minister's Office Singapore. Speech by PM Lee Hsien Loong at the 5GO Appreciation Reception on 1 September 2019. https://www.pmo.gov.sg/Newsroom/PM-Lee-Hsien-Loong-at-5GO-Appreciation-Reception.

[42] Chung, S., Kim, J. and Hong, Y. "The Effects of Bilateral Intergenerational Program on Intergenerational Perceptions of the Participants," *Journal of Intergenerational Relationships*, 19(1), 2021, 56–77.

Converting social capital to collective efficacy

In interacting with older adults, the SGO staff and volunteers will get to hear views and feedback on their perspectives of government policies, schemes and services. The feedback is valuable in contributing to identifications of gaps in service delivery and policies. For example, when the PGP was first rolled out, the volunteers learnt from older adults that key medications for common medical conditions, such as high cholesterol, diabetes and high blood pressure, were not subsidised. The feedback was forwarded to the authorities for attention.[43] The mechanism of feedback loop to policy makers could strengthen the level of trust with the state and enhance social cohesion, particularly if citizens feel that their voices are heard and the actions taken are of benefit to them. Cagney and Wen (2008)[44] made a distinction between social capital and collective efficacy. While social capital is about relationships, collective efficacy converts those relationships into actions that would bring benefit to everyone. With mutual trust and attachment to the community, collective efficacy will take these relationships further as citizens in the community feel empowered to do something and act on each other's behalf, so that everyone could better their lives. Older adults in general would prefer to age in place and are likely to live in the same community for as long as possible due to familiarity with the environment and bonds formed with the people around them. Living in a cohesive community with collective efficacy will enhance and promote healthy ageing of older people at the community level. The promotion of collective efficacy between the community (including older persons themselves) and the SGO would uplift the level of the helping relationship to one of empowering the community to be actively involved in creative problem solving and not just being reliant on the SGO or the state for solutions. In addition, the SGO could utilise the information it captures through the outreach efforts to identify potential

---

[43] Oei, C. "Going the Last Mile for Pioneers: Communicating the Pioneer Generation Package Differently," *Challenge*, Public Service Division, 11 May 2016. https://www.psd. gov.sg/challenge/ideas/feature/going-the-last-mile-for-pioneers-communicating-the-pioneer-generation-package-differently.

[44] Cagney, K. A. and Wen, M. "Social Capital and Aging-Related Outcomes," in I. Kawachi, S. V. Subramaniam and D. Kim, (eds.), *Social Capital and Health*, (Springer Publishing Company).

gaps in policies and service delivery and contribute to policy planning and service development.

Some Issues on Building a Support Network

The issues pertaining to building a social network can be challenging. First, the success of building a social network hinges on abilities to manage the complexity of human relationships. Beyond systems and structures, building of trust and relationship is critical as this dictates if the individuals feel connected and safe to open up to share their thoughts and concerns, and in turn are motivated to lend a helping hand to others. Dealing with the intangibles is often far more challenging than working with tangibles like providing specific services, as results cannot be easily quantified. Next, there is a need to deal with multiple levels of stakeholders, including with the older adults and their families, the neighbours, community, service providers and the governmental agencies. This requires knowledge and skills in community development and abilities to facilitate, negotiate, problem solve, manage conflict and mobilise resources to meet needs. Finally, there is often a lack of community leadership to direct, facilitate and energise the social network. The lack of leadership can result in the social network becoming deficit in nature, providing unidirectional help to people in need and not capitalising on community assets to resolve issues at the ground.

Moving Forward

Deepening trust, promoting reciprocity and increasing density of social network

The building of social capital entails norms of trust, reciprocity and social network.[45] In reaching out to older adults to communicate benefits of the government policies and schemes that would benefit them, the SGO helps bridge the relationship between older citizens and the state and provides

---

[45] Putnam, R. D. "Tuning In, Tuning Out: The Strange Disappearance of Social Capital in America," *Political Science and Politics*, 28, 1995, 664–683.

assurance that their welfare matters. In this regard, the building of trust with demonstration of how help is delivered to older adults in need is evident through actions taken by the SGO in activating formal services like health and social services, to support the vulnerable older adults. Located within each community setting are informal resources and assets that could be tapped to better the quality of life of older persons. These informal resources include businesses and corporations, self-help groups, faith-based organisations and interest groups, which the SGO could capitalise on to further its work and mobilise support for the cause of supporting older persons within the community. The SGO through the satellite offices located in the heartland of Singapore is best placed to identify community assets and link the resources with older adults to better their lives.

There is a need to continue to deepen trust and enhance the density of social networks of older adults so that the socially isolated individuals are willing and able to reach out to the community in times of need. The density of social networks is made up of individuals who have strong ties to many other individuals, and this forms a strong network of support and would not fall apart easily.[46] The density of social network would mean that the respective communities are the eyes and ears at the ground level to raise concerns to the SGO if the welfare of older adults is compromised. The building of a density of social network for vulnerable older adults will serve as a protective factor in enabling the vulnerable older individuals to be connected with the wider community so that there is early detection of vulnerabilities and risks, and support can be provided early. In particular, older adults who are from the lower socio-economic background would require greater attention as they are at higher risk of health problems due to their social circumstances.[47] The building of a dense social network

---

[46] Bekkers, R., Volker, B., van der Gaag, M. and Flap, H. "Social Networks of Participants in Voluntary Associations," in N. Lin and B. Erikson (eds.), *Social Capital: An International Research Program*, (Oxford University Press, 2008).

[47] Low, L. L., Wah, W., Ng, M. J., Tan, S. Y., Liu, N. and Lee, K. H. "Housing as a Social Determinant of Health in Singapore and Its Association with Readmission Risk and Increased Utilisation of Hospital Services," *Frontiers in Public Health*, 4, 2016, Article 109.

would mitigate the risk factors of mortality, physical and psychological health.[48] The SGO could pay greater attention to deepening the density of social networks of older adults.

Promoting volunteerism and volunteer management

The opportunities for volunteerism at the SGO present strengths of building inter-generational connections as well as in encouraging senior volunteerism, which is a potential growth area in productive ageing. With the ageing of the population and demographic changes, it is anticipated that the pool of younger adults who can be tapped to be volunteers will continue to decline.[49] This is because the younger generation will have less discretionary time to volunteer as they will be heavily involved in supporting the older family members and have other commitments. For the SGO to continue its work in a more sustainable manner, it would be tactical to have a comprehensive plan to tap into the expertise of retired older persons and encourage them to be volunteers. Volunteer management requires knowledge and skills in recruitment, selection, training, supervision, motivation, recognition and retention. Managing senior volunteerism especially requires flexibility and innovative measures to meet diverse needs of older volunteers and their aims in volunteering. In a survey conducted with volunteers above 50 years of age, some challenges pertaining to the physical stamina needed to make house visits, the intellectual abilities to explain the various schemes and stresses in managing rejections from the older adults surfaced as issues for the older volunteers.[50] The findings showed the need to design volunteering tasks that are manageable for the profile of volunteers and provide training support and supervision so that

---

[48] Litwin, H. and Shiovitz-Ezra, S. "Network Type and Mortality Risk in Later Life," *Gerontologist*, 46, 2006, 735–743.

[49] Vasoo, S. "Some Challenges on Managing Volunteers and Enhancing Their Participation in the Social Service Sector," in S. Vasoo, B. Singh and X. J. Chan (eds.), *Community Development Areas in Singapore*, (World Scientific Publishing Co. Pte. Ltd, 2019).

[50] Mokhtar, I. A. "Engaging and Helping Seniors: The Case of the Pioneer Generation Ambassadors in Singapore," *International Journal of Academic Research in Business and Social Sciences*, 10(2), 2020, 439–451.

older volunteers continue to find meaning and fulfilment in their services at the SGO.

Use of strengths-based and empowerment approaches

There is a need to balance meeting the needs of the frail and vulnerable older adults and empowering them to be active agents in the helping process. The current narrative seems to focus much on helping and providing support to the older adults. The SGO should safeguard that it does not unintentionally promote a sense of dependency of the older adults on its officers and volunteers. The use of strengths-based and empowerment approaches would encourage the older adults, their families and the community to play an active role in co-creating solutions to the identified needs and be part of the helping process.

For older adults who were beneficiaries and have regained their levels of independence, they could reciprocate and join in as volunteers to support others. The norm of reciprocity in social capital[51] would encourage older adults to be active agents and not be mere recipients of help. The SGO should promote the norm of reciprocity amongst the volunteers and older adults such that there is common understanding of mutual help and support. Over time, the SGO could develop specialised groups of volunteers and tap into the reservoir of active older adults who can provide care and support to older adults living alone or older couples living on their own.

Technological advancement

During the COVID-19 situation, the SGO had to embrace technology to reach out or maintain contact with vulnerable older adults. More older adults, too, have embraced the use of digital devices to connect with the SGO and service providers. The innovative use of technology should continue so that older adults who are socially isolated and lonely can capitalise on digitalisation to build social networks like virtual support groups.

---

[51] Putnam, R. D. "Tuning In, Tuning Out: The Strange Disappearance of Social Capital in America," *Political Science and Politics*, 28, 1995, 664–683.

Research

With the scope of outreach of about half a million older citizens, the SGO has valuable data on the profiles of older adults, their needs and strengths. More research can be done to examine the needs and abilities of the older persons and contribute to policy planning and development.

Conclusion

From the public health perspective, the investment in building a social network for older adults will contribute to reducing health costs as the support networks can counter the negative effects of social isolation and loneliness as the population ages. Furthermore, support networks can open new pathways for productive ageing as the citizens are mobilised towards common goals in problem solving and in providing mutual support and help. Solutioning can be creative in meeting the diverse needs of people within the community and be culturally sensitive. Older adults are themselves valuable assets to be tapped given their years of experience and expertise in life and they have much to offer in designing their lives in later years. However, there is a need for community leadership to facilitate, mobilise and inspire citizens towards the building of social capital and social networks.

The SGO has begun the journey to be the agent of support for older adults who are socially isolated, in vulnerable situations and lacking social support. Having such a structure with governmental support helps to scale the outreach efforts and connect with older citizens, particularly in the building of trust and relationship. There is good potential for the SGO to further its work in mobilising older adults and the community at large to play a part in co-creating solutions to problems of ageing. Moving forward, the SGO will have to build its capabilities in community leadership, volunteer management and community development. Finally, there is scope for more research to be done so that the inputs on the ground are channelled meaningfully to policy planning and service development and for the enhancement of social cohesion.

Chapter 6

Issues and Challenges of Digitalisation in Ageing Singapore

Tan Tai Kiat

Abstract

Digitalisation is potentially a new social determinant of health and can affect ageing. From a gerontological perspective, digitalisation can affect ageing biologically, socially and psychologically. Digitalisation covers digital literacy and connectivity and can be an enabler or a disenabler. Enabling and disenabling people from communities can mean physically and virtually, and even through resources like information and services. Using Singapore's case, this chapter discusses how effects of digitalisation can present policy implications in the politics of ageing. This includes implications on future politics of ageing, taking into consideration the political force of ageing coupling with digitalisation as another political force.

Introduction

Politics can be defined as activities aimed at improving one's status, and ageing can be defined as the chronological life span leading to senior age and health status. There are policy implications driving the politics of ageing. While ageing is commonly understood as a concept and process of growing old, this discussion focusses particularly on seniors as a group because of the impact of digitalisation on them, evinced during the Coronavirus Disease (COVID-19) pandemic. It is reckoned that such an impact can be politicised when not managed well. This is coupled with digitalisation, potentially as a new social determinant of health that can digitally divide society and even drive political forces.

Digitalisation and Social Determinants of Health

It has been argued that digitalisation potentially is a new social determinant of health.[1] This recognition was evident during COVID-19. The pandemic has showed how digitalisation can affect ageing of different cohorts, and from a gerontological perspective, particularly the seniors. The World Health Organization[2] has defined social determinants of health as the conditions influencing health status from how people live, work and age, plus the wider forces shaping conditions of daily life such as politics, education, sustenance and the environment. Unlike digitisation, that is, the conversion of information into digitalised format, digitalisation is about utilisation of digitised information with technologies. Digitalisation can enable social determinants of health and even improve one's health status; hence, there are implications on the politics of ageing. The effects of digitalisation can be enabling and disenabling. From what has been reported during the COVID-19 lockdown periods, digitalisation has become the primary means to access services, and disenabling this may lead to social isolation. Indeed, digitalisation has changed how we run our lives, even running our lives. From smartphone applications to online services and even social connections, digitalisation has featured prominently and influenced what we do these days. This phenomenon is likely to normalise and perpetuate in the new-normal post-COVID-19 world, as a new way of life.

---

[1] Sieck, C., Sheon, A., Ancker, J. S., Caster, J., Callahan, B. and Siefer, A. "Digital Inclusion as a Social Determinant of Health," *NPJ Digital Medicine*, 4(52), 2021. https://www.nature.com/articles/s41746-021-00413-8.

[2] World Health Organization, "Social Determinants of Health: Key Concepts," *World Health Organization*, 7 May 2013. https://www.who.int/news-room/questions-and-answers/item/social-determinants-of-health-key-concepts.

Digitalisation — Affordability, Accessibility and Adaptability

When was our last digital touch, on the hand phone, computer or kiosk? It is likely that many would attest that it would be within a day and even minutes earlier, accessing WhatsApp, email and internet banking services. More than a technological enabler in our lives, digitalisation as a new social determinant of health has the potential of a political force to drive digital divide, wedging the haves and have-nots who are not able to jump onto the digitalisation bandwagon. What is generally observable is that the haves and have-nots may not only be digitally divided materially and technologically, in terms of affordability and accessibility, but also divided due to adaptability to digitalisation.[3] This becomes an important last-mile consideration which can move the have-nots to become haves.

Accessibility and affordability are necessary for digitalisation but not sufficient without adaptability. Having the means to own a smartphone and free Wi-Fi access does not imply the person is digitally connected. Digitalisation must appeal and adapt to the needs and wants of the users, failing which, this triumvirate recipe of affordability, accessibility and adaptability is likely incomplete and can further divide the haves and have-nots. Where one is not already acculturated in digitalisation, this person is likely to engage in the politics of ageing differently. The person is likely to engage with people whom he is familiar with, who in turn, can be his facilitator to digitalisation. But this engagement really depends on who his fellow natives are and whether they could be intermediaries. Otherwise, the have-nots could be plugged out of digitalisation and could even group together as a political force advocating their interest not in support of digitalisation, jettisoning the digitalisation drive and eroding trust in the system.

Is a cookie-cutter approach to digitalisation the way forward or will a mass customisation approach work better in the politics of ageing,

---

[3] Tan, T. K. "How to Help Seniors be More Digitally Connected," *Today*, 8 December 2020. https://www.todayonline.com/commentary/how-help-seniors-be-more-digitally-connected.

ensuring diversity of needs are accommodated?[4] Perhaps fusing a hybrid online–offline model into a mosaic way could be the way for the future politics of ageing with digitalisation, such that, one that has the native elements to support adaptability and sustainability. Digitalisation is commonly viewed as more than an enabler, and the converse is true that being without it can lead to a disenabling effect. It has the potential to change our lives for the better and worse depending on how digitalisation is exploited. The potential of digitalisation as a new social determinant of health thus belies its influence over our health status.

Biopsychosocial Health

The World Health Organization[5] has defined health as a state of social, mental and physical well-being beyond the usual biomedical understanding of health. Juxtaposing this broad definition of health onto gerontology and life course study, ageing can be meaningfully framed in the gerontological process of ageing.[6] Gerontology looks at biological, psychological and social dimensions, or biopsychosocial in short.[7] Some would say age is just a number, but with chronological lifespan intersecting the idiosyncratic life course, this would demand a more contextual, processual and gerontological understanding of ageing. It is not only the biological cellular differences that matter but also psychological and social differences from accumulated experiences over time. This discussion on politics, ageing and digitalisation thus uses a gerontological frame as the focus is on ageing, with politics and digitalisation.

[4]Gandhi, A., Magar, C. and Roberts, R. "How Technology Can Drive the Next Wave of Mass Customization," *McKinsey on Business Technology*, 32(Winter), 2013. https://www.mckinsey.com/~/media/mckinsey/dotcom/client_service/bto/pdf/mobt32_02-09_masscustom_r4.ashx.
[5]World Health Organization, Basic Documents (49th edition), 2020. *World Health Organization*. https://apps.who.int/gb/bd/.
[6]Elder, G. H. J. "Review: Models of the Life Course," *Contemporary Sociology*, 21(5), 1992, 632–635. https://doi.org/10.2307/2075543.
[7]Engel, G. "The Need for a New Medical Model: A Challenge for Biomedicine," *Science*, 196(4286), 1977, 129–136.

How does the biopsychosocial aspect of ageing interact with digitalisation? From a gerontological perspective, the impact of movement restrictions, like safe management measures in Singapore during pandemic, has led to profound effects on seniors. Biologically, their exercise routines with friends have been disrupted and physical health would be affected over time. Socially, the seniors would miss out the physical social gatherings, and this can affect mental health psychologically due to loneliness and social isolation. But it has been shown that digitalisation can enable seniors to maintain or even improve their social determinants of health during this pandemic period, by keeping fit with group exercises through Zoom sessions, staying connected through WhatsApp and getting psychological support online. The underlying assumption of these enabling effects of digitalisation is that the seniors can afford, access and adapt to these. What if they are not able to do so? Does it then point to a disenabling effect for the have-nots, such as the effect to emerge as a political force and even be perceived as a political force driving this divisive digitalisation policy? If it is the latter, trust in the system could be affected as the have-nots are disadvantaged due to their inability to keep up with digitalisation. If the policy safeguards and safety nets are lacking, the have-nots can be the digital underdogs, an emerging new force and challenge in the politics of ageing. There are policy implications. Mass customised nudges, including digital evangelisation are necessary to appeal to the bio-psychosocial needs of seniors and digitalisation can cater to this diverse needs of the ageing population.

The argumentation in this discussion therefore premises on three aspects: firstly, with politics as activities; secondly, ageing as a process; and thirdly, digitalisation as the environment, physically and virtually. These simplified premises for politics, ageing and digitalisation, by no means simplistic, imply that digitalisation is a digital-environmental aspect of life, which will interact with daily activities and influence life course and ageing over time. The politics of this is in relation to the policy implications as digitalisation could be perceived as a policy move and even a product of politics. The arguments on the forces of the haves and have-nots of digitalisation then would be whether these will emerge as political forces wedged in society or politics inadvertently wedging these forces. The call for action lies in the policy implications to manage digitalisation in ageing, such that digitalisation does not cause an inevitable displacement effect, dividing society and becoming a political issue.

Digitalisation and COVID-19

Digitalisation can present itself in a disruptive manner from how it has interacted with COVID-19, changing the way of life. The life course perspective recognises idiosyncratic experiences, notwithstanding that all may have similar lived experiences like COVID-19, and the experiences again vary by cohorts or age groups. For example, during COVID-19, school-at-home was as common as work-from-home. Regardless of age groups, those who do not have the material and technological means to do so would be disadvantaged not only in terms of learning but also future employability. At the workplace, the employment of robotic technologies in usually manual work like cleaning and security also requires workers to relearn new processes and digitalisation applications. Otherwise, these workers could face risks of redundancy and advance to gig economy for freelance employability. Even for gig economy, a level of digitalisation knowledge is still necessary to work online, be it freelance work or support on-demand services like transport and food delivery. From ordering to processing and payment, the digitalisation touch at a click of a button can be challenging to some like the seniors. The seniors may have the ability to afford and access digitalisation, but they may not have the adaptability to use it. The disenabling effect on the have-nots, unable to adapt to digitalisation, can perpetuate and sustain over time as society moves fast with digitalisation. Therefore, digitalisation can be the emergent political force in ageing from the division between the haves and have-nots.

The digital force on ageing is ostensible for those without technological means to utilise online services. This became apparent during the COVID-19 lockdown periods, where seniors were affected in accessing basic needs like sustenance and they also faced the risks of social isolation due to lockdown movement restriction measures. It is imperative that the accelerated push towards digitalisation during COVID-19 considers adaptive policy calibrations, such that digitalisation does not become an unintended consequence of widening digital divide, driving a deep wedge between the haves and have-nots. The changes from COVID-19 are likely to persist after the pandemic or in the new-normal state and will have lasting implications on the politics of ageing with digitalisation. Digitalisation potentially is a social determinant of health and a political force. Recognising them now as more than a technological enabler could reframe the policy imperative and narrative, to forestall deepening the digital divide wedge in future politics of ageing.

Digitalisation as an Enabler and Disenabler

Digitalisation is more than technological devices and it encompasses digital literacy and connectivity, where the absence of any of these elements can be disenabling. Furthermore, this enabler is premised on the affordability, accessibility and adaptability of digitalisation for users. Paradoxically, this enabler can present unintended disenabling consequences. For example, a senior who has the means to access WhatsApp is inundated with daily COVID-19 news forwarded by their contacts, including unauthenticated news feeds. Without authenticating them, and re-forwarding these to more contacts, the effects of digitalisation could be legitimising such news and promoting mindshare. This enabling yet disenabling effect of digitalisation would usher a new political force, like the unprecedented information flow of COVID-19 vaccination information shared over the social media affecting the pace of the vaccination drive.

Some forms of mass customisation may facilitate more seniors plugging in to digitalisation, such that the masses can still have affordable and accessible digitalisation, and a mosaic way beyond a hybrid approach to engender a diversity of adaptation. This mosaic way may disengage apathy to digitalisation due to accessibility, affordability and, more importantly, adaptability considerations. Mass customisation can be analogised as appealing to the targeted masses of the different age groups, where mass can be regarded as the age groups and customisation to the needs of the individuals. The needs and wants of the individuals can be uncovered from biological, psychological and social perspectives. For instance, a senior interested in health and wellness may want push advisories to age well and manage chronic health conditions. They could be activated to plug into digitalisation that can help them track these conditions proactively. Likewise, there is a need for psychosocial support through an online support and interest group to combat loneliness, where social isolation has been a commonly reported concern during COVID-19.[8]

Digitalisation can be enabled by different strokes for different folks, and these strokes can be visualised in a mosaic way. It is imperative to customise and contextualise to what seniors need and want to ensure adaptability of digitalisation, stickiness and sustainability. This mosaic way would also enable seniors to have a choice of how to adopt to digitalisation, and thereafter adapting their lifestyle with digitalisation. If the intuitive first-touch appeal of digitalisation is not present, even the presence of incentives, albeit not sustainable in the long run, may not move the needle of seniors adapting to digitalisation due to habits formed over time. Proffering the choice to seniors to do so would mean a more deliberate and proactive engagement. The humanistic nature of compassion and empathy would still demand a human touch over digitalisation, and the verdict is open of how politics and ageing would evolve with the forces of digitalisation. Human touch is also critical for mass customisation. It is not about the ability to own the most sophisticated smartphone, but the ability of customising the apps from a generic smartphone to the needs and wants of the seniors.

During COVID-19, there were concerns that exclusion from resources like online services and timely information on policy changes has affected those seniors without the skills and capabilities to access resources.[9] Conversely, the inclusion to some networks, as the source of information, could lead to unfettered propagation of unsolicited plus unverified materials. While it can be argued that the have-nots who do not have such remote access could be protected from such materials, the greater implication is that they can be further isolated and divided socio-digitally. Digitalisation

[8] Nanda, A. "Seniors Stuck at Home, Caught Between Loneliness and Fear of COVID-19," *The Straits Times,* 9 October 2021. https://www.straitstimes.com/singapore/seniors-stuck-at-home-caught-between-loneliness-and-fear-of-covid-19.

[9] Chan, C. M. L. "Commentary: Encourage Seniors in Digitalisation Drive Instead of Forcing Tech Adoption on Them," *Channel News Asia,* 13 January 2021. https://www.channelnewsasia.com/commentary/digital-transformation-smart-nation-can-leave-seniors-behind-401921.

itself can gradually splinter divides if left unmanaged, and, building from COVID-19, enabling and disenabling people from communities and resources. The next-best support for the have-nots may garner political sentiments against digitalisation, especially among the groups most affected like seniors. Depending on the politics of the day, digitalisation could be construed as a political good wedging and dividing society. Hence, there are policy implications to manage politics of ageing with digitalisation, perhaps by adaptive policies that can support a diversity of needs and wants in a mosaic way, while nudging the masses to adapt digitalisation. The passage of time can change the mindset to digitalisation and the seniors' adaptation. It is expected that this mindset change will be irreversible and once this change is made and habits formed, it will stick. Therefore, government policies should be forward looking to engender mindset change and habit forming, while still providing choices.

Singapore's Case and Policy Implications

COVID-19 has presented a serendipitous opportunity to drive digitalisation in Singapore. This is necessitated by pandemic management measures such as safe management and entry restriction. Digitalisation has inevitably seeped into daily life, from regular COVID-19 updates through WhatsApp, to TraceTogether token, to redemption of free masks at kiosks and electronic vouchers provided by the government. Scanning QR codes on a token or tapping the TraceTogether device has become a daily affair for all as it is mandatory to do so for purposes of vaccination verification to facilitate entry access. Digitalisation suddenly becomes a way of life in Singapore, and this disrupted change has affected some, especially seniors, who may not be able to keep up with the pace of change.

To help seniors overcome digital challenges, SingHealth Community Hospitals (SCH) has implemented digital social prescribing to teach seniors how to use smartphone, as the ubiquitous smartphone is widely recognised as the gateway to the digital space.[10] The concept of social prescribing is to connect people to assets within their community and to

---

[10] Lee, K. H. "Digital Social Prescribing," *Defining Med 2021,* 23 February 2021. https://www.singhealth.com.sg/rhs/news/defining-med/digital-social-prescribing.

improve their social determinants of health. SCH also recognises digitalisation as a new social determinant of health. By teaching seniors how to connect to Wi-Fi, use WhatsApp and scan QR codes, SCH has equipped them with these basic digital functions to cope with COVID-19 safe management measures so that they can still be socially engaged. The ability to use WhatsApp also enables the seniors to be informed of daily COVID-19 news updates on the latest new measures, border closures and movement restrictions. Distance caregiving is facilitated by digitalised communication; while it cannot replace the physical touch, it can still be a good substitute for online psychosocial support.[11] The interface for digital devices should consider the characteristics of seniors. By using more pictures and fewer words in digital formats, it would be helpful and appealing to their senses. From a gerontological perspective, such mass customisation also caters to the sensory accommodations for seniors, for both hardware and software in terms of visual, auditory and tactile touches. Fewer clicks to reach services and webpages should also increase online engagement.

The enabling effects of digitalisation on politics of ageing can reinforce a virtuous circle of active ageing and lifelong learning and promote inter-generational interaction. With more activities streaming and even free educational materials online, the ability of seniors to adapt to digitalisation enables ready access to such digitalised services, resources and networking to keep them active and healthy. For sustainability, more face-to-face volunteer opportunities could be set up as a one-stop digitalisation helpdesk for seniors, as their last-mile concierge to nudge and support adaptation. This helpdesk would be useful for seniors who may have digitalisation issues as they explore new applications and need guided advice. It can even present new opportunities for inter-generational mutual mentoring to build new communities which can strengthen social capital and the local ecosystem.[12]

---

[11] Tan, T. K. "Humanising Technology for Older Adults," *Ethos,* Issue 20, 28 January 2019, Civil Service College Singapore. https://www.csc.gov.sg/articles/humanising-technology-for-older-adults.

[12] Mehta, K. K. "Social Integration and Creating an Age-inclusive Community in Singapore," *SUSS – Researchers @ Work,* Issue 3, 2021. https://www.suss.edu.sg/about-suss/centres/centre-for-applied-research/researchers-at-work/issue-3/social-integration-and-creating-an-age-inclusive-community-in-singapore.

On the contrary, the disenabling effects of digitalisation can be a vicious cycle with disenfranchisement impact. It is conceivable that seniors who cannot afford, access and adapt to digitalisation risk being locked out from digitalised services, resources, networking and even opportunities from online applications. This could spiral into an insular view over time with implications for the overall system and the politics of ageing. How the politics of ageing can be impacted through the disenabling effect could be through the aggregated political force of the have-nots. They can rally as an alternative voice to the mainstream, potentially challenging the system because the digitalisation policies do not take into consideration the diverse needs and wants, leaving them with no choice to buy in or drop out.

This perspective can be balanced with the view that the enabling effect can be disenabling too. Unsolicited and unverified information widely circulated can be perceived as truth, possibly creating ripple effects that can be difficult to control. This was seen at the onset of COVID-19 vaccination on the claims shared on social media, which affected the initial vaccination take-up rate. Singapore has enacted the Protection from Online Falsehoods and Manipulation Act in 2019 to safeguard against use of online falsehood communication and information manipulation. It is necessary to have such safeguards as there are online reported radicalisation activities in Singapore and even propagation of untrue information regarding COVID-19 vaccination.[13] Digitalisation is a double-edged sword as information can flow freely in a borderless virtual world. Depending on how it is used, the prevalence of online scams and cybercrimes can cause seniors to be concerned about digitalisation and still affect adoption. Would a hybrid online–offline approach then be the way forward, one that can tip the balance and nudge more seniors to adapt to digitalisation? Or a mosaic way incorporating the hybrid approach which can cater to the diverse needs of seniors, enabling them the guided choice to adapt to digitalisation amenable to their pace? This may sound oxymoronic, but a human-guided digital choice could shed some light.

---

[13] POFMA Office, "Issuance of Correction Direction Under the Protection from Online Falsehoods and Manipulation Act on Falsehoods of COVID-19 Vaccines," 29 November 2021, POFMA Office, Singapore. https://www.pofmaoffice.gov.sg/media-centre/.

Implementation matters in the politics of ageing with digitalisation, and one that is at a managed pace for the seniors given their biopsychosocial characteristics. The crux is on human touch to guide seniors to select, optimise and compensate the digitalisation means they need and want, such that they have a choice.[14] Such a guided selective, optimisation with compensation, and a more community gerontology inquiry of the seniors' needs and wants, is a step towards mass customisation.[15] By matching needs and wants to guided adaptability, possibly through native digital evangelists and a last-mile digitalisation helpdesk, one can ensure stickiness and sustainability of digitalisation measures. This is necessary for seniors who require the personal touch with constant nudging and a safety net in place so that they do not fall through the digital cracks. While this could take more time and effort to implement, this time–space deliberation of effectiveness over efficiency with respect to policy implementation must be weighed politically. There may be political costs if the have-nots are disadvantaged by digitalisation due to policy implementation, and digitalisation can become a political issue.

Hence, targeting the have-nots by presenting guided choices to them could be the secret sauce to start the digitalisation conversation with seniors, instead of a one-size-fits-all approach regardless of age. Digitalisation can empower the elders to optimise the various options to enhance their health status through better information. For example, the seniors could be nudged to use the national identity electronic barcode or TraceTogether QR at brick-and-mortar kiosks by printing out vouchers themselves. The next step can be to enable them to select the types of vouchers available, check balance and a guided choice on whether to print out or use the QR code for redemption. The incentive for using the QR code may be accumulating bonus points for future redemptions. Implementation also matters in going native, by advancing from digital ambassadorship to native

[14] Baltes, M. M. and Carstensen, L. L. "The Process of Successful Ageing," *Ageing and Society*, 1996, 16, 397–422. https://www.cambridge.org/core/services/aop-cambridge-core/content/view/C1E6F81ADC2C4D91484A8819C7BED061/S0144686X00003603a.pdf/the-process-of-successful-ageing.pdf.

[15] Ma, C. "Applied Research in Singapore's Ageing Society: Methods, Philosophies, and Approaches," *SUSS — Researchers @ Work*, Issue 3, 2021. https://www.suss.edu.sg/about-suss/centres/centre-for-applied-research/researchers-at-work/issue-3/applied-research-in-singapore-ageing-society.

digital evangelist. A native digital evangelist would be a close and recognisable contact of the seniors, such that they can evangelise digitalisation and be proactive in helping seniors identify and nudge their needs and wants, coupled with the invisible hand of top-down support from local communities. This will allow diversity in use and adoption of a mass approach to reach out and meet the digital needs of the seniors. Another measure to ensure stickiness is to have a multilingual online platform, appealing to the linguistic needs of the seniors.

With an inverse population pyramid due to the rapidly ageing population in Singapore[16], it is crucial to segmentise provision of services to appeal to different cohorts. Hence, a mass customisation instead of one-size-fits-all approach is necessary; otherwise, this could lead to politics of ageing between cohorts. This mass customisation also takes into consideration that some seniors are more digitally savvy, and some require a brick-and-mortar last-mile IT helpdesk safety net. The native digital evangelist can be the younger cohorts, like their grandchildren and student volunteers in their community, by educating and socialising the young on the needs and challenges of the aged. This can be a virtuous circle beyond inter-generational interactions, enabling the younger cohorts to plan for future ageing and caring for the aged now.

Future Politics of Ageing with Digitalisation

COVID-19 has presented new opportunities to define and even redefine the future politics of ageing with digitalisation. Digitalisation, accelerated due to COVID-19, will be commonplace in the new-normal state. How would the future politics of ageing with digitalisation be, from what we see and experience now?

Cultural Theory can be applied onto future politics of ageing with digitalisation with the interpretation of the grid-group matrixes of regulation and choice from a native perspective.[17] It will be informative to determine the existential state and proportion of the native sub-

---

[16] Vasoo, S., Ngiam, T. and Cheung, P. "Singapore's Ageing Population: Social Challenges and Responses," in D. R. Philips (ed.), *Ageing in the Asia-Pacific Region: Issues, Policies and Future Trends*, (London: Routledge, 2000).

[17] Douglas, M. "A History of Grid and Group Cultural Theory," 2007. https://www.project. chass.utoronto.ca/semiotics/cyber/douglas1.pdf.

populations of these four matrixes, generally categorised as fatalist, hierarchist, individualist and egalitarian. This determination can guide policy implementation to target measures taking into consideration the general characterisation of the matrixes. The question asked would be the desired matrix for future politics of ageing with digitalisation. Perhaps some form of regulation would still be required now for data protection and cybersecurity in the technology space until it stabilises. But in the long run, where digitalisation is expected to be the omnipresent, there is a need to mainstream digitalisation as group interest. This seems to point to hierarchist as the desired matrix now, with other matrixes coexisting. At a future state, can those in the other matrixes be moved or move to this desired state, and what if they do not move?

What if the future politics of ageing with digitalisation is closer to egalitarian when technology stabilises with possibly light-touch regulation as it matures, then the other matrixes would present implications to policy makers to ensure the haves and have-nots by choice are not digitally isolated by policy. The policy challenge is how to move those in these matrixes to a common state, such that digitalisation aspects can be as ubiquitous as travel cards and hand phones today and only a minority do not own them, but this does not isolate them from travel and communication. The future state of digitalisation is imaginable where wearable is the norm, and a digital concierge would remind the wearer of their health status, including medical appointments, optimal exercise and even social time for that personal biopsychosocial charge and refresh. Table 1 shows the matrixes corresponding to the four cultural grid-group matrixes.

Table 1   Grid–Group Matrix

HIGH Grid (Rigid Regulation)	Fatalist	Hierarchist
LOW Grid (Flexible Regulation)	Individualist	Egalitarian
Regulation versus Choice	LOW Group (Individual Choice)	HIGH Group (Group Choice)

It is also thinkable that a fully digitalised world lacking human touch, compassion and empathy may not be completely tenable.[18] A mosaic way may be the way forward, and from Culture Theory it is not hybrid but a mosaic matrix of grid-groups that can probably decipher the future politics of ageing with digitalisation. It is not about hybrid combining the digital haves and have-nots, but a diverse yet liveable mosaic way of a digitalised world, enabling customisation to fit the needs and utility of digitalisation. There are implications to policy implementation in this mosaic way of guided choices, such that the measures targeting the fatalist matrix would be different from the other matrixes. The digitalisation policies should be adaptive to mass customise to the needs and wants of the future seniors, who are in the younger cohorts now, yet coexisting with the seniors of today as they are likely to live longer due to better life expectancy.

A gerontological life course view to ageing is useful to plan the way forward. What matters in new politics of ageing? The gerontological biopsychosocial approach can be expanded to include spirituality as a new dimension separate from biopsychosocial. Spirituality in the new-age realm can be wellness and mindfulness which are popular with the younger cohorts. With better life expectancy, spiritual engagement through digitalisation can present new opportunities to nudge seniors to adopt and adapt digitalisation.[19] Spirituality could be the new dimension in the new politics of ageing with digitalisation, symbiotically promoting active ageing and digital inclusivity. There will still be some have-nots. The politics for ageing therefore should still cater safety nets so that this group is not left behind and disadvantaged due to digitalisation policy design and implementation.

---

[18] Faculty of Arts and Social Sciences, "An Interview with Emeritus Prof S. Vasoo and Assoc Prof Winston Goh on the Strange Start of Psychology at the National University of Singapore," 8 December 2021. Faculty of Arts & Social Sciences, National University of Singapore. https://fass.nus.edu.sg/news/2021/12/08/an-interview-with-emeritus-prof-s-vasoo-and-assoc-prof-winston-goh-on-the-strange-start-of-psychology-at-the-national-university-of-singapore/.

[19] Tan, T. K. "Humanising Technology for Older Adults," *Ethos,* Issue 20, 28 January 2019, Civil Service College Singapore. https://www.csc.gov.sg/articles/humanising-technology-for-older-adults.

Conclusions

COVID-19 has indeed revealed the importance of mental health and is likely to draw more people to digitalisation engagement on spirituality. What this means is for digitalisation measures to duly consider the inter-sections of one's lifespan and life course. In the politics of ageing, digi-talisation measures must be more adaptive, calibrated and intentional with causes that relate to the cohorts. This would mean digital native evange-lists to actively identify the needs and wants of seniors, not a one-size-fits-all approach, pushing digital resources to them instead of them pulling services. Such an implementation mechanism can be intuitive and a guided process as well: intuitively appealing to senses, needs and wants, but involuntarily guided by incentives and nudges to reach a start of group cohesiveness. Otherwise, digitalisation would not be an equitable lever but a political wedge dividing the haves and have-nots.

Digitalisation is an enabling and disenabling force in the new politics of ageing. The post-COVID-19 new-normal world and the future state will have digitalisation features as our way of life. The politics of digitalisation with digitalisation is vested in guided choices in the new mosaic way of life. Having a gerontological biopsychosocial understanding of seniors is crucial to guide adaptation. Similarly, policy implementation must be adaptive as the seniors in the new normal world can be unintentionally displaced by digitalisation policies. With better life expectancy and an ageing population, the seniors, collectively, can be a political force. With digitalisation potentially dividing the haves and have-nots, this could cre-ate another new political force. The policy implications are to step up native digital evangelism advancing from digital ambassadorship, taking on a more native evangelistic drive to address the needs and wants of sen-iors in the digital space. The mosaic way of life is to allow guided choices for digitalisation buy-in. Politics is about choices, and this is what the politics of ageing with digitalisation is all about.

https://doi.org/10.1142/9789811265198_0008

Chapter 7

Reaching Out to the Elderly Living Alone: Tightening the Nodes

R. Jai Prakash

Abstract

Singapore is experiencing significant demographic changes. By 2030, it will progress to be one of the world's demographically oldest countries. With increasing singlehood and low fertility rates, the incidence of the elderly living alone is also on the rise. Given an ageing population and an increased risk of social isolation amongst the elderly due to the recent pandemic, it is crucial to strengthen the ecosystem of support networks for the elderly living alone, particularly at the community level. A pragmatic model of community intervention is thus needed to augment social connectedness for the elderly living alone in Singapore.

Introduction

Singapore is one of the most rapidly ageing societies in Asia. The number of residents aged 65 years and above made up 16% of the total resident population in Singapore in 2021, a sharp increase from 2010 (7.2%).[1]

---

[1] Department of Statistics Singapore, "Population trends," 2021. https://www.singstat.gov.sg/-/media/files/publications/population/population2021.pdf.

By 2030, 25% of the Singapore resident population would be 65 years and older. In absolute numbers, the number of elderly will increase from about 637,800 in 2021 to over 900,000 in 2030. This increase in the ageing population will have socio-economic implications.

Over the last decade, the number of elderly living alone in Singapore has been rising and this trend is expected to continue. The proportion of couple-based households with children has declined from 56% in 2010 to 47.7% in 2020. On the other hand, households without children increased from 13.7% to 16.6%, and one-person households increased from 12.2% to 16% over the same period. Amongst households with persons aged 65 years and over, the proportion of the elderly living alone has increased from 17.4% in 2010 to 21.6% in 2020. In 2020, there were about 63,800 single-person elderly households in Singapore.[2] By 2030, this is projected to increase to 83,000 single-persons elderly households.

While there is a strong focus on successful ageing in Singapore, the statistics on the number of the elderly who die alone is concerning.[3] This chapter will examine theoretical concepts of successful ageing and draw lessons from a community initiative that is aimed at reducing the incidence of the elderly dying alone in Singapore. Recommendations to increase social connectedness for the elderly living alone are also discussed.

Impact of the Elderly Living Alone

There is a need to endeavour towards and ensure successful ageing for the elderly, given the context of a rapidly ageing population. In theory, the successful ageing model proposed by Rowe and Kahn (1997) advocates

---

[2] Ministry of Health Singapore, "I Feel Young in My Singapore! Action Plan for Successful Ageing," 2016. https://www.moh.gov.sg/ifeelyoungsg/how-can-we-build-stronger-ties/care-for-a-senior.

[3] Ng, T. P., Jin, A., Feng, L., Nyunt, M. S. Z., Chow, K. Y., Feng, L. and Fong, N. P. "Mortality of Older Persons Living Alone: Singapore Longitudinal Ageing Studies," *BMC Geriatrics*, 15(1), 2015, 1–9; Ang, S. "Five Cases of Seniors in Singapore Who Died Alone at Home," *The Straits Times*, 6 September 2021. https://www.straitstimes.com; and Hui, Y. S. and Soh, G. "From Welfare to Funeral Services: Seniors in Singapore Who Live Alone Get Help," *The Straits Times*, 12 September 2021. https://www.straitstimes.com.

that positive ageing comprises three factors: avoiding illness and limiting disability (the physical factor), sustaining high levels of mental functioning (the cognitive factor), and remaining meaningfully and actively engaged in life (the social factor).[4] This is further maintained by Erikson's final stage of psychosocial development where old age is recognised by a struggle between integrity and despair.[5] Feelings associated with integrity versus despair are favoured amongst the elderly. With integrity, the elderly can accept their positive and negative aspects of life and that their lives are meaningful. Conversely, feelings of despair will lead the elderly to lack a sense of completeness and perceive that their lives are meaningless.[6] Such feelings could further lead to the elderly feeling helpless, a deep sense of regret in their lives and in serious circumstances have a sense of being done with life and suicidal tendencies.

Social isolation as a construct is an objective state of having few associations of irregular social contact with significant others.[7] Based on an ecological framework, the elderly who live alone can be socially isolated from different levels of micro, meso and macro systems of their environment.[8] Essentially, they are likely to have limited family and peer connections at a micro level, lack of access to community services at a meso level which will in turn further alienate them to macro-level services from government touchpoints such as healthcare and social services. The lack of social connectedness poses a serious risk to physical, social and mental well-being. The elderly who live alone are more likely to be socially isolated and at increased risk of chronic illness and premature mortality.[9]

[4] Rowe, J. W. and Kahn, R. L. "Successful Aging," *The Gerontologist*, 37(4), 1997, 433–440.

[5] Erikson, E. *Childhood and Society* (2nd ed.), (New York: Norton, 1963/1987).

[6] Blando, J. *Counseling Older Adults*, (London: Routledge, 2011).

[7] National Academies of Sciences Engineering Medicine, *Social Isolation and Loneliness in Older Adults: Opportunities for the Health Care System*, (Washington, DC: The National Academies Press, 2011).

[8] Bronfenbrenner, U. *The Ecology of Human Development: Experiments by Nature and Design*, (Cambridge, MA: Harvard University Press, 1979).

[9] Lee, J. M. G., Chan, C. Q. H., Low, W. C., Lee, K. H. and Low, L. L. "Health-seeking Behaviour of the Elderly Living Alone in an Urbanised Low-income Community in Singapore," *Singapore Medical Journal*, 61(5), 2020, 260.

Physical Well-being

As a first consequence of social isolation, a threat to physical well-being could occur at several fronts including self-rated health, the number of chronic illnesses, existence of pain and the capacity to do activities of daily living (ADLs). Linton *et al.* (2018) found that elderly Singaporeans not living alone had a likelihood of reporting better self-rated health and independence in all ADLs and instrumental activities of daily living (IADLs), as compared to the elderly living alone.[10] Likewise, Malhotra *et al.* (2021) found that loneliness contributes to poorer physical health and the elderly are more likely to demonstrate reduced functioning in ADLs.[11] The elderly living with their spouses or children likely have better family support and interdependence on family members, especially so in Singapore's communal culture and an emphasis on values such as family piety where adult children can be expected to support their parents financially and emotionally.[12]

Social and Mental Well-being

Second, social isolation and a lack of social participation could reduce perceptions amongst the elderly that they are less valued and are not part of a community. These perceptions could in turn lead to adverse effects on the elderly's mental health. Ng *et al.* (2015) found that depressive symptom scores were higher amongst elderly Singaporeans living alone than those elderly living with children.[13] Stronger social networks were also found to be associated with lower depression scores. The consequences of

[10]Linton, E., Gubhaju, B. and Chan, A. *Home Alone: Older Adults in Singapore, Singapore*; Centre for Ageing Research and Education (CARE) Research Brief Series: 4, 2018, pp. 1–13.

[11]Malhotra, R., Tareque, M. I., Saito, Y., Ma, S., Chiu, C. T. and Chan, A. "Loneliness and Health Expectancy Among Older Adults: A Longitudinal Population-based Study," *Journal of the American Geriatrics Society*, 69(11), 2021, 3092–3102.

[12]Lim, L. L. and Kua, E. H. "Living Alone, Loneliness, and Psychological Well-being of Older Persons in Singapore," *Current Gerontology and Geriatrics Research*, 2011.

[13]Ng, T. P., Jin, A., Feng, L., Nyunt, M. S. Z., Chow, K. Y., Feng, L. and Fong, N. P. "Mortality of Older Persons Living Alone: Singapore Longitudinal Ageing Studies," *BMC Geriatrics*, 15(1), 2015, 1–9.

weaker social networks could lead to less social support such as having fewer people to speak to about their problems, to depend on for social and financial support or simply to go out for recreational purposes. Such a lack of social participation from family, friends and the community would hurt mental well-being.

Impact on Mortality

Third, loneliness is a significant risk factor for mortality amongst the elderly.[14] Several international studies have pointed out that loneliness had consistently been shown to be linked to mortality. Loneliness might increase mortality risk through several pathways, ranging from biological responses and perceptions to social interactions and environmental factors. Malhotra *et al.* (2021) found that the elderly who are lonely can expect to have a shorter life.[15]

Current Services for the Elderly Living Alone

The Singapore government had continually reviewed the needs of the elderly and responded swiftly. This began with the Inter-Ministry Committee report on ageing in 1999 and since then, there had been several reviews to address the evolving needs of the ageing population and to enable Singaporeans to age successfully. There was a greater recognition for health and social services to be in sync and for services to take an integrated approach to respond to both the health and social needs of the elderly. In line with this move, the Agency for Integrated Care (AIC) was incorporated in 2019 to take the lead as a national care integrator, a developer and a facilitator of community health and social services for the elderly. The formation of the Regional Health Systems (RHS) by the Ministry of Health (MOH) was another attempt to provide a seamless

---

[14] Chan, A., Raman, P., Ma, S. and Malhotra, R. "Loneliness and All-cause Mortality in Community-dwelling Elderly Singaporeans," *Demographic Research*, 32, 2015, 1361–1382.

[15] Malhotra, R., Tareque, M. I., Saito, Y., Ma, S., Chiu, C. T. and Chan, A. "Loneliness and Health Expectancy Among Older Adults: A Longitudinal Population-based Study," *Journal of the American Geriatrics Society*, 69(11), 2021, 3092–3102.

transition of care in different geographical locations. Each RHS is anchored by an acute general hospital which is linked to community health and social services such as community hospitals, nursing homes, home care, day rehabilitation services as well as polyclinics and private general practitioners to deliver preventive and comprehensive health management.[16]

Specifically, for the elderly living alone, the government takes a three-pronged strategy to meet their needs.[17] First, at a preventive level, outreach efforts are stepped up by Silver Generation Ambassadors (SG Ambassadors). This is on top of the efforts of the Senior Activity Centres (SACs) that befriend and carry out programmes to keep the elderly meaningfully engaged in the community. SG Ambassadors proactively reach out to assess the elderly's health and social needs and educate the elderly about the services, including active ageing programmes, available to support them. Second, there is an active community befriending programme whereby the befrienders conduct physical visits with the elderly. These visits are regularly supplemented with phone calls to look out for distress signs amongst the elderly who live alone. The elderly could also tap into a 24-hour care hotline (CareLine) that provides tele-befriending services and support in the community. Third, both at a remedial and developmental level, different agencies coordinate casework and case management services for the elderly who present themselves with more complex needs. Community resource, engagement and support teams provide the elderly at risk for dementia or depression with information on services, emotional support and coping strategies. Family Service Centres provide counselling and support services to manage family relations, financial and emotional difficulties. The elderly with care needs, and who have no or little family support, are supported by senior group homes, sheltered homes and nursing homes, and day-care services which provide residential and socio-emotional support.

---

[16] Agency for Integrated Care, *Care Services*. 2021. https://aic.sg/care-services.

[17] Ministry of Health Singapore, "Elderly Living Alone and Undetected Deaths," 6 June 2020, https://www.moh.gov.sg/news-highlights/details/elderly-living-alone-and-undetected-deaths.

A Community Case Study: The Elderly Living Alone Project

In 2014, when social services for the elderly were under the purview of the Ministry of Social and Family Development (MSF), a community initiative known as the "the elderly living alone project" was led by me in my capacity as a General Manager of a Social Service Office (SSO). The impetus to the project was reported incidences of the elderly passing away alone at home and going unnoticed. Ang (2021) similarly reported five such deaths of the elderly during the period 2016–2021, who passed on alone at home and their deaths were discovered many months later.[18] As a start, local planning officers (who were tasked to coordinate unmet social needs in the community) in the SSO did a ground sensing of the needs of the elderly living alone. Forty community walks were carried out and the sensing gathered from the conversations with the elderly pointed to the need for a more systemic assessment of the issue at hand. In terms of the scale of the issue, there were higher numbers of elderly living in rental blocks in the mature estate. On the high side, in one location of four rental blocks, based on data triangulated from social service agencies then, there were about 800 elderly residing in them. Of this, community partners expressed concern that there were about 100 elderly living alone. Close to 50% of the SSO's clients then were also above the age of 60 years old.

The primary objective of the project was to understand the needs of the elderly living alone. The secondary objective was to get the elderly integrated into social networks by building an ecosystem of support for vulnerable elderly living alone. Community development and design thinking approaches were taken to tap into the strengths of the different community partners and empower them to design sustainable solutions. The SSO collaborated with eight community partners from the health, mental health and social service agencies in providing eldercare services to the local community.

The data-gathering phase involved a needs assessment conducted via one-to-one in-depth interviews with 100 elderly who were living alone.

---

[18]Ang, S. "Five Cases of Seniors in Singapore Who Died Alone at Home," *The Straits Times*, 6 September 2021. https://www.straitstimes.com.

Topics covered in interviews comprised questions on six domains of elderly well-being. They were physical, psychological, social functioning and networks, living environment, economic and financial status, and access to social services. Findings from the interviews were analysed and key challenges were identified in reaching out to the elderly. The four key challenges were firstly, the limited resources from a single agency to engage and monitor the elderly living; secondly, the low take-up rate of services or a high proportion of rejection of help by the elderly despite their needs and a lack of ability to care for themselves; thirdly, wellness and medical issues of the elderly were not actively followed up; and lastly, the lack of a holistic assessment of the needs of the elderly by any one agency.

These challenges were subsequently discoursed at an ideation workshop attended by 20 participants from different health and social agencies. As illustrated in Figure 1, three questions were deliberated at the ideation based on three tiers of need; first, how can we help the elderly living alone better integrate into the community; second, how do we help the elderly meet their basic needs; and third, how can we better render help to the vulnerable elderly in times of crisis.

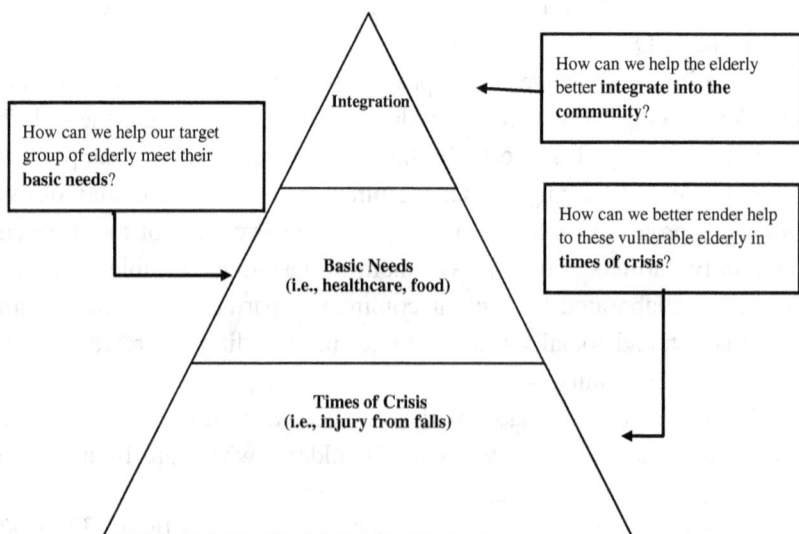

Figure 1.   Different Tiers of Needs for the Elderly

As part of the recommendations from the ideation workshop participants, a screening checklist (Table 1) was developed. The checklist could be used by any practitioner from any agency to assess the needs of an elderly person living alone. This would enable the social service or healthcare professional or a befriender of an elderly person living alone to do a

Table 1.   Screening Checklist for the Elderly Living Alone

Physical Health
✓ When was the previous medical check-up?
✓ Do they suffer from any chronic illnesses?
   o   If they are, are they going for regular check-ups?
   o   Are they consuming their medication regularly?
✓ Do they look underweight? This could be a sign of malnutrition.
✓ Are they able to carry out their basic and instrumental ADLs?
✓ If they are assessed to be prone to falls, do they possess walking aids?

Psychological health
✓ How do they react to unfamiliar people?
✓ Check for common signs of mental health challenges, e.g., dementia, depression, suicidal thoughts.

Social functioning and networks
✓ How many living children do they have?
✓ How involved is the family in the elderly's life?
✓ What is the frequency and quality of interaction with friends and neighbours?
✓ Do they participate in activities within the community?
✓ What languages are they able to communicate in?

Home environment
✓ What is the general state of cleanliness in their house?
✓ Is there elder-friendly infrastructure, e.g., handlebars, gentle slopes, in the place where they stay?
✓ Do they have symptoms of hoarding disorder?
✓ Check for pest infestations.

Economic status
✓ Are they keen and able to be employed?
✓ Are they receiving financial support from children?
✓ Are they receiving financial hand-outs from the SSO/other community partners?

Social services
✓ Are they known to any organisations/groups?
   o   What forms of assistance are provided?
✓ Do they have knowledge about sources of help to turn to during times of need?

quick one-stop holistic triaging and make a referral to relevant agencies for the services required by the elderly. In addition to the screening, the social service or healthcare professional or befriender was encouraged to collate a list of emergency contact numbers that could be used by the elderly for future caregiving or support purposes, in times of need or crisis. The emergency contact numbers were collated and managed by different SACs in the neighbourhood. Finally, a mobile phone chat application (WhatsApp) was used for ease of communication. A group chat was created amongst key service providers to facilitate easier networking, exchange information and, more importantly, to ensure there were no broken links in referrals or case management of the elderly living alone. The key case manager in such situations was assigned to the SAC Cluster Support. Cluster Support, appointed by MOH, is a step-up service for vulnerable elderly with no or weak family support. The services provided included social support through monitoring, casework management and counselling services.

Recommendations

Given the continued changes in the demographics in Singapore, its impact on population ageing and risks to the elderly living alone would be increasingly visible. Apart from demographic impact, global health crises such as the Coronavirus Disease 2019 (COVID-19) posed further challenges to social isolation. While the effects of safe management measures such as social distancing and limitations of group size on socialising are not unique to the elderly population, its impact could be worse on them. In America, it was found that before COVID-19, about one-quarter of Americans over age 65 were socially isolated, and more than 40% of people over age 60 reported feeling lonely. With the COVID-19 pandemic, more elderly people who lived alone felt even more isolated.[19] While similar local research in Singapore could be limited, it is likely the impact would be similar. In a study by Malhotra and Visaria (2020), the

---

[19] Frueh, S. "Pandemic Isolation and the Elderly: A Doctor Reflects on the Impacts," in National Academies of Sciences Engineering Medicine. (2020). *Social Isolation and Loneliness in Older Adults: Opportunities for the Health Care System*, (Washington, DC: The National Academies Press, 2022).

researchers alluded that technology should be used to address social isolation of the elderly during the time of COVID-19 as there had been worldwide concerns of social restriction measures and their impact on the elderly's risk of social isolation.[20]

In March 2020, Singapore issued an advisory for the elderly to avoid social gatherings and crowded places as much as possible and to go out only for essential purposes such as to buy food. Subsequently, family interactions were limited and activities conducted by government agencies were suspended. During those phases, several befrienders and grassroots organisations had immense challenges reaching out to the elderly. The social distancing measures would have also limited the opportunities for the elderly to come together to meet their peers or join social programmes organised by social service agencies such as the SACs. However, it is in these instances that there is a greater need to closely follow up with the elderly living alone. Unlike the younger generation, the elderly are more estranged from technology. As such, the anxiety levels and issues faced by the elderly living alone can be more neglected when their social connections are reduced by social distancing measures. It is important that befriending should continue, observing safe management measures to ensure basic daily needs such as delivering groceries, food or caring for their existing illness and having sufficient medications are met. The outreach is also needed to ensure the elderly can maintain their ADLs such as by teaching them basic exercises that they can do at home or equipping them with coping strategies to help with their social well-being, such as using technology to keep in touch with their friends or who to contact if they need help.

Community Coordination

There are several national efforts to coordinate and put systems and structures in place to enable successful ageing. These resulted in stronger health-social integration efforts, which is a commendable move. As illustrated in the "elderly living alone project", what is needed is more

---

[20] Malhotra, R. and Visaria, A. "Social Isolation in the COVID-19 Pandemic — Is Maintaining Social Connections Online a Viable Option for All Older Persons: Insights from Singapore," 2020. Available at SSRN 3609081.

---

ground-up community ownership and "solutioning". Greater efforts are essential to tighten the nodes so that no elderly person living alone is cut off from the community services they require and, in unfortunate adverse circumstances, has to die alone.

There is a need for different stakeholders working with the elderly in the community to come together at a local geographical level, strengthen their relationships, exchange information, have a deeper understanding of the needs of the elderly in their community and co-create solutions to address them. Each locality and neighbourhood would be made up of different profiles of the elderly. In 2021, Outram, Rochor, Ang Mo Kio, Bukit Merah and Kallang were some of the neighbourhoods in Singapore which had higher proportions of residents aged 65 years and over. For each of these areas, at least one in five residents was aged 65 years and over.[21] While there are macro programmes at the national level, the elderly population in each of these communities would have unique needs and depending on the ecosystem of help services, community stakeholders would face unique challenges. As such, locality-based conversations and "solutioning" are critical amongst community stakeholders. As implemented in the "elderly living alone project", each locality could have community partners tightening the connections, starting with the screening for needs, conducting overall all-inclusive assessments into the physical, social, mental health needs, aiming towards providing integrated community services and eventually evaluation.

Yi et al. (2021) established a comparable community-based integrated service (CBIS) model of care for the elderly living alone in Siheung City, Korea.[22] CBIS was developed by a multi-disciplinary team comprising public officials and community stakeholders. Through regular meetings and feedback gathered from opinions of the local community, connecting links between existing services were reviewed, improved and included in the CBIS model. Eventually, the elderly who participated in the CBIS rated their overall satisfaction with the services as 9 out of 10. A similar

[21] Department of Statistics Singapore, "Population trends," 2021. https://www.singstat.gov.sg/-/media/files/publications/population/population2021.pdf.

[22] Yi, Y. M., Park, Y. H., Cho, B., Lim, K. C., Jang, S. N., Chang, S. J., Ko, H., Noh, E.Y. and Ryu, S. "Development of a Community-based Integrated Service Model of Health and Social Care for Older Adults Living Alone," *International Journal of Environmental Research and Public Health*, 18(2), 2021, 825.

model can be replicated in mature estates in Singapore where different stakeholders in the community can come together, assess the unique needs of the elderly in the specific estate and develop interventions by integrating the different existing services and using local resources. Examples of such interventions can be as micro as meeting basic food or medical needs to macro programmes such as dementia care or to facilitate ageing in place.

Practitioner Coordination

At the social worker level, competencies would need to be continued to be built to raise the practitioner's knowledge and skills to serve the elderly in the community. Attempts by the Nanyang Technological University and the Singapore University of Social Sciences to offer further education programmes in gerontology are noteworthy proactive efforts to meet the evolving needs of the sector. More of such efforts or short micro-certificate courses could be delivered by tertiary institutions.

Apart from competency, health and social service practitioners must embrace core service principles such as no wrong door policy, practice a single point of assessment when they get in touch with an elderly person beyond their agency functions, ensuring effective warm transfers between agencies, ensuring follow-ups are done by agencies referred to and for referral agencies to close the loop, thereby increasing communication amongst professionals, volunteers and any others such as grassroots members who come into contact working with the elderly. MSF has developed guidelines for case master action planning to facilitate coordinated case planning approaches when multiple agencies are involved to assist a client with complex needs. Information sharing amongst agencies could also be enhanced by consolidated data systems such as One Client View and Case Connect for agencies to make referrals to each other and track case progress.[23] Each person encountering an elderly living alone can be the starting point of the node of community services that the elderly might require.

---

[23] Ministry of Social and Family Development Singapore, "Building Capabilities, Deepening Partnerships and Leveraging Technology to Strengthen Social Service Delivery" [Fact sheet]. 2021. https://www.msf.gov.sg/media-room/Pages/Building-Capabilities-Deepening-Partnerships-and-Leveraging-Technology-to-Strengthen-Social-Service-Delivery.aspx.

Technology as an Enabler

Given the uncertain future pandemic outlook where living with social restrictions might become a norm at different phases of a health crisis, technology adoption in the landscape of elderly service provision would be another area that requires urgent attention. Social restriction measures could further limit the access to the social networks of the elderly and lead to more adverse psycho-social impacts on the elderly living alone. Apart from increasing communication between the elderly and his/her social networks, technology could also be used to monitor the safety and well-being of the elderly living alone. Digital platforms such as tele or video conferencing could help to deliver basic health consultation and telemedicine services when there is a need to maintain social distancing. The Mobile Access for Senior Scheme ensures that the elderly can get subsidised smartphones and phone plans in Singapore.[24] However, it is for low-income elderly and elderly will need to for it themselves. To enhance digital literacy amongst the elderly, especially those living alone, more intentional effort is required to help them to procure mobile phones and internet-based tools including Wi-Fi support in their homes to increase social connectivity. Subsequently, elder-friendly language and training are necessary to coach the elderly to navigate the devices and the Internet. At the end of the continuum, the provision of technical support should also be considered. Sum *et al.* (2008) found that internet use by the elderly as a communication technology was associated with a lower level of social loneliness.[25] Sen *et al.* (2021) found that mobile technology-based applications that help families stay connected also link the elderly to resources in healthcare and encourage physical and mental well-being, which was particularly helpful in the implementation of the social distancing measures during the COVID-19 pandemic.[26] In the elderly living alone project, technology was also an enabler to facilitate communication amongst stakeholders.

[24] Infocomm Media Development Authority, "Mobile Access for Seniors," 2022. https://www.imda.gov.sg/programme-listing/Mobile-Acess-for-Seniors.

[25] Sum, S., Mathews, R. M., Hughes, I. and Campbell, A. "Internet Use and Loneliness in Older Adults," *Cyberpsychology Behaviour*, 11(2), 2008, 208–211.

[26] Sen, K., Prybutok, G. and Prybutok, V. "The Use of Digital Technology for Social Wellbeing Reduces Social Isolation in Older Adults: A Systematic Review," *SSM-Population Health*, 2021, 101020.

Conclusion

There is substantial evidence that the incidence of the elderly living alone is on the rise in most parts of the world, especially in rapidly developing societies.[27] Ageing issues and the consequences of social isolation are an impact of several social challenges that many developing societies face. Health pandemics and social distancing measures further amplify the problem of social isolation. Researchers further questioned whether the elderly living alone should be considered a vulnerable segment of the society with abundant data that social isolation of the elderly living alone could be linked to declining health and mortality and a negative impact on physical, social and mental well-being.

In many societies, especially in Asian countries like Singapore, there was a traditional emphasis on strong families and family solidarity. Many of Singapore's policies including looking after the elderly are based on the first principle of the family as the first line of support. However, this principle is coming under increasing pressures from modernisation and urbanisation.[28] It would be tougher to base it as the foundation for the provision of social services with new social phenomena. These changes include lower marriage rates, a delay in forming families by couples, an overall decline in fertility rates, shrinking family sizes and changing family composition.

The Singapore government has constantly reviewed policies and services, adapting them regularly to ensure successful ageing. Policy and government resources would continue to form the backbone of health and social services. However, without a strong community network and intervention, such services may not be easily accessible to those who need the services and the policy intentions would be hard to achieve. The definition of a family or a pseudo-family also needs to be widened to include stakeholders within each community or locality. Apart from trained professionals, in light of the shortage of manpower in the social service sector, volunteers from schools, grassroots organisations and even

---

[27]Reher, D. and Requena, M. "Living Alone in Later Life: A Global Perspective," *Population and Development Review*, 2018, 427–454.

[28]Mehta, K. K. and Vasoo, S. "Organization and Delivery of Long-term Care in Singapore: Present Issues and Future Challenges," *Journal of Aging & Social Policy*, 13(2–3), 2002, 185–201.

neighbourhoods in specific localities can augment the outreach to the elderly. This increased social interaction through community stakeholders revisits the belief of community spiritedness or what is called the "Kampong Spirit" in Singapore, where there is a strong emphasis on looking out for each other and providing mutual help and support in a community. With a rich extensive ecosystem of diverse individuals comprising professionals and volunteers, which can be further enhanced using technology, the needs of the elderly through each touchpoint or outreach can be banked into a virtual social exchange system that can be matched with different community resources. There is further potential for such a system to tap into corporate resources. Such a system could strengthen the inter-organisational partnership and maximise the social impact of individual entities in helping the elderly living alone. Each social connection can tighten the nodes in the entire ecosystem designed to support the elderly, particularly the elderly living alone.

Chapter 8

Information Technology's Role in Ageing and Community Service

Jedi Pan Zhengxiang

Abstract

As information technology is having a revolutionary impact all-round, be it in the political, economic or social arena, its mining and consequences for the "silver generation" cannot be ignored. In this regard, many programmes, under the ambit of the "silver technology", have been rolled out for the ageing of Singapore's society over the years such as unobtrusive monitoring, digital companionship and assistive technology for "silver productivity". There are also wellness games for early detection, intervention and rehabilitation such the *Ping Ping Pong Pong* game that serves as an iterative design process of modern health technology. This chapter demonstrates that long-term tech-enabled solutions will play a key role in dealing with the aged in the coming years.

Information technology has left a mark on society with a plethora of exciting applications. New methods of data collection complement human senses, new methods of information management consolidate immense amounts of knowledge that the human brain cannot and "telepathy" is now realised with wireless technology, greatly enhancing our communication capabilities. As good as these inventions may sound, the bridge to translate digital technology into social good still depends on how people embrace, utilise and innovate in this rapidly evolving field. This chapter provides an overview on how the Singapore community is bridging its social needs with digital technology, namely, age-friendly silver technology for the ageing population, and information technology's role in enhancing community service.

Silver Technology for Health and Wellness

Singapore is currently faced with a rapidly ageing "silver population". The first half of this chapter presents research and innovations in silver technology that have taken place in Singapore.

Singapore's Long-term Care Framework for the Ageing Population

The Singapore government has constantly kept in view the importance of *social support for the elderly*. Back when Singapore was made up of mainly immigrants, the elderly depended on their village or immigrant clan members, which differed across ethnic groups.[1] As the influx of immigrants subsided, with resettlement of residents into high-rise public housing estates and the breakup of village communities, the government needed to design a different elderly support system. In the 1980s, direct funding towards senior welfare was limited with more emphasis placed on informal support from family and neighbours. However, to support the ageing of baby boomers between 1947 and 1964,[2] the government soon began to set up policies in anticipation of a demand surge in elderly long-term care, such as setting up statuary boards and encouraging voluntary

---

[1] Cheung, P. L., Ngiam, T. L., Vasoo, S. and Chan, Y. Y. "Social Support Networks for the Elderly in a High-rise Public Housing Estate in Singapore," in *Social Services and Aging Policies in the U.S. and Asia*, (International Exchange Center on Gerontology, University of South Florida, 1988), pp. 305–340.

[2] Roy, S. "Baby Boom Generation in Singapore and Its Impact on Ageing," *International Journal of Humanities and Social Sciences*, 8(3), 2014, 809–817.

welfare organisations (VWOs) to step in.[3] The emerging long-term care framework places a similar emphasis on support from neighbours and community partners.

On the primary front, informal family-based care is now bolstered with support from semi-formal care from community organisations and VWOs, such as island-wide Active Ageing Hubs. On the secondary front, formal care support systems are institutionalised into community hospitals, nursing homes and hospices. These facilities with more expensive, specialised staff and equipment are meant for elderly who require more intensive care, or as a last resort for those without family or communal ties. Families, communities-at-large, and institutions thus form a care network to distribute the caregiving workload, a paradigm for senior care that is more sustainable, diverse and unique to Singapore.[4]

The deep intertwinement between informal and formal care support systems allows innovation of new services to reach a wide array of the elderly. Development of such innovations to combat ageing challenges is, coincidentally, at the height of its time thanks to the advent of technology. The Singapore society is poised to be among the frontiers of tech-enabled ageing.

Silver Technology: The State of the Art in Singapore

While elderly care has always been a physical-oriented affair, the rapid advance of technology has uncovered many new, unheard methods to assist caregivers and healthcare workers, so much so that research centres for silver technologies are set up with dedicated manpower and resources for performing translational research.

While the field of medicine is concerned mainly with providing reactionary treatment to diseases, silver technology can be used for developing both preventative and reactive measures, extending beyond hospitals and clinics into community and home-based applications (see Figure 1).

---

[3] Mehta, K. and Vasoo, S. "Organization and Delivery of Long-term Care in Singapore: Present Issues and Future Challenge," *Journal of Aging & Social Policy*, 13(2–3), 2002, 185–201.

[4] *Ibid.*, 187.

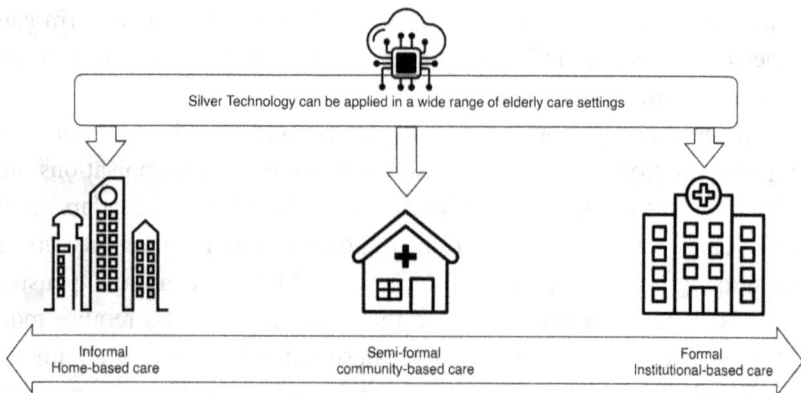

Figure 1.   Silver Technology's Role in Singapore Context

Research on silver technology is multi-disciplinary in nature; designing interventions requires deep understanding of the specific problem at hand as well as meticulous trials and revisions. After all, health complications caused by ageing are multifaceted and each problem may be caused by many factors. Sensors require advancements in hardware technology to better capture physical phenomena, information utilises big data techniques like knowledge graphs and natural language processing to generate insights, and digital interfaces apply Human–Computer Interaction research findings to communicate with humans effectively. To top it off, emerging artificial intelligence (AI) technologies allow many new innovative approaches to be taken when tackling ageing issues. The crossover between many of these different disciplines has one common goal in mind: perform research that can be translated into impactful innovations. A few examples are highlighted below.

Unobtrusive Monitoring and Digital Companions

Harnessing Internet-of-Things (IoT) technology, smart sensor grids were designed to unobtrusively track odd behaviour, compute wellness indices[5]

---

[5]Gao, S., Wang, D., Tan, A.-H. and Miao, C. "Progressive Sequence Matching for ADL Plan Recommendation," *IEEE/WIC/ACM International Conference on Web Intelligence and Intelligent Agent Technology (WI-IAT)*, 2015, pp. 360–367.

and compose report summaries in form of easy-to-understand stories thanks to the design of a unique storytelling engine. Special attention was placed on monitoring for events that need immediate attention, such as coupling deep learning algorithms with infrared sensors for accurate fall detection.[6] By averting use of cameras, user privacy is preserved without compromising prediction accuracy. Further research aims to hitch on popular commercial health monitoring devices such as smart watches and mobile phones to minimise number of wearables and increase proliferation of such unobtrusive monitoring.[7]

An AI companion is also developed in tandem with the smart sensor grid.[8] The design features two separate intelligent agents harnessing behavioural information from the smart sensor grid as well as advancements in persuasive AI to provide realistic and context-aware interactions.[9] A backend proxy is employed to coordinate with two virtual avatars — a butler and a nurse — in persuading the elderly to adopt health recommendations that are personalised based on readings from the smart sensor grid.

Assistive Technology for Silver Productivity

A multitude of assistive technologies were introduced to help the elderly function better against the odds of ageing. To combat cognitive decline which may cause the elderly to forget future time-sensitive tasks, a

---

[6]Fan, X., Zhang, H., Leung, C. and Shen, Z. "Robust Unobtrusive Fall Detection Using Infrared Array Sensors," *IEEE International Conference on Multisensor Fusion and Integration for Intelligent Systems (MFI)*, (Daegu, South Korea, 2017), pp. 194–199.

[7]Wang, D., Candinegara, E., Hou, J., Tan, A.-H. and Miao, C. "Robust Human Activity Recognition Using Lesser Number of Wearable Sensors," *International Conference on Security, Pattern Analysis, and Cybernetics (SPAC)*, (Shenzhen, China, 2017), pp. 290–295.

[8]Wang, D., Subagdja, B., Kang, Y. and Tan, A. "Silver Assistants for Aging-in-Place," *IEEE/WIC/ACM International Conference on Web Intelligence and Intelligent Agent Technology (WI-IAT)*, Vol. 3, (Singapore, 2015).

[9]Kang, Y., Tan, A. and Miao, C. "An Adaptive Computational Model for Personalized Persuasion." *Proceedings of the 24th International Conference on Artificial Intelligence (IJCAI'15)*, (Buenos Aires, Argentina, 2015), pp. 61–67.

prospective memory aid based on Fuzzy Cognitive Map (FCM)[10] predictions is implemented for a reminder app, enabling smartphones to automatically plan the optimal number of reminders and schedule delivery of notifications.[11] The reminder application has received positive feedback in its pilot study; subsequent revisions are looking into incorporating Self-determination Theory (SDT) to craft motivational reminder messages for more defiant users to improve their medication adherence.[12]

The next piece of assistive technology aims to bridge seniors with e-commerce platforms, enhancing their trust and ability to navigate online storefronts by themselves. Having identified seniors' limited ability to scroll through websites and read product text, researchers opted to implement three accessibility features: speech recognition, multimodal search and personalised speech feedback.[13] A follow-up usability study with a prototype of the above features[14] presented findings to refine how the features should be presented to the elderly: presenting one input option at a time, eliciting a coherent interaction method and removing designers' assumptions that user interface icons are self-explanatory.

It is anticipated that the elderly can enjoy more productivity, becoming more independent as the development of assistive technologies progresses.

[10]FCM is a modelling method for neural networks, which is one of the branches in AI.

[11]Hou, J., Zeng, Z., Miao, C. and Liu, Y. "Prospective Memory Aid: A Reminding Model Based on Fuzzy Cognitive Maps," *IEEE International Conference on Fuzzy Systems (FUZZ-IEEE)*, (Vancouver, BC, Canada, 2016), pp. 170–177.

[12]Zhang, Y., Qiu, Y., Pan, Z., Yu, X. and Miao, C. "Infusing Motivation into Reminders for Improving Medication Adherence," *Social Computing and Social Media: Applications in Marketing, Learning, and Health*, (Springer, Cham, 2021), pp. 456–471.

[13]Meng, L., Nguyen, Q. H., Tian, X., Shen, Z., Chng, E. S., Guan, Y., ... Leung, C. "Towards Age-friendly E-commerce Through Crowd-improved Speech Recognition, Multimodal Search, and Personalized Speech Feedback," *Proceedings of the 2nd International Conference on Crowd Science and Engineering (ICCSE'17)*, (Beijing, China, 2017), pp. 127–135.

[14]Yu, X., Meng, L., Tian, X., Fauvel, S., Huang, B., Guan, Y., ... Leung, C. "Usability Analysis of the Novel Functions to Assist the Senior Customers in Online Shopping," *International Conference on Social Computing and Social Media (SCSM)*, (Springer, Cham, 2018), pp. 173–185.

Wellness Games for Early Detection, Intervention and Rehabilitation

Digital games mark a milestone for the advent of information technology, and the booming commercial games industry likewise served as a testament that digital technology can be made to be fun and engaging. Researchers were quick to notice that they can gamify desirable, beneficial activities into digital tasks for increasing players' level of engagement. Health games focus on activities that are good for health and can benefit the elderly through a number of different functions such as cognitive assessment, cognitive training, physical activity stimulation, early detection of ailments and rehabilitation.[15] Thus, health games have been gaining more research attention over the years. This section provides a case study of a health game that has engaged thousands of the elderly in Singapore.

Ping Ping Pong Pong Wellness Game for Cognitive Inhibition and Exercise

Having received awards from the Singapore Book of Records,[16] the *Ping Ping Pong Pong* game serves as a case study for the iterative design process of modern health technology. Developed on the Microsoft Kinect[17] platform, this game launches ping pong balls in the player's direction. The player is required to physically move either hand to hit back the ball.

The *Ping Ping Pong Pong* game that applies the rules of familiarity design was designed using elements familiar to many elderly in Singapore. Firstly, the gameplay emulates a table tennis game, a popular sport among the Singapore population. This allows most seniors to simply associate

---

[15] Zhang, F. and Kaufman, D. "Physical and Cognitive Impacts of Digital Games on Older Adults: A Meta-analytic Review," *Journal of Applied Gerontology*, 35(11), 2016, 1189–1210.

[16] *First Interactive Gaming Kiosk Equipped with Personal Wellness Analytics*. (2015, August 30). Retrieved January 11, 2021, from Singapore Book of Records: https://singaporerecords.com/first-gaming-kiosk-equipped-with-wellness-analytics/.

[17] Microsoft Kinect integrates camera and depth sensor technology to recognize body posture and gestures.

their knowledge of hitting balls with a paddle to understand the game, thereby perceiving the game as playable. Secondly, playing the game is as simple as swinging the arm as if holding a paddle thanks to the Microsoft Kinect camera and depth sensors. In contrast to a desktop table tennis game where the mouse is used to control the paddle, swinging the arm is a more familiar action associated to table tennis, thus allowing seniors to feel more comfortable with the game the first moment they play. Thirdly, the game was decorated with background elements that conform to the cultural familiarity of seniors in Singapore.

A focus group study was then conducted with 10 seniors to find out whether the aforementioned familiar elements improve their gameplay experience.[18] The experiment group played with the gesture-based *Ping Ping Pong Pong* game, while the control group played with a desktop table tennis game using the computer mouse to control the paddle. The experiment group reported significantly higher satisfaction and adoption likelihood in the post-game survey questionnaires.

In a subsequent pilot study, the game performance of three different age groups was compared: *youngsters* below 20 years old, *adults* between 45 and 55 years old, and *elderly* above 65 years old.[19] This study also contains three slightly different tasks that recreate the Go/No-go structure, a common design pattern for cognitive tests.[20] The performance difference between the three age groups is as expected where the elderly group has lowest accuracy and takes slightly longer to respond. The pilot study concluded that lowered cognitive inhibition ability has caused their performance to be lower than other age groups.

---

[18]This publication received the "Best Demo Award" in the 2015 International Joint Conference on Web Intelligence and Intelligent Agent Technology. See Pan, Z., Miao, C., Yu, H., Leung, C. and Chin, J. J. "The Effects of Familiarity Design on the Adoption of Wellness Games by the Elderly," *IEEE/WIC/ACM International Conference on Web Intelligence and Intelligent Agent Technology (WI-IAT)*, (Singapore, 2015), pp. 387–390.

[19]Liu, S., Shen, Z., Yu, H., Lin, H., Guo, Z., Pan, Z., ... Leung, C. "A Kinect-based Interactive Game to Improve the Cognitive Inhibition of the Elderly: (Demonstration)," *International Conference on Autonomous Agents & Multiagent Systems (AAMAS)*, 2016, pp. 1479–1481. https://dl.acm.org/citation.cfm?id=2937219.

[20]Nosek, B. A. and Banaji, M. R. "The Go/No-go Association Task," *Social Cognition*, 19(6), 2001, 625–666.

A follow-up five-week-long study[21] was carried out in collaboration with a community centre, aimed at evaluating if playing the game regularly[22] helped the elderly improve their cognitive inhibition. In this study, cognitive inhibition is measured once before the first game session, and once after the last game session using the Flanker Task, Simon Task and Stroop Task. All three tests unanimously showed improvement of elderly response time after playing the game for five weeks. Improvement in accuracy is less pronounced but still present; one test showed high degree of confidence while two other tests did not. Deeper analysis revealed that the elderly who frequently play digital games started with significantly higher accuracy before playing the exergame, narrowing the improvement margin. The accuracy improvement remains consistent among the elderly with little to no prior experience with digital games. Results show promising outcomes that engaging with digital games can improve cognitive inhibition.

The game has been deployed in many different community centres during senior events and health festivals as part of the programme to engage seniors and, at the same time, to conduct larger-scale user testing. Through collaboration with hospitals and commercial partnerships, the game is also being developed to accommodate for institutional-based and home-based settings, catering to the wider care network.

In a nutshell, the *Ping Ping Pong Pong* Wellness Game is shown to improve cognitive inhibition[23] among older adults through fun and engaging gameplay. Through the use of familiar elements in game design, elderly players are willing to engage with the gameplay without the usual digital barriers and have fun from the novel experience, at the same time providing performance and postural logs for future analysis. The game can be tailored to complement the elderly care framework in Singapore, providing the elderly in different settings with a beneficial recreational activity.

---

[21]Zhang, H., Shen, Z., Liu, S., Yuan, D. and Miao, C. "Ping Pong: An Exergame for Cognitive Inhibition Training," *International Journal of Human–Computer Interaction*, 37(12), 2021, 1104–1115.
[22]Participants are required to complete six in-game rounds which is about 15 minutes long, at least once per week for five consecutive weeks.
[23]Inhibition describes the ability to keep thoughts and attention in line with task goals, and away from distractions. See https://www.ncbi.nlm.nih.gov/pmc/articles/PMC4738960/.

Enhancing Game Experience to Promote Benefits of Health Games

It is well agreed that digital games can have a positive impact when specifically designed and engineered for non-entertainment purposes.[24] In the case of improving elderly health, interactive elements of digital games help attract and encourage the elderly to participate in activities that stimulate their cognitive and physical well-being. Therefore, games can fill up the elderly's free time with fun, immersive activities that keep them engaged and happy if they are willing to engage with the digital medium.

To bridge the digital gap for the elderly, many existing research studies focus on age-friendly game design. Elderly-specific preferences when interacting with digital games (i.e., the elderly health game experience) have also been investigated. Affective designs in health games that appeal to these preferences can potentially encourage seniors to embrace technology and play more often, enabling future health games and health tech to reach more elderly. Thus, in the quest to uncover what makes the elderly enjoy health games, the author has befriended and accompanied several elderly people with Parkinson's Disease to learn and understand their game experience of playing a health game designed for improving their health. After briefing them on game benefits, the elderly were guided step by step to complete the in-game tasks, after which they shared parts of the game experience that they enjoyed. Three unique aspects of the elderly health game experience are summarised as follows[25]:

1. Familiarity — Observations were consistent with the author's proposed framework of familiarity design for elderly games.[26]

---

[24] Zayda, M. "From Visual Simulation to Virtual Reality to Games," *Computer*, 38(9), 2005, 25–32.

[25] Pan, Z., Zhang, Y., Zhang, H. and Miao, C. "Health Games Adoption among Elderly: A Depiction of the Elderly Health Game Experience," *International Journal of Information Technology*, 2021.

[26] Pan, Z., Miao, C., Yu, H., Leung, C. and Chin, J. J. "The Effects of Familiarity Design on the Adoption of Wellness Games by the Elderly," *IEEE/WIC/ACM International Conference on Web Intelligence and Intelligent Agent Technology (WI-IAT)*, (Singapore, 2015), pp. 387–390.

Symbolic familiarity is invoked via the in-game farmland theme, and actionable familiarity is invoked via the usage of a digital stylus pen in the gameplay. Similar to the Ping Pong wellness game, intuitive gameplay allows the elderly to play.

2. Health Values — Healthy aspects of games such as fine motor skills training and cognitive stimulation are generally valued alongside the fun. By bringing out health games' health values to the elderly as part of the introduction, they are more enticed to try out the game for the health benefits.

3. Human Interactions — Elderly players feel at ease and are more confident to engage the health game with the researcher's assurance and encouragement. Even during less demanding parts of the game, the elderly rely much on a human game companion when attempting to learn how to play unfamiliar digital games, citing the companionship as a major source of encouragement for them to try new things. The human presence also gave them an avenue to express affection comfortably, opening up their minds to learn new digital skills.

Based on these findings, a storytelling-inspired coaching model was developed to improve the elderly's health game experiences and acceptance towards digital technology. The coaching model proposes to generalise playing health games into four scenarios: Introduction, Completing a Game Task, Persuading Player to Continue and Final Challenge. Each scenario draws analogies from storytelling elements to lay out a step-by-step guide for the game coach, enabling them to react appropriately to the elderly throughout the gameplay session. The scenarios were also piloted tested and refined in a focus group study with five elderly players.[27]

The four scenarios are then modelled using Goal Net methodology to formalise a coaching model for tailoring health games to elderly players. The coaching model was applied onto an existing health game and was further compared with an unstructured gameplay session in a subsequent

---

[27] Pan, Z., Zhang, H., Zhang, Y., Leung, C. and Miao, C. "A Goal Oriented Storytelling Model for Improvement of Health Game Experiences among Older Adults," *Human Aspects of IT for the Aged Population. Supporting Everyday Life Activities (ITAP)*, (Springer, Cham, 2021), pp. 135–152.

study.[28] Results suggest the coaching model outperforms conventional unstructured gameplay sessions, helping elderly players attain better performance, improve their game literacy and also their health game experiences.

Future studies will look into using the coaching model to implement affective AI-driven health game companions that can effectively guide the elderly to play and enjoy health games. When used together with new technology that adjusts game difficulty to the elderly's varying abilities,[29] the coaching model may also potentially help the elderly overcome their digital barriers, increase technology acceptance and ultimately enable technology to benefit more elderly users. This preserves the human touch in a rapidly digitalising society, building digital inclusivity among the elderly in Singapore.

In summary, research in silver technology has taken on a translational approach that aims to create tangible and impactful real-world applications. An interdisciplinary approach is taking shape to bring together the best technology in each field to create innovations that can benefit the ageing population. These innovations help advance the mission to create an age-friendly environment in Singapore. Technology applications designed to benefit the community at large also benefit heavily from age-friendly features. The next section examines a few case studies of technology that are inclusive to people from all walks of life, capable of helping individuals who are digitally illiterate.

Harnessing Information Technology Innovations for Community Service

The second half of this chapter presents several avenues for information technology to contribute to the community service arena, further tightening Singapore's social fabric amidst challenges posed by the pandemic.

[28] Pan, Z., Zhang, Y., Zhang, H. and Shen, Z. "Coaching Older Adults in Health Games: A Goal Oriented Modelling Approach," *Social Computing and Social Media: Applications in Marketing, Learning, and Health (SCSM)*, (Springer, Cham, 2021), pp. 424–442.

[29] Zhang, H., Miao, C. and Yu, H. "Fuzzy Logic Based Assessment on the Adaptive Level of Rehabilitation Exergames for the Elderly," *IEEE Global Conference on Signal and Information Processing (GlobalSIP)*, (Montreal, QC, Canada, 2017), pp. 423–427.

Digital Vouchers for Post-pandemic Resource Allocation

Information technology is immensely helpful in scaling up welfare programmes through automating administrative work and speeding up transactions. The ability to upscale such programmes is timely to counteract effects caused by the COVID-19 pandemic. Businesses of heartland neighbourhood shops are taking a hit as residents — especially seniors who frequent the shops — head out less often. As such, funds are being allocated for needy households to encourage them to purchase their daily needs from neighbourhood shops and hawkers.

While food aid programmes have always been around in the Singapore community, the pandemic has spurred the expansion and digitalisation of such programmes. Several ground-up initiatives sharing the title "Belanja A Meal" were started across several divisions. The more traditional approach involves volunteers buying food from hawkers and distributing them to beneficiaries. Other meal programmes take a slightly different operational model that uses digital technology and smartphones: Beneficiaries were given cards or coupons with QR codes and bring them to participating hawker stalls to redeem food of their choice, while volunteers focus on teaching hawker stall owners to accept the meal cards using their smartphones. In Woodlands, the digital implementation of "Belanja A Meal" has also been used to substitute other food programmes to disperse queuing crowds at collection points, such as Ramadan food distribution.[30]

The concept of digital vouchers has also been expanded to benefit neighbourhood mom-and-pop shops, at the same time broadening residents' choice to include groceries and provisions. For example, the Yuhua division has launched its own Yuhua Voucher programme for residents to buy their daily needs products at neighbourhood shops and hawkers.[31]

---

[30] Yuen, S. "Ramadan Free Meal Scheme in Woodlands Goes Digital," *The Straits Times*, 18 April 2021, Singapore. Retrieved January 10, 2022, from https://www.straitstimes.com/singapore/ramadan-free-meal-scheme-in-woodlands-goes-digital.

[31] Low, D. "Mom-and-pop Shops and Coffee Shop Stalls in Yuhua Get Their Own Shopping Platform," *The Straits Times*, 31 October 2021, Singapore. Retrieved January 10, 2022, from https://www.straitstimes.com/singapore/community/mom-and-pop-shops-and-coffeeshop-stalls-in-yuhua-get-their-own-shopping-platform.

Unlike traditional one-time-use vouchers, these vouchers can be spent at any denomination, helping residents avoid the compulsion to finish using up the voucher in one go and focus on what they really need for the day.

The Community Development Council (CDC) also launched their digital version of shopping vouchers shortly after, issuing $130 million to 13 million households across Singapore.[32] Both implementations of the digital voucher have adopted several measures to ensure no resident is left out of the assistance scheme. Voucher QR codes are available physically as an option for residents unable to own or use a smartphone. As such, shop owners are trained to scan residents' voucher QR codes, unlike prevailing e-payment platforms that require residents to scan the shop's payment QR code. The practice empowers shops to support future digital community initiatives and allows less digitally savvy residents to still benefit from those initiatives.

Knowledge Management for Resident Engagement, Volunteer Training and Cross-agency Collaboration

Aside from directly improving workflows of welfare programmes, information technology can also positively transform how social services work and coordinate as noted below:

> Information technology is becoming more important to social work. The growth of information technology has to be taken advantage of by social workers. As new information about demographic profiles and behaviours is generated, it is cogent that such information be tapped quickly to chart organizational plans and strategies. Since information on demographic profiles and behaviours is scattered, it will be useful to develop a more coordinated information system on these aspects for social workers and other interested groups to utilize.[33]

---

[32] Goh, Y. H. "$100 Worth of CDC Vouchers for Each S'porean Household Available for Collection Online," *The Straits Times*, 23 December 2021, Singapore. Retrieved January 10, 2022, from https://www.straitstimes.com/singapore/100-worth-of-cdc-vouchers-for-each-sporean-household-available-for-collection-online.

[33] Vasoo, S. "The Social Work Profession in Response to Challeging Times: The Case of Singapore," *Asia Pacific Journal of Social Work and Development*, 23(4), 2013, 315–318.

Access to a wide range of information is therefore crucial in deriving insights, knowledge and evidence for improving the way we serve our community. This section describes an overview of a digital knowledge hub that aims to provide an integrated, streamlined information retrieval process for use of the community and social services.

Applications of a Community-Based Digital Knowledge Hub

Communications and engagement

In today's era with many communication platforms available, a dedicated smart profiling system can be built to record profiles of residents' households (e.g., hobbies, children in school, ailing parents) as well as preferred mode of contact, which enables outreach to be personalised (e.g., birthday, wedding anniversary). A solid communication channel with residents also helps in keeping them informed and updated with assistance programmes that may benefit them.

Multi-agency ticketing system

The knowledge hub can serve as a ticketing system for mobilising help across different agencies to solve resident's problems. Effort needs to be made to collate feedback from house visits, social media, emails and phone calls into a central ticketing system, and tagged with relevant agencies for appropriate follow-up. The system may also analyse keywords and tags across tickets across a time span to spot recurring requests that may be due for wider-scale mobilisation (e.g., more job fairs in response to more elderly residents looking for odd jobs).

Volunteer management

Transparent, accessible information should be made available across various community organisations as the data are essential to paint the proper context for volunteer training. Organisations can also readily tap into up-to-date trends to make adjustments to their social services and volunteer training programmes, creating a healthy evidence-based revision framework. Demographically targeted volunteer recruitment efforts would also

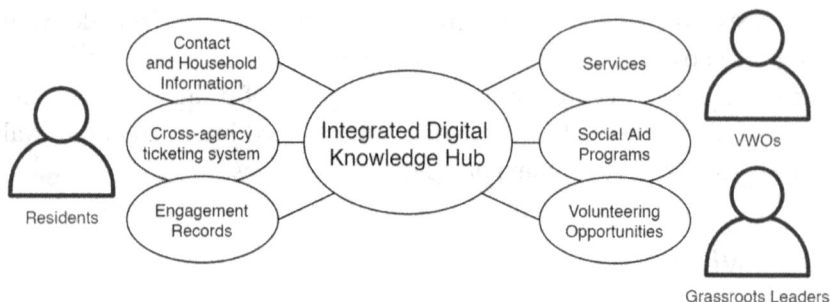

Figure 2.   Community-based Integrated Digital Knowledge Hub

become a new possibility; residents who are in capacity to give back to society can be encouraged to step up and do so.

The knowledge hub in its digital form enables a wide array of seamless integration with existing communication platforms (see Figure 2). Targeted messaging can be made as easy as crafting a message, filtering the intended audience and clicking "send", while the system automatically disseminates the message in different communications platforms according to each resident's preference. For example, a notification can be sent to residents in a specific block prior to a house visit, an online talk for youth can be broadcasted to residents below a certain age, and an upcoming job fair can be advertised to unemployed individuals. Updates in ticketed issues raised by residents may also be disseminated via this platform, beefing up communications and giving residents more community involvement throughout the process of community improvement.

Building and maintaining such a comprehensive knowledge hub may not be a small undertaking, however the potential benefits are well justified with the endless new possibilities that can stem from this new method of getting to know our community.

Emerging Crowdsourcing Technologies for Community Mobilisation and Silver Productivity

The previous two sections have described how information technology helps upscale existing welfare programmes, and how community leaders might harness IT to analyse residents' profiles and deepen engagements to build trust and goodwill. This last section presents promising emerging technologies that can look further beyond — crowd mobilisation of residents with varying backgrounds and skillsets for different communal needs. The term Social Exchange Bank (SEB) is aptly coined to describe the vision for crowd mobilisation:

> Through aggregative technology, we will be able to set up a Social Exchange Bank (SEB) wherein people can offer services and expertise to those who need services and expertise to help meet social needs. Through such a SEB managed via artificial intelligence, we can efficiently respond to those who need social services. An affordable fee could be charged for the services rendered to meet a social need. The setting up of the SEB is cost-effective, and it can be a new social exchange vehicle to reach out efficiently and cost-effectively to the people in need of services in the community.[34]

SEBs can particularly benefit the elderly or underprivileged population who may have niche skills to contribute but fall short from actually contributing, due to difficulty of finding recipients for their craft. The setting up of SEBs calls for the application of crowdsourcing technology.

Crowdsourcing refers to the act of massing effort from a large group of workers to accomplish a task as a collective. The advent of crowdsourcing technologies has significantly improved task allocation methods, taking into consideration work quality, punctuality and fair compensation for workers. While issuing identical sub-tasks to different workers is common crowdsourcing practice, it is often not possible to break up complex problems into identical sub-tasks. Current algorithms are looking into dynamic assembly of teams with diverse skillsets, enabling more complex problems to be solved using crowdsourcing methods.[35] These emerging algorithms can open new frontiers to future crowdsourcing initiatives, especially for mobilising seniors in the Singapore community.

---

[34] Vasoo, S. *Community Development Arenas in Singapore*, (Singapore: World Scientific, 2019), p. xvii.

[35] Pan, Z., Yu, H., Miao, C. and Leung, C. "Efficient Collaborative Crowdsourcing," *Proceedings of the 30th AAAI Conference on Artificial Intelligence (AAAI'16)*, Phoenix, Arizona, USA, 2016, pp. 4248–4249.

166   *J. Z. Pan*

Crowd computing can be re-contextualised as potential solutions for issues raised in gerontology research.[36] As seniors need to stay active to enjoy better health, encouraging silver productivity can be a key research focus in crowd computing. The author has worked on a productive ageing mobile app that allows seniors to actively contribute their knowledge and past experiences in helping organise historical photos of Singapore.[37] This implementation serves as proof of concept of how seniors' collective knowledge and wisdom may be crowdsourced to contribute to a common cause.

A potentially more impactful paradigm for crowd computing is for seniors to passively contribute to research without requiring any particular skillset. Research on affective computing, realistic AI companions, persuasive agents and prospective memory agents (i.e., personalised reminders) can only be improved based on elderly test users' behavioural data. Crowd computing technologies are important in these research efforts for gathering and organising large amounts of behavioural data. For example, the SG50 Wish Mobile App harnesses such technology to collate user-generated content. SG50 Wish[38] is an app designed for residents to personalise and share their well wishes during Singapore's 50th anniversary celebrations. In promotion of inter-generational interactions, youngsters use the app to take pictures of seniors holding the SG50 logo while Augmented Reality technology generates a new image with birthday cakes on the logo, symbolising birthday wishes for Singapore.[39]

---

[36]Yu, H., Pan, Z., Miao, C. and Leung, C. "Crowd Computing for Population Aging Challenges," *Proceedings of the 1st International Conference on Crowd Science and Engineering (ICCSE'16).*

[37]Yu, H., Miao, C., Liu, S., Pan, Z., Khalid, N. S., Shen, Z. and Leung, C. "Productive Aging through Intelligent Personalized Crowdsourcing," *Proceedings of the 30th AAAI Conference on Artificial Intelligence (AAAI'16),* (Phoenix, Arizona, USA, 2016), pp. 4405–4406. Retrieved from https://dl.acm.org/doi/abs/10.5555/3016387.3016616.

[38]Tan, T. H. *SG50 Wish,* 2015. Retrieved from Androidblip https://www.androidblip.com/android-apps/com.LILY.MKrapid.html.

[39]Pan, Z., Miao, C., Tan, B. T., Yu, H. and Leung, C. "Agent Augmented Inter-generational Crowdsourcing," *IEEE/WIC/ACM International Conference on Web Intelligence and Intelligent Agent Technology (WI-IAT),* (Singapore, 2015), pp. 237–238.

The crowdsourced findings will be used to conduct further studies on persuasion and designing technologies for promoting inter-generational bonding.

All in all, emerging crowdsourcing technology provides avenues to identify strengths and excavate wisdom from the elderly, at the same time empowering them to contribute to silver technology research, achieving fuller community mobilisation. The technology is promising in realising an SEB where people can give and take based on their skills and needs. Exciting applications that can be done with such a system include job matching, volunteer training and interest group bonding / skills exchange workshops.

Summary

As Singapore recovers from the effects of COVID-19, the nation needs to be well prepared to face the challenges brought about by an ageing society. Unlike the pandemic, the effects of ageing are here to stay, and long-term tech-enabled solutions play a pivotal role in paving the social landscape ahead for Singapore. This chapter has hopefully shed light on how state-of-the-art technology has been applied to combat short- and long-term societal issues, and ways forward for human-centric technology applications to continue benefitting the Singapore community.

Chapter 9

Productive Ageing: Examining Conceptual and Empirical Issues

Peter Sun and Nancy Morrow-Howell

Abstract

As population ageing is a global phenomenon, dealing with declining birth rates is likewise a rising global issue. This will have a momentous knock-on political, economic and social impact on all societies, and dealing with this trend will become a key national and international political issue. This will involve issues involving employment and healthcare, especially for the chronically ill. Against this backdrop, a key issue is how to deal with productive ageing in terms of research, programmes and policies. This in turn will involve the issue of productive engagement of the ageing in a society. As ageing transforms the world in older societies, issues of health, education, employment and social programmes will change, in turn, requiring our attitudes and expectations to alter likewise.

Introduction on the Productive Ageing Perspective

Population ageing is a global phenomenon. Lower birth rates and mortality rates are transforming age distributions. There are increasing numbers

169

of people over the age of 60 but fewer children are being born. The biggest challenges facing most societies are economic security and healthcare. Consequently, public and private budgets are strained to provide support to people who live into the seventh, eighth and ninth decade of life. These trends put pressure on societies to modify physical and social structures to accommodate longer lives. Clearly, policy and programme developments are in the longer term needed to provide post-employment income and healthcare for chronic conditions. Additionally, long-term care is needed for the growing number of older adults who need assistance with daily living.

These demographic realities have led government officials, professionals and academics alike to focus on the problems of ageing societies — how to address issues of poverty, morbidity and the social care needs of people over the age of 60. These are challenges never faced before in human history, because the extension of human life has been so dramatic and so rapid. Yet, these challenges have created a narrative that "problematises" longer lives. Older adults are seen as burdens to economies, as drains to families and communities' resources, and as a strain to the health and social care system. The phrase "silver tsunami", often used to describe the demographic revolution, depicts the public's attitudes about old age and longer life. Population ageing is seen as a disaster and older people will drown younger people and society as we know it.

This focus on "age as problem" or the "age drain perspective" fails to recognise the successes of global demographic shifts. Medical and public health advances have doubled the human span in the last 150 years, a huge success for humankind. Further, people are in general living healthier lives within those extended years. As seen in many chapters of this book,[1] in many places in the world, adults who reach the age of 60 can expect to live 20–30 years more. Additionally, educational levels continue to grow for subsequent cohorts. In sum, not only are the numbers and percentage of older adults increasing but the human capital of this segment of the population is increasing as well. This human capital has been deemed the

---

[1] Vasoo, S., Singh, B. and Chokkanathan, S. S. (eds.), *Singapore Ageing: Issues and Challenges Ahead*, (Singapore: World Scientific, 2023).

only growing natural resource.[2] Yet, this aspect of population ageing has received limited attention.

In response to the predominance of the age drain perspective, Dr. Robert Butler, the first head of the National Institute on Aging in the United States, introduced the term "productive ageing".[3] Butler called for the redirection of attention from the dependencies associated with later life to the contributions of older adults.[4] Further, he suggested that society could not continue to dismiss the growing capacity of the older population, and that productive engagement of older people was a necessity, not a luxury.[5] From these early advocacy efforts came a new paradigm for population ageing where the capacity of older adults is not only recognised but seen as a resource to be used to offset the demands associated with population ageing. In sum, productive ageing is an important perspective, because it shifts away from a paradigm centred on ageing as problematic to an empirically driven paradigm that recognises and promotes the contributions of older adults.

Challenges and Concerns

From its beginning, the concept of productive ageing was criticised in several ways.[6] There was concern that productivity might be viewed as the most important element of later life. Productive activities would be valued

---

[2] Freedman, M. *The Big Shift: Navigating Midlife and Beyond*, (New York, NY: Perseus Books Group, 2011).

[3] Butler, R. N. and Gleason, H. *Productive Aging: Enhancing Vitality in Later Life*, (New York: Springer, 1985).

[4] Butler, R. N. *Why Survive? Being Old in America, 1st edn, (New York:* Harper & Row, 1975).

[5] Butler, R. N. "Living Longer, Contributing Longer," *The Journal of the American Medical Association*, 278(16), 1997, 1372–1374.

[6] Moody, H. "Productive Aging and the Ideology of Old Age," in N. Morrow-Howell, J. Hinterlong and M. Sherraden (eds.), *Productive Aging: Concepts and Challenges*, (Baltimore: Johns Hopkins University Press, 2001), pp. 175–196; and Holstein, M. B. and Minkler, M. "Critical Gerontology: Reflections for the 21st Century," M. Bernard and T. Scharf (eds.), *Critical Perspectives on Ageing Societies*, (Buckingham, UK: Open University Press, 2007), pp. 12–26.

over artistic, leisure, spiritual and other types of important human endeavours. There was also the charge that calling certain aspects of ageing productive implied that other facets of ageing were unproductive. In fact, the word productive itself can carry negative connotations when tied closely to the idea of factory labour and forced output of service and products. There is also the fear that older people will be judged by their ability to be productive. There may be expectations that older adults with impaired function or low resources should engage in work, volunteering or caregiving. People who have experience in being disadvantaged, discriminated and marginalised across their life course will continue to be excluded in these respected roles.

In light of these valid concerns, it is important to articulate values to guide research, programmes and policy development regarding the productive participation of older adults. The agenda should be about increasing opportunity and choice as well as about eliminating barriers to engagement. Participation of older adults cannot be coerced, and there must be the recognition of various levels of health, education and income. Participation cannot be exploited, and both paid and unpaid work needs to be recognised and valued. Diversity and inclusion are important values for preventing disparities in engagement and health outcomes.[7] In sum, the productive ageing concept should be about tapping the growing human capital of the older population, creating opportunities and choices for productive engagement in later life, and supporting older adults in these valued roles for the benefit of the individual, the family and society. All these efforts will motivate older adults to be involved in meaningful social and economic activities for family and community betterment.

Defining Productive Engagement and Potential Outcomes

The term "productive ageing" has been operationalised to mean the engagement of older persons in roles that make economic contributions to society. Most often, scholars have focused on paid and unpaid work, including working, volunteering and caregiving. Other scholars have

---

[7] Gonzales, E., Matz-Costa, C. and Morrow-Howell, N. "Increasing Opportunities for the Productive Engagement of Older Adults: A Response to Population Aging," *The Gerontologist*, 55, 2015, 252–261.

included all types of paid employment, formal and informal volunteering, family caregiving, custodial grandparenting and educational/training activities. Gerontologists have noted the value of other types of activities to older adults, including recreational, artistic, spiritual and social, and have argued that all forms of activities can and should be studied and facilitated.

The productive ageing argument is that productive activities have the potential to benefit families, communities and societies as well as individual older adults. That is, working, volunteering and caregiving are valued functions in society, and there may be increased demands for these activities. Labour shortages due to declining birth rates are requiring longer working lives; the reliance on unpaid labour in non-profit and public organisations remains high in certain socio-political contexts, and family caregiving is in increasing demand in response to the growing number of people over the age of 85 who need assistance. At the same time, for many older adults, this vital engagement promotes physical, cognitive, social and mental health. Indeed, it is the "win-win", the positive outcomes in multiple domains, that characterises the productive ageing perspective.

Scholars have proposed that a wide range of outcomes may be associated with productive engagement of older adults and that these outcomes can be specified at the societal, community or individual level. At the societal level, with older adults engaged in paid or unpaid jobs, there will be a larger supply of experienced employees, volunteers and caregivers. Organisations have already begun to support older workers to facilitate longer working lives, given labour supply issues, and longer working lives may lead to more earned income and savings and, therefore, less reliance on post-retirement income and less strain on public and private income support programmes.[8] In certain socio-political cultures, older adults volunteer more hours than younger adults, and the value of their contributions has been assessed at US$44.3 billion a year in the U.S.[9]

---

[8] Munnell, A. and Sass, S. A. *Working Longer: The Solution to the Retirement Income Challenge*, (Washington, DC: Brookings Institute Press, 2008).

[9] Johnson, R. W. and Schaner, S. G. *Value of Unpaid Activities by Older Americans Tops $160 Billion Per Year* (No. 4; The Retirement Project: Perspectives on Productive Aging). Urban Institute, 2005.

There are a growing number of inter-generational volunteer programmes, with older adults tutoring and mentoring children and youth. The growth of these efforts could improve inter-generational understanding and increase inter-generational reciprocity. Inter-generational and family relationships could be strengthened through caregiving activities, which have been valued at US$470 billion annually in the US.[10] Indeed, the active engagement of older adults in their communities has seldom been considered as an economic asset. Thus, increasing the involvement of older adults as volunteers and caregivers may lead to a stronger civic society.

On the individual level, most older adults express the desire to remain meaningfully engaged, to make contributions, to "matter".[11] Volunteering, the most discretionary of the activities, is associated with improved well-being outcomes.[12] While paid work has been associated with improved health and mental health, there are older people who are negatively affected by these roles.[13] Similarly, both positive and negative outcomes of caregiving have been documented.[14] Clearly, the context and nature of engagement affect outcomes for the individual.[15] For example, some

---

[10] AARP, *Valuing the Invaluable 2019 Update: Charting a Path Forward* (Insight on the Issues), AARP, 2019.

[11] Flett, G. L. and Heisel, M. J. "Aging and Feeling Valued Versus Expendable During the COVID-19 Pandemic and Beyond: A Review and Commentary of Why Mattering is Fundamental to the Health and Well-being of Older Adults," *International Journal of Mental Health Addiction*, June 2020, 1–27.

[12] Anderson, N. D., Damianakis, T., Kröger, E., Wagner, L. M., Dawson, D. R., Binns, M. A., Bernstein, S., Caspi, E. and Cook, S. L. "The Benefits Associated with Volunteering Among Seniors," *Psychological Bulletin*, 140(6), 2014, 1505–1533.

[13] Wickrama, K. (K. A. S.), O'Neal, C. W., Kwag, K. H. and Lee, T. K. "Is Working Later in Life Good or Bad for Health? An Investigation of Multiple Health Outcomes," *The Journals of Gerontology: Series B*, 68(5), 2013, 807–815.

[14] Bom, J., Bakx, P., Schut, F. and van Doorslaer, E. "The Impact of Informal Caregiving for Older Adults on the Health of Various Types of Caregivers," *The Gerontologist*, 59(5), 2019.

[15] Gonzales, E., Matz-Costa, C. and Morrow-Howell, N. "Increasing Opportunities for the Productive Engagement of Older Adults: A Response to Population Aging," *The Gerontologist*, 55, 2015, 252–261; and Matz, C., Sabbath, E. and James, J. "An Integrative Conceptual Framework of Engagement in Socially-Productive Activity in Later Life: Implications for Clinical and Mezzo Social Work Practice," *Clinical Social Work Journal* [special issue on productive aging], 48, 2020, 156–168.

workers have less positive outcomes because of the work environment and lack of choice. Volunteering produces better health outcomes for adults with fewer socio-economic resources, and the negative outcomes of caregiving can be mediated by policies that support caregiving activities.

In sum, while productive engagement may benefit society, it has both positive and negative effects on older people. If productive engagement is important for society and, in many circumstances, good for older adults, researchers should seek to build knowledge about how to increase participation, minimise negative effects and maximise positive outcomes. Operationalising productive ageing is important, because it creates a research agenda that can translate into programme and policy interventions. The productive engagement perspective highlights the many determinants of productive activities, with a focus on extra-individual factors such as on programme, policies and organisational factors. This focus differentiates the productive ageing paradigm from successful ageing, where individual behaviours are highlighted.[16] Three components of successful ageing have been proposed: low probability of disease, high functioning and active engagement with life. Active engagement with life includes close personal relationships with family and friends and continued involvement in productive activities. Productive engagement can thus be viewed as a key element of the larger vision of successful ageing, because it expands and interrogates the types of productive activities that are most conducive to successful ageing.

Development of Conceptual Frameworks

Bass *et al.* presented the first conceptual framework to understand antecedents of engagement in these productive activities.[17] They identified four sets of factors: individual factors (motivation, attitude, gender, etc.), situational factors (roles, responsibilities, health, family situation, etc.), environmental factors (economy, culture, cohort, etc.) and social policy factors (employment policies, pensions, programmes, etc.). They proposed that increasing participation of older adults in activities that have

---

[16] Rowe, J. and Kahn, R. *Successful Aging*, (New York, NY: Pantheon Books, 1998).
[17] Bass, S. A., Caro, F. G. and Chen, Y. P. (eds.) *Achieving a Productive Aging Society*, (Westport, CT: Auburn House, 1993).

economic value to society can best be achieved through programme, policies and regulations.

Sherraden *et al.* presented another conceptual framework that indicated that institutional capacity, social policies and programme developments should be targeted to increase the productive involvement of older
adults.[18] They proposed that productive engagement is a function of both
individual and institutional capacity. Given current demographic shifts,
the individual capacity of older adults is growing while the institutional
capacity has not been updated to support engagement. Institutional capacity includes the ability of social institutions, such as colleges/universities,
businesses and workplaces, civic clubs, public or private agencies, and
religious organisations to provide productive roles for older adults.
Organisations vary in their ability to attract and support older adults as
workers, volunteers and caregivers, and interventions to improve these
capacity are feasible.[19]

Morrow-Howell, Mui and Wang refined the model to emphasise the
importance of culture[20] (see Figure 1). They recognised the important
influences that socio-political and cultural factors have on definitions of
productive activities, attitudes about older adults and programme/policy
options. For example, volunteering rates vary widely between countries,[21]
explained by cultural traditions and the size and strength of non-govern-
mental agencies. Regarding work, mandatory retirement ages exist in
most but not all countries, and currently, there are important debates
about raising the retirement age or eliminating age restrictions all

---

[18] Sherraden, M., Morrow-Howell, N. and Hinterlong, J. "Productive Aging: Theoretical
Choices and Directions," in *Productive Aging: Concepts and Challenges*, (John Hopkins
University Press, 2001), pp. 260–284.

[19] Hong, S., Morrow-Howell, N., Tang, F. and Hinterlong, J. "Engaging Older Adults in
Volunteering: Conceptualizing and Measuring Institutional Capacity," *Nonprofit and
Voluntary Sector Quarterly*, 38, 2009, 200–219.

[20] Morrow-Howell, N. and Mui, A. C. "Introduction," in N. Morrow-Howell and A. C. Mui
(eds.), *Productive Engagement in Later Life: A Global Perspective*, (London: Routledge,
2012).

[21] United Nations Volunteers (UNV) programme, *The Scope and Scale of Global
Volunteering: Current Estimates and Next Steps*, (United Nations Volunteers, 2018).

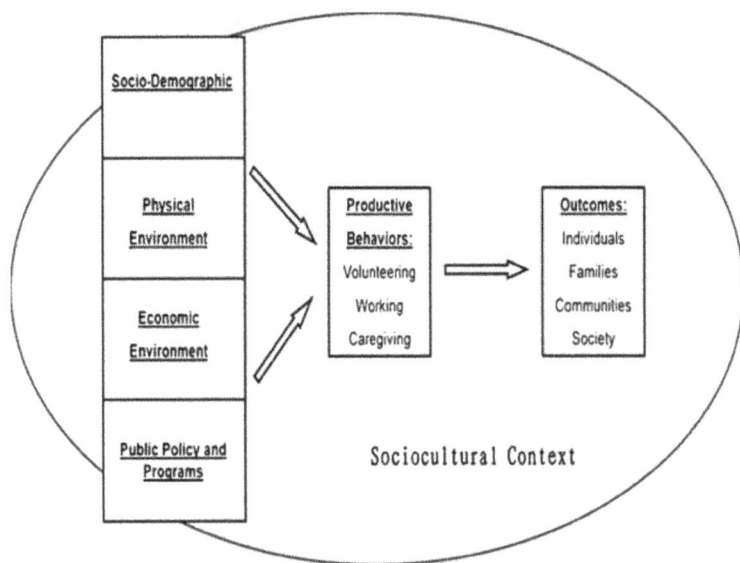

Figure 1. Cross-cultural Framework on Productive Engagement in Later Life

Source: Morrow-Howell, N. and Wang, Y. "Productive Engagement of Older Adults: Elements of a Cross-cultural Research Agenda", *Ageing International*, 38, 2018, 159–170.

together.[22] Caregiving and grand parenting are important roles in most societies but cultures vary in terms of expectations and support for these activities.

Figure 1 shows the four types of antecedents for productive engagement — socio-demographic, economic, physical environment, and public policies and programmes. These determinants relate to the productive activities of working, volunteering, and caregiving; and these activities are viewed as intermediate outcomes with effects on individuals, families, communities, and society as more ultimate outcomes. Noteworthy, the socio-cultural context is included as an underlying, foundation background to understanding productive engagement. Sociocultural variations exist in expectations about later life, family structures, labour market

---

[22] Hofäcker, D., Hess, M. and König, S. *Delaying Retirement: Progress and Challenges of Active Ageing in Europe, the United States and Japan*, (London: Palgrave MacMillan, 2016).

supply and demands, physical and social infrastructures, and existing pro-grammes. These contexts clearly shape the antecedents, the outcomes and the relationships between all these variables.

Volunteering

The United Nations' "2018 State of the World's Volunteerism Report" found decreasing rates of formal, organisation-based volunteering as a function of age in some countries and relatively high rates in other coun-tries. In Hungary, Poland, Portugal and Canada, formal volunteering rates decreased with age, with the proportion of volunteers aged 65 and above ranging between 1% in Hungary and 40% in Canada. Formal volunteering rates increased with age in the United States, Italy and South Africa but peaked in midlife, with the proportion of volunteers aged 65 and above at 25%, 22% and 5%, respectively. Rates of volunteering are relatively high among all age groups in both Australia and Japan; roughly 30% of popula-tions aged 65 and above volunteered in an organisation. A fairly even distribution between the sexes in formal volunteering was also found, though when factoring in direct volunteering, women carry out a majority (57%) of volunteer work.[23]

A number of socio-cultural and political factors are related to the vari-ability in global volunteerism. In the United States, older adults who have a higher educational level, higher income, work part time and are married are more likely to volunteer.[24] Further, older adults in the U.S. benefit from a wide array of federal and state policies and programmes that pro-mote civic service. A study of 13 European countries found that the increased likelihood of volunteering was related to education, retirement and participation in religious activities but not related to chronic diseases.[25] In predominantly Catholic countries, such as Mexico, participation in

---

[23] United Nations Volunteers (UNV) programme, *The Scope and Scale of Global Volunteering: Current Estimates and Next Steps*, (United Nations Volunteers, 2018).

[24] Bureau of Labor Statistics, *Volunteering in the United States, 2015*. Economic News Release, 25 February 2016. See https://www.bls.gov/news.release/volun.htm.

[25] Papa, R., Cutuli, G., Principi, A. and Scherer, S. "Health and Volunteering in Europe: A Longitudinal Study," *Research on Aging*, 41(7), 2019, 670–696. See https://doi.org/10.1177/0164027519834939.

religious-based organisations is related to social solidarity and group cohesion.[26] Research on older adults in Hong Kong and China shows that their cultural traditions have emphasised post-retirement leisure, which may explain lower levels of volunteerism. At the same time, Chinese scholars have noted a growing enthusiasm for extending helping behaviour beyond kith and kin to their own communities.[27] Research in Australia has found that the reluctance to volunteer among older adults may be attributed to negative perceptions of volunteering, which can be changed via trialing volunteering for a short period of time.[28]

The link between formal volunteering among older adults and positive physical and psychological outcomes is well established in the literature. Experience Corps, a randomised controlled trial in the U.S., has demonstrated that a high-intensity volunteering programme with elementary school students can lead to increased physical activity, strength, walking speed, cognitive functioning and self-rated health.[29] Consistent with the Experience Corps findings, older adults in Japan involved in an intensive volunteering programme had better self-rated health than controls, in addition to increased social networking with grandchildren or neighbours.[30] In a longitudinal study of Taiwanese older adult volunteers, Li *et al.* found better self-rated health and higher life satisfaction

---

[26] United Nations Volunteers (UNV) programme, *The Scope and Scale of Global Volunteering: Current Estimates and Next Steps*, (United Nations Volunteers, 2018).

[27] Morrow-Howell, N. and Mui, A. C. "Introduction," in N. Morrow-Howell and A. C. Mui (eds.), *Productive Engagement in Later Life: A Global Perspective*, (London: Routledge, 2012).

[28] Jongenelis, M. I., Jackson, B., Warburton, J., Newton, R. U. and Pettigrew, S. "Improving Attitudes to Volunteering Among Older Adults: A Randomized Trial Approach," *Research on Aging*, 42(2), 2020, 51–61. https://doi.org/10.1177/0164027519877476.

[29] Brydges, C. R., Carlson, M. C., Andrews, R. M., Rebok, G. W. and Bielak, A. A. M. "Using Cognitive Intraindividual Variability to Measure Intervention Effectiveness: Results from the Baltimore Experience Corps Trial," *The Journals of Gerontology: Series B*, 76(4), 2021, 661–670. https://doi.org/10.1093/geronb/gbaa009.

[30] Fujiwara, Y., Sakuma, N., Ohba, H., Nishi, M., Lee, S., Watanabe, N., Kousa, Y., Yoshida, H., Fukaya, T., Yajima, S., Amano, H., Kureta, Y., Ishii, K., Uchida, H. and Shinkai, S. "Effects of an Intergenerational Health Promotion Program for Older Adults in Japan," *Journal of Intergenerational Relationships*, 7(1), 2009, 17–39. https://doi.org/10.1080/15350770802628901.

among volunteers versus non-volunteers; they also show that volunteering may attenuate or even reverse physical and psychological decline over time.[31] Ayalon's study of Israeli older adults confirmed prior findings that volunteering is associated with a reduced mortality risk; but not all types and lengths of volunteering resulted in the same outcomes.[32]

Work

Over the past few decades, an increasing proportion of older adults globally are participating in the labour force. Between 2019 and 2021, the employment rates of individuals aged 55 to 64 were 77% in Japan, 72% in Germany, 62% in Canada, 61% in the United States, 56% in France, 53% in Italy and 31% in Turkey.[33] In 2015, there were also significant regional differences in employment rates among older adults aged 65 and over: about 7% in Europe and Central Asia, 10% in the Arab States, 20% in the Americas, 25% in Asia and the Pacific, and 40% in Africa. Compared to the rates in 2005, the 2015 rates in the Americas, Europe and Central Asia increased, while the rates in Africa, the Arab States, and Asia and the Pacific decreased. While overall employment rates are on average increasing, the long-term unemployment rates (i.e., being unemployed for a year or more) of older adults aged 65 and over in most countries (82% of countries with data) tend to be greater than the overall unemployment rates.[34] Self-employment is another growing trend among older adults; an estimated 31 million older adults in the U.S. have some interest in

[31] Li, Y.-P., Chen, Y.-M. and Chen, C.-H. "Volunteer Transitions and Physical and Psychological Health Among Older Adults in Taiwan," *The Journals of Gerontology: Series B*, 68(6), 2013, 997–1008. https://doi.org/10.1093/geronb/gbt098.

[32] Ayalon, L. "Volunteering as a Predictor of All-cause Mortality: What Aspects of Volunteering Really Matter?" *International Psychogeriatrics*, 20(5), 2008, 1000–1013. https://doi.org/10.1017/S1041610208007096.

[33] OECD, *Employment Rate by Age Group*. OECD Data, 2021. http://data.oecd.org/emp/employment-rate-by-age-group.htm.

[34] ILO, "What about Seniors? A Quick Analysis of the Situation of Older Persons in the Labour Market," 4 May 2018. https://www.ilo.org/global/statistics-and-databases/publications/WCMS_629567/lang--en/index.htm.

entrepreneurship.[35] Other patterns of work are also becoming more prevalent: bridge jobs, phased retirement and unretirement (that it, labour market reentry following retirement).

The global extension of work in later life may be partially explained by demographic changes, such as greater life expectancy, lower fertility rates and the consequent ageing of the population. Economic changes, such as inadequate pensions to support retirement, may also play a role in the greater share of older adults in the working-age population. Regional differences in employment rates highlight differences in social protection systems, which, in turn, affect labour force participation decisions in later life. For example, compared to the employment rate of older adults aged 65 and over in Europe (7%), the much higher employment rate of older adults in Africa (39%) implicates a weaker safety net and hence fewer labour market exits.[36] Socio-cultural and political factors also affect work in later life. Researchers have found that older adults in Hong Kong are less likely to work if they live with married children.[37] In Singapore, older adults may face the push of a strong Chinese work ethic to extend their working lives, but also a simultaneous pull away from work owing to the traditional concept of *xiang qin fu* or "enjoying the fortune of doing nothing".[38] Similarly, the promotion of Active Ageing policy and reforms in Poland may also result in a dual tension for older workers: an acceleration of work opportunities in tandem with a widening lag in care infrastructure.[39]

[35] Halvorsen, C. J. and Chen, Y.-C. "The Diversity of Interest in Later-life Entrepreneurship: Results from a Nationally Representative Survey of Americans Aged 50–70," *PLOS One*, 14(6), 2019, e0217971. https://doi.org/10.1371/journal.pone.0217971.

[36] ILO, "What about Seniors? A Quick Analysis of the Situation of Older Persons in the Labour Market," 4 May 2018. https://www.ilo.org/global/statistics-and-databases/publications/WCMS_629567/lang--en/index.htm.

[37] Ko, P.-C. and Yeung, W.-J. J. "Contextualizing Productive Aging in Asia: Definitions, Determinants, and Health Implications," *Social Science & Medicine (1982)*, 229, 2019, 1–5. https://doi.org/10.1016/j.socscimed.2019.01.016.

[38] Thang, L. L. "Experiencing Leisure in Later Life: A Study of Retirees and Activity in Singapore," *Journal of Cross-cultural Gerontology*, 20(4), 2005, 307–318. https://doi.org/10.1007/s10823-006-9010-6.

[39] Zbyszewska, A. "Active Aging through Employment: A Critical Feminist Perspective on Polish Policy," *International Journal of Comparative Labour Law & Industrial Relations*, 32(4), 2016, 449–472.

Research has documented both the benefits and potential hazards of working in later years. As mentioned in the case of Poland, the absence of a case infrastructure for older workers may translate into deleterious working conditions and living standards. Indeed, results from the Survey of Health, Ageing and Retirement in Europe (SHARE) have established a strong correlation between poor job quality and poor health.[40] On the other hand, paid work has been linked with happiness, less depressive symptoms, increased cognitive capacities and slower mental health decline.[41] In both China and India, it was found that paid employment had limited but positive mediating effects on the well-being of older adults.[42] Finally, it is important to recognise that older workers may represent a select group of workers with a higher baseline of health and economic security nets.[43]

Caregiving

In 2020, an estimated 29 million American caregivers aged 50 and over cared for an adult or child with special needs.[44] Estimates of informal

[40] Börsch-Supan, A., Brugiavini, A., Jürges, H., Mackenbach, J., Siegrist, J. and Weber, G. (eds.) *Quality of Employment and Well-being: First Results from the Survey of Health, Ageing and Retirement in Europe*, (Mannheim Research Institute for the Economics of Aging, MEA, 2005).

[41] Calvo, E., Haverstick, K. and Sass, S. A. "Gradual Retirement, Sense of Control, and Retirees' Happiness," *Research on Aging*, 31(1), 2009, 112–135. https://doi.org/10.1177/0164027508324704; Fisher, G. G., Chaffee, D. S., Tetrick, L. E., Davalos, D. B. and Potter, G. G. "Cognitive Functioning, Aging, and Work: A Review and Recommendations for Research and Practice," *Journal of Occupational Health Psychology*, 22(3), 2017, 314–336. https://doi.org/10.1037/ocp0000086; and Wickrama, K. (K. A. S.), O'Neal, C. W., Kwag, K. H. and Lee, T. K. "Is Working Later in Life Good or Bad for Health? An Investigation of Multiple Health Outcomes," *The Journals of Gerontology: Series B*, 68(5), 2013, 807–815. https://doi.org/10.1093/geronb/gbt069.

[42] Ko, P.-C. and Yeung, W.-J. J. "Contextualizing Productive Aging in Asia: Definitions, Determinants, and Health Implications," *Social Science & Medicine (1982)*, 229, 2019, 1–5. https://doi.org/10.1016/j.socscimed.2019.01.016.

[43] Li, C.-Y. and Sung, F.-C. "A Review of the Healthy Worker Effect in Occupational Epidemiology," *Occupational Medicine*, 49(4), 1999, 225–229. https://doi.org/10.1093/occmed/49.4.225.

[44] AARP and NAC. *Caregiving in the United States 2020*. AARP, 2020. https://doi.org/10.26419/ppi.00103.001.

caregivers aged 50 and over in Europe range from 13.5% to 25.6%. By country, the share of informal caregivers is nearly 13% in Portugal and Spain, about 18% in Central European countries such as Austria, Germany, Italy and Greece, and more than 22% in Luxembourg, Belgium and Denmark.[45] In Asian societies, there is considerable variability in the percentage of grandparent caregivers. India has the highest proportion of grandparental caregivers (56%), whereas Vietnam (34%), Myanmar (33%) and Thailand (28%) have lower percentages.[46] In China, 42% of older adults in urban areas took care of grandchildren in 2006, compared to 35% of older adults in rural areas.[47]

Older adult caregivers in the US tend to be White, married and caregivers of older adults.[48] Research has compared differences between minority and White caregivers, with agreement on the significance of ethnicity on service use but conflicting results on whether one group uses more services than the other.[49] A study on Chinese American caregivers' service use, which varied based on the timing of their migration and subsequent acculturation, showed that there is also variability within minority groups.[50] In Europe, informal caregivers tend to be female and among the

---

[45] Tur-Sinai, A., Teti, A., Rommel, A., Hlebec, V. and Lamura, G. "How Many Older Informal Caregivers Are There in Europe? Comparison of Estimates of Their Prevalence from Three European Surveys," *International Journal of Environmental Research and Public Health*, 17(24), 2020, 9531. https://doi.org/10.3390/ijerph17249531.

[46] Ko, P.-C. and Yeung, W.-J. J. "Contextualizing Productive Aging in Asia: Definitions, Determinants, and Health Implications," *Social Science & Medicine (1982)*, 229, 2019, 1–5. https://doi.org/10.1016/j.socscimed.2019.01.016.

[47] Sun, J. "Chinese Older Adults Taking Care of Grandchildren: Practices and Policies for Productive Aging," *Ageing International*, 38(1), 2013, 58–70. https://doi.org/10.1007/s12126-012-9161-4.

[48] AARP and NAC. *Caregiving in the United States 2020.* AARP, 2020. https://doi.org/10.26419/ppi.00103.001.

[49] Kosloski, K., Schaefer, J. P., Allwardt, D., Montgomery, R. J. V. and Karner, T. X. "The Role of Cultural Factors on Clients' Attitudes Toward Caregiving, Perceptions of Service Delivery, and Service Utilization," *Home Health Care Services Quarterly*, 21(3–4), 2002, 65–88. https://doi.org/10.1300/J027v21n03_04.

[50] Liu, J., Lou, Y., Wu, B. and Mui, A. C. Y.-S. "I've Been Always Strong to Conquer Any Suffering: Challenges and Resilience of Chinese American Dementia Caregivers in a Life Course Perspective," *Aging & Mental Health*, 2020, 1–9. https://doi.org/10.1080/1360786 3.2020.1793900.

middle and higher educated populations. More highly educated caregivers tend to have better health, which may explain why they are more involved in informal caregiving.[51] In India, cultural values such as filial piety and gendered societal roles are important influences on older adult caregiving.[52] In China, caregiving and other forms of productive engagement are related to health, social and human capital, which are being promoted through national professional organisations and social entrepreneurship.[53]

Grandparent caregivers in China help alleviate young adults' childcare stress, but nearly half of grandparent caregivers in China reported caregiver burden, in part due to not feeling competent in their caregiving role.[54] Geography and access to resources also affect caregiving outcomes. Bedard *et al.* found that Canadian rural caregivers' self-reported burden was associated with fewer health behaviours, compared to urban caregivers.[55] In a review of the literature, Goins *et al.* also found a positive association between caregiver burden and depression among rural caregivers.[56] Some studies have found that the positives of caregiving outweigh the negatives. A sample of Australian caregivers aged 65 and older had a

[51] Tur-Sinai, A., Teti, A., Rommel, A., Hlebec, V. and Lamura, G. "How Many Older Informal Caregivers Are There in Europe? Comparison of Estimates of Their Prevalence from Three European Surveys," *International Journal of Environmental Research and Public Health*, 17(24), 2020, 9531. https://doi.org/10.3390/ijerph17249531.

[52] Ugargol, A. P. and Bailey, A. "Family Caregiving for Older Adults: Gendered Roles and Caregiver Burden in Emigrant Households of Kerala, India," *Asian Population Studies*, 14(2), 2018, 194–210. https://doi.org/10.1080/17441730.2017.1412593.

[53] Mui, A. C. "Productive Ageing in China: A Human Capital Perspective," *China Journal of Social Work*, 3(2–3), 2010, 111–123. https://doi.org/10.1080/17525098.2010.492634.

[54] Sun, J. "Chinese Older Adults Taking Care of Grandchildren: Practices and Policies for Productive Aging," *Ageing International*, 38(1), 2013, 58–70. https://doi.org/10.1007/s12126-012-9161-4.

[55] Bédard, M., Koivuranta, A. and Stuckey, A. "Health Impact on Caregivers of Providing Informal Care to a Cognitively Impaired Older Adult: Rural Versus Urban Settings," *Canadian Journal of Rural Medicine: The Official Journal of the Society of Rural Physicians of Canada = Journal Canadien De La Medecine Rurale: Le Journal Officiel De La Societe De Medecine Rurale Du Canada*, 9(1), 2004, 15–23.

[56] Goins, R. T., Spencer, S. M. and Byrd, J. C. "Research on Rural Caregiving: A Literature Review," *Journal of Applied Gerontology*, 28(2), 12009, 39–170. https://doi.org/10.1177/0733464808326294.

higher quality of life than non-caregivers.[57] A cross-sectional study of informal caregivers in the U.S. also found that caregivers had higher processing speed and memory performance than non-caregivers.[58]

Future Directions

Countries around the globe are in the process of transforming into older societies. Health, educational and social systems are changing, as well as attitudes and expectations about later life. In these formative times, researchers, government officials and professionals must determine the extent to which older adults can be, want to be and need to be engaged in paid and unpaid work for the sake of families, communities and the individuals themselves. At the same time, programmes and policies that support this engagement must be designed, implemented and evaluated.

Ongoing research needs to inform basic and applied knowledge about productive ageing. It is important to note that productive activities have largely been studied separately, when clearly they do not happen in isolation of other activities. Research needs to focus on activity patterns and balances of activities. For example, a study from the Czech Republic found that older adults aged 50–70 have on average seven different roles, and the grandparent role was associated with the highest levels of happiness.[59] In addition, the number of productive activities among U.S. older adults (employment, volunteering, attending meetings and caregiving) was associated with reduced levels of bodily inflammation, particularly among individuals aged 70 and above.[60]

[57] Ratcliffe, J., Lester, L. H., Couzner, L. and Crotty, M. "An Assessment of the Relationship Between Informal Caring and Quality of Life in Older Community-dwelling Adults — More Positives Than Negatives?" *Health & Social Care in the Community*, 21(1), 2013, 35–46. https://doi.org/10.1111/j.1365-2524.2012.01085.x.

[58] Bertrand, R. M., Saczynski, J. S., Mezzacappa, C., Hulse, M., Ensrud, K. and Fredman, L. "Caregiving and Cognitive Function in Older Women: Evidence for the Healthy Caregiver Hypothesis," *Journal of Aging and Health*, 24(1), 2012, 48–66.

[59] Vidovićová, L. "New Roles for Older People," *Journal of Population Ageing*, 11(1), 2018, 1–6. https://doi.org/10.1007/s12062-017-9217-z.

[60] Kim, S. and Ferraro, K. F. "Do Productive Activities Reduce Inflammation in Later Life? Multiple Roles, Frequency of Activities, and C-reactive Protein," *The Gerontologist*, 54(5), 2014, 830–839. https://doi.org/10.1093/geront/gnt090.

Leisure, religious and social activities are also important to well-being, and it is probably the mix of productive and other types of activities that is most beneficial to individuals. Future research should inquire what balance or patterns of activities in later life would produce the most benefit to the older person and to society as a whole; how policies and programmes can facilitate this participation; and how socio-political and cultural factors shape productive engagement in later life. To facilitate comparisons within and across countries, researchers should clearly operationalise the activities studied or use well-established definitions from harmonised datasets.

Changing contexts for productive ageing: Digital, environmental and community care

Future attention on productive engagement will need to adapt to the changing technological, environmental and community landscape. Increasingly, technology is a key component of new opportunities for engagement, such as virtual volunteering, remote employment, and online support and educational programmes for caregivers. Promoting the digital literacy of older adults will be essential for bridging the "digital divide" between older and younger generations and ensuring that older adults are not left out.[61] Likewise, the growing threat of climate change and environmental degradation may stymie the chance for all people, including older adults, to be fully engaged; yet, older adults may be more sensitive to environmental influences, due to increased physical and social vulnerabilities. Thus, practitioners and policy makers must intervene at the intersection of older adults and their physical environment.[62] From another perspective, public and non-profit organisations focussing on the

---

[61] Seifert, A., Cotten, S. R. and Xie, B. "A Double Burden of Exclusion? Digital and Social Exclusion of Older Adults in Times of COVID-19," *The Journals of Gerontology: Series B*, gbaa098, 2020. https://doi.org/10.1093/geronb/gbaa098.

[62] McDermott-Levy, R., Kolanowski, A., Fick, D. and Mann, M. "Addressing the Health Risks of Climate Change in Older Adults," *Journal of Gerontological Nursing*, 45, 2019, 21–29. https://doi.org/10.3928/00989134-20191011-04.

environment can benefit from the commitment of older volunteers.[63] Finally, current efforts to develop long-term services and supports (LTSS) in the home and community should be informed by a productive ageing perspective. That is, supporting people with functional limitations in any setting includes facilitating engagement in meaningful roles, and programmes and policies can include people with disabilities at any age as caregivers, workers and volunteers.

In conclusion, global demographic shifts are presenting great opportunities for longer, fulfilling lives. To achieve this promise, societies must take a strengths-based perspective on the older population, seek ways to increase the productive engagement of older adults and maximise outcomes to families, communities and the older people themselves. We must design programmes and policies to support older people as workers, volunteers and caregivers, and we must confront ageism and age stereotyping that limits the potential of ageing societies.

---

[63] Pillemer, K., Wells, N., Meador, R., Schultz, L., Henderson, C. and Tillema Cope, M. "Engaging Older Adults in Environmental Volunteerism," *The Gerontologist*, 57, 2017, 367–375. https://doi.org/10.1093/geront/gnv693.

Chapter 10

Data Management and Analysis in Social Service Sectors

Leong Chan-Hoong and Angelica Ang Ting Yi

Abstract

This chapter will introduce how data from the social service sector can be obtained, managed and analysed. We will first describe the different genres and classifications of databases and how they can be harnessed to make policy or programme decisions. The types of data include information derived from ethnographic research, quantitative surveys, primary versus secondary databases, administrative data and location-based information. Following this, we will discuss the limitations of data management. It should be emphasised that this chapter is not aimed to demonstrate the full range of statistical models and data analytics, but to give readers a flavour of the diverse possibilities in the field of data management and analysis, such that they may be more cognisant of the potential to harness reliable data from their current and future work.

Introduction

Singapore is a rapidly ageing society with a significant socio-economic disparity. The social service sector, with support from the state, offers ground-up initiatives and programmes in aid of vulnerable individuals and

189

families. While this partnership underscores the spirit of collective reliance and social capital, there is nevertheless a need to ensure that the resources devoted to these community-based projects are utilised meaningfully and efficiently. This necessitates a procedural, systematic assessment of the inputs, outcomes and other collateral changes. In other words, sound corporate governance and public accountability in the social service sectors are all but expected compliance.

To achieve this goal, social service agencies need to maintain and keep track of their financial accounts, administrative records on the beneficiaries, volunteers and management teams, and the outcomes of programmes, services, and/or new initiatives. Importantly, these data provide organisations a compass for strategic planning and accountability. Specifically, which measure works and what do not? What is the social impact? Where are the gaps if any? What is the opportunity cost? While these considerations determine social impact, the value of programme evaluation, however, is contingent on the credibility and reliability of the methodology, data and the analytical techniques. The quality of the information matters as much to social service delivery. In summary, data management and analysis serve to meet a range of objectives; they include but are not limited to the following purposes.

Programme evaluation

Social service agencies provide services to cater to the needs of their constituents. The outcome and impact of these activities, however, may not be evident and service gaps may arise due to blind spots or oversights. As such, an objective, evidence-based evaluation is necessary to help improve existing programmes, plan new interventions, inform service gaps and to calibrate existing policies.

Accountability and justification

Social service agencies received funding from the state agencies and other philanthropic organisations to fulfil a mission. As such, there is a financial obligation to ensure that the resources are accountable, and the outcome of programme and spending is justifiable. It is a means to demonstrate to the stakeholders, donors and the community at large the areas in which their contributions have been utilised.

Types of Data

What are the different data types and sources? Due to the wide range of programmes, services and policies practised across the social service sector, different types of statistics are produced, each serving a different purpose, and with varying degrees of reliability and validity. In other words, the data collected by any one agency is constrained by the genre of interventions, programmes or services. It is thus important to appreciate the cost/benefits, limitations and efficacy of each dataset to make informed decisions on the type of data to collect. There are several ways by which we can classify the different types of data.

Group-level data vs individual-level data

One approach to the classification is based on group-level (i.e., secondary) versus individual-level (i.e., primary) data types. Table 1 outlines the different characteristics and examples of the two levels of data.

Table 1.   Types of Data and Analysis

Level of Data	Sources of Data	Representation	Data Analysis
Group level (secondary data)	**Census data** (e.g., age, income, gender, residence location) **Government administrative records** (e.g., wealth, taxation, family structure, % of school attrition, delinquency, criminal records, criminal records, election records) **Big data** (e.g., density and mobile phone location, tweets, bank transactions, search records, Google Analytics) **Spatial data** (e.g., locations of amenities, geographical features)	Population	No inferential statistics needed
Individual level (primary data)	**Surveys/In-depth interviews** **Observer participants** **Focus group discussions** **Experimental designs** (e.g., pre- and post-intervention)	Sample	Inferential statistics needed, e.g., *t*-test

There are two key differences between the group-level and individual-level data. Firstly, group-level data are representative of data at a larger, population-wide scale. On the other hand, individual-level data refer to data at a smaller scale, and are only representative of individuals of the sample group from which data were collected. Secondly, when analysing group-level data, there is no need for inferential statistic testing since data are already collected at the population level. However, when analysing individual-level data, further inferential statistic testing (e.g., *t*-test) is often required. For instance, if there is a survey with a few hundred people (individual-level data) on an intervention programme, we may need to conduct statistical testing on data collected from pre- and post-intervention groups to see if the differences are statistically significant. However, as we go about collecting data to justify the programmes our organisations have, in many cases, we do not just use one type of data. Instead, we may choose to use a mixed method design, whereby both group-level and individual-level data are utilised — for instance, in our evaluation, we could choose to have a survey, as well as to look at census data.

Objective and subjective data

Apart from group-level and individual-level distinction, data can also be categorised into objective and subjective measurements. For objective indicators, information is very clear-cut and does not require further interpretation (e.g., financial expenses, observable activities, amount of time taken, budget spent on housing rental). These are data that we can unanimously agree to be high or low, or good or bad. On the other hand, subjective data often require some deliberation and interpretation (e.g., personal, user experiences) after being collected.

Observable behaviours and objective data tend to paint a more powerful portrait than evaluative, latent opinions. This is due to the fact that subjective data are prone to social desirability bias; that is, people provide an answer that will cast them in a positive light. For instance, for a question on volunteering for charitable causes, a respondent may be inclined to inflate his or her contribution to be seen as likeable by societal standards. This might lead to biasness and inaccuracies in the data. Several examples of objective and subjective data are listed in Table 2.

Table 2.   Objective Versus Subjective Data for Impact Evaluation

Objective	Subjective
• Financial expenses, donation, consumption • Observable behaviour, e.g., pro-social actions, delinquency • How time is spent, e.g., work 14 hours a day • Big data/Spatial data, e.g., human mobility, transactions, online login	• Personal, user experience • Questions using Likert scale "agree/disagree" • Focus group discussions

In the next section, we will showcase examples of the different data types. The following is an example of spatial data, an objective measure of residential neighbourhoods that reveals ethnic concentration, i.e., residents are clustered according to their racial background.[1] When looking at the data below, one might ask the following: What is the policy implication of this data? What does it mean for ethnic-based service delivery? Further points of analysis may include the following: Does residential proximity to places of worship or social service centres have any potential correlations to residents' physical or mental health, or to levels of social trust amongst members of the community? Is there a presence of amenities that may aid in alleviating social vulnerability amongst socially disadvantaged residents and clients? (See Figure 1.)

We will move on to the next example, which is of Big Data. In this study by Yan *et al.* (2021), data were collected on the emotions expressed in Tweets during the COVID-19 "lockdown" (i.e., Circuit Breaker) in Singapore and used to give a birds-eye view of the sentiments amongst different subgroups in the local populace.[2] As observed in the two graphs in Figure 2, when comparing 2019 and 2020, significantly more

---

[1] Leong, C. H., Teng, E. and Ko, W. "The State of Ethnic Congregation in Singapore Today," in C. H. Leong and L. C. Malone-Lee (eds.), *Building Resilient Neighbourhoods: The Convergence of Policies, Research, and Practice*, (Singapore: Springer, 2020), pp. 29–49.

[2] Yan, Y., Chin, W. C. B., Leong, C. H., Wang, Y.-C. and Feng, C.-C. "Emotional Responses Through COVID-19 in Singapore," in S. L. Shaw and D. Sui (eds.), *Mapping COVID-19 in Space and Time: Understanding the Spatial and Temporal Dynamics of a Global Pandemic*, (Singapore: Springer, 2021), pp. 61–79.

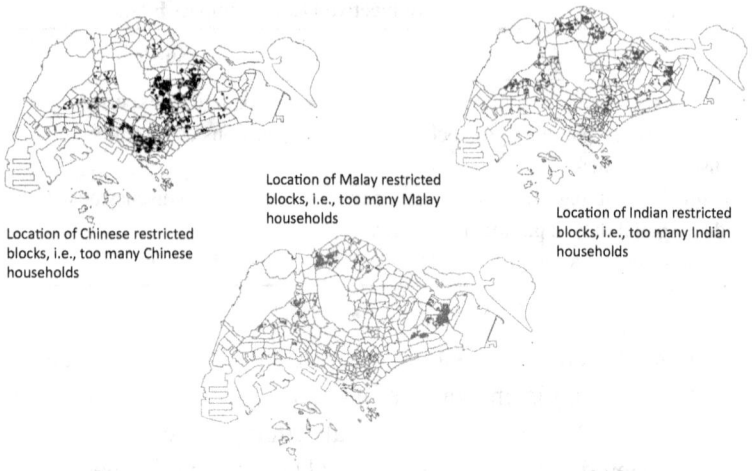

Figure 1.   Ethnic Segregation in Public Housing in Singapore

Source: Leong C. H., Teng, E. and Ko, W., (eds.), *The State of Ethnic Congregation in Singapore Today*, in *Building Resilient Neighbourhoods: The Convergence of Policies, Research, and Practice*, (Singapore: Springer, 2020), pp. 29–49.

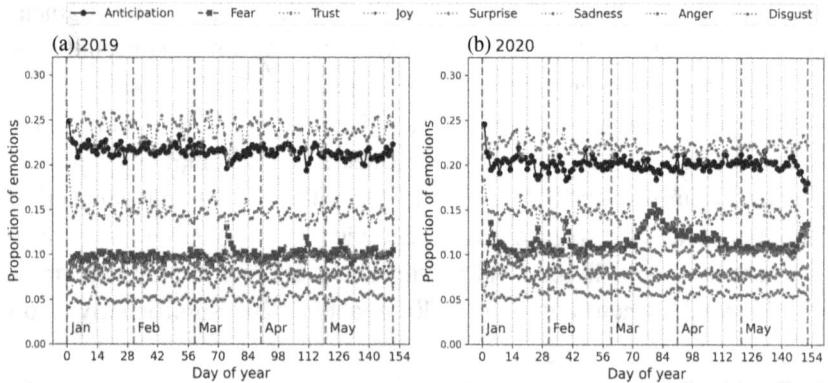

Figure 2.   Emotion Proportion by Types During COVID-19 (a) 2019 and (b) 2020.

"fear"-related tweets were posted during the COVID-19 "lockdown" in Singapore in 2020, as indicated by the spike in the square dotted line of the graph on the right.[3]

---

[3] *Ibid.*

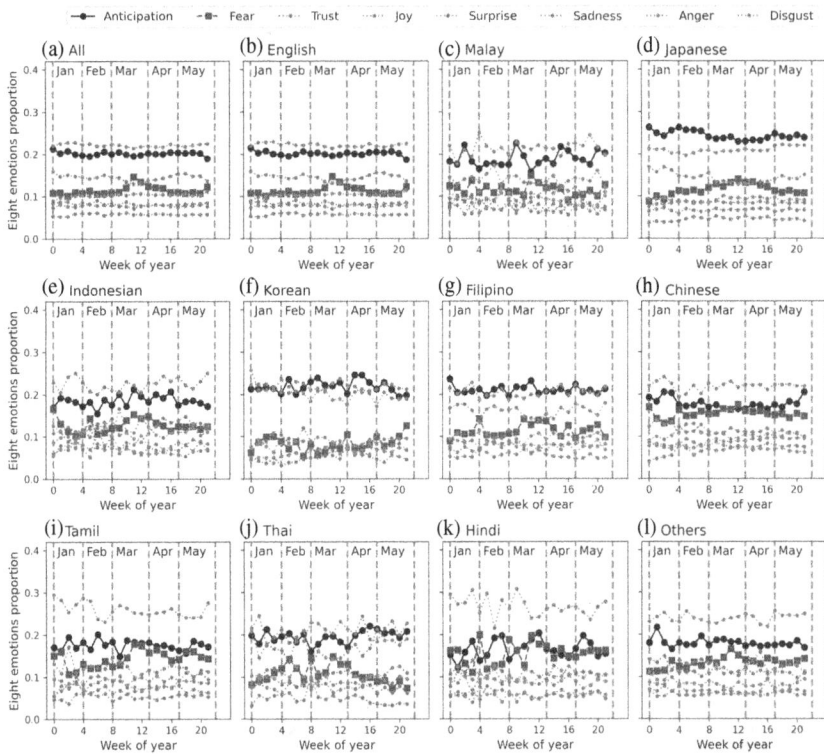

Figure 3.   Sentiment Analysis of Tweets During COVID-19 Lockdown in 2020

Source: Yan, Y., Chin, W. C. B., Leong, C. H., Wang, Y.-C. and Feng, C.-C. "Emotional Responses Through COVID-19 in Singapore," in S. L. Shaw and D. Sui (eds.), *Human Dynamics in Smart Cities*, (Singapore: Springer, 2021).

In Figure 3, the tweets were then sorted according to the language they were posted in, and sentiment analysis was conducted. From the data, researchers were able to identify differences in the sentiments of individuals from different subgroups in Singapore, with certain communities being more affected by the lockdown than others. Using Twitter's data, we could see that there are significant variations in the pandemic experiences amongst different subgroups in Singapore, such as the Japanese subgroup, which had significantly higher levels of sentiments on "anticipation", as compared to other subgroups in Singapore. The data may serve to inform policy and programme decisions, allowing the evidence-based allocation of resources to subgroups which may need it most.

Table 3.   The Top 10 Languages Used in COVID-19 Related Tweets in Singapore

Rank	Language	Number of Tweets	Percentage (%)
1	English	5,433,782	84.51
2	Malay	259,485	4.04
3	Japanese	170,802	2.66
4	Indonesian	151,604	2.36
5	Korean	84,960	1.32
6	Filipino	61,019	0.95
7	Chinese	48,855	0.76
8	Tamil	40,946	0.64
9	Thai	30,894	0.48
10	Hindi	18,578	0.29
	Other languages	128,524	1.99%
	Total	6,429,449	100.00%

A surprising finding arose when COVID-19-related tweets originating from Singapore were ranked from highest to lowest in number, according to the language in which they were published. Following English, which 84.51% of quotes were published in, the next top three languages with the highest number of tweets were Malay (4.04%), Japanese (2.66%) and Indonesian (2.36%), all of which were groups which constituted a relatively smaller percentage of the local populace (i.e., minority groups).[4] This analysis also reflected the kind of communication platforms on which members of different communities may engage in conversations and discuss current issues (see Table 3).

To round up this section, let us recall our example of the Child Aid programme that was mentioned in the previous chapter. In this example, what individual-level or group-level data can one collect? Based on the context of the community that this organisation serves, what would be the data that would be the most relevant to have? (See Table 4.)

Table 5 lists a few examples of individual-level and group-level data that can be collected for this hypothetical example. Can you think of other individual-level and group-level data to collect?

---

[4] Ibid.

Table 4. Distilling the Purpose, Target Audience, and Measurement Indicators

Hypothetical Example: Child Aid	
Clarity of Purpose	Child Aid — provide food, uniform and other allowance for children from low-income families to stay afloat
Scope	Promote education and uplift welfare of children from poverty households
Stakeholder Engagement	Work with schools, VWOs and family counsellors
Materiality	Monetary cost of provision, manpower, etc.
Comparative	School dropout rate, % child labour in province, duration of programme, location of schools, % completed primary education
Transparency	Getting credible data from Government, NGOs
Verification	Independent audit
Embeddedness	Annual budget, buy-in from local authorities, NGOs

Table 5. Potential Types of Data for Child Aid Example

Examples of Individual-level Data	Examples of Group-level Data
• In-depth child interview • In-depth parent interview • Amount of money received by child • School attendance of child • Academic grade of child • Number of friends child has • Health status of child • Feedback from social workers	• Dropout rate of schools • Socio-economic status of schools • % child-labour in province • % completed primary education

Data Measurement

In this section, we discuss data measurement, how data should be managed and the impact on social impact evaluation. It is crucial that data are measured and captured accurately, so as to accurately reflect the social impact that needs to be examined. There are four areas to take note in data measurement.

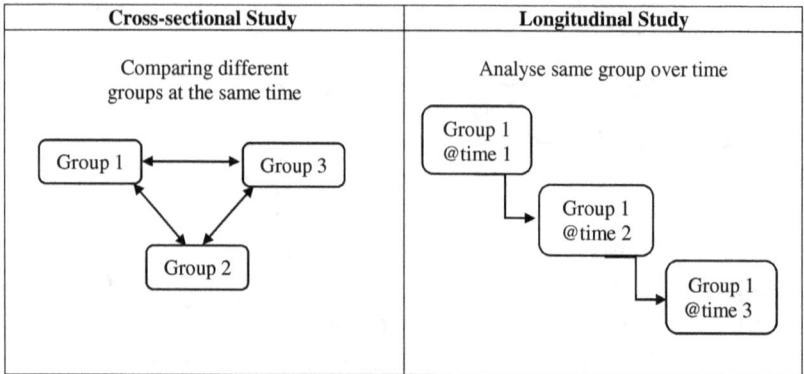

Figure 4.   Comparison Between Cross-sectional and Longitudinal Studies

Cause and effect

Can the outcome be attributed to the social service agency's programme or intervention, or has it come about due to natural changes that occur over time? For instance, a country may over time report a reduction in the sentiments of fear or anxiety related to COVID-19 — this might not be attributed to the implemented lockdown measures, but to the populace growing more accustomed to a pandemic life as it wears on.

Generally, there are two research designs in empirical research — cross-sectional studies and longitudinal studies (see Figure 4). Cross-sectional studies take place at one specific point in time, during which they enable the comparison of different groups at the same time. On the other hand, longitudinal studies extend beyond one time point, and allow the same group to be compared over time.[5] Hence, despite longitudinal studies being more costly and having their fair share of challenges (e.g., manage participant dropouts by keeping them interested and engaged throughout the study duration — possibly by offering remuneration to them for their time), they are deemed to be more robust than cross-sectional studies. As longitudinal studies enable the researcher to draw

---

[5]Rindfleisch, A., Malter, A. J., Ganesan, S. and Moorman, C. "Cross-sectional versus Longitudinal Survey Research: Concepts, Findings, and Guidelines," *Journal of Marketing Research*, 45(3), 2008, 261–279.

conclusions about cause and effect, they are hence generally deemed to be more preferable than cross-sectional studies.

Reliability

Another important point to consider is the concept of reliability or precision, i.e., does the measurement provides us a consistent reading? One example would be the contactless forehead scan thermometers that are often used at the entrances of buildings (e.g., shopping malls and educational institutions) during the COVID-19 pandemic in Singapore. One might wonder if the readings taken are reliable. If a person's measured temperature fluctuates widely every time it is taken by the thermometer, this would suggest that the equipment is not reliable. Recall the example of the Child Aid programme that was cited in the current and previous chapters. In this case, unreliability may be attributed to human factors: if there is a high turnover rate of teachers at a particular school, the record of a child's attendance in class may not be reliable as different teachers may embrace different standards in recording class attendance. It may also be noted that the concept of "reliability" in social sciences is similar to that of "precision" in the "hard" social sciences.

Validity

The third notable point is the concept of validity, i.e., are you measuring what you intend to measure? While reliability seeks to understand consistency of reading, validity aims to find out if the reading is an appropriate representation of the measure we intend to assess. Using the previous example of a scan thermometer, a question of validity may be as follows: Does the temperature taken on the forehead using a scan thermometer provide a good indication of fever or body temperature? The instrument may produce a reliable (i.e., consistent) reading of temperature on the forehead, but is it a valid measure of a fever? In general, there are a few types of validity, which are as listed in order of least to most robust:

1. *Face validity*: Face validity offers some form of superficial affirmation that the instrument measures what it intends to measure. For instance,

to find out if an individual is trustworthy, we could ask the person if they have ever "cheated in an examination" or "knowingly short changed another person". This will have at least some aspects of face validity, though one may argue that an untrustworthy person will not be forthcoming about their past misbehaviours.

2. *Conceptual validity*: Conceptual validity offers more concrete, robust insights to the underlying measurement or latent dimensions that we want to capture. For example, monetary incentives offered to children from vulnerable families to remain in school provide an assessment of direct educational support. Questions can also be posed indirectly with the aim of reducing desirability bias; for instance, instead of asking if an individual considers himself or herself as extrovert, we could ask how much they enjoy travelling, meeting new people or engaging in outdoor activities.

3. *Convergence validity*: Measurement validity can also be discussed in the form of convergence validity. In a nutshell, does the measurement converge with other instruments for similar constructs? We should expect a significant correlation if the measurements are tapping on the same dimension. The measurement of extroversion, for instance, would expectedly echo findings from similar instruments that assess a person's proclivity to outdoor activities, social engagement or appetite for adventures.

4. *Predictive validity*: Predictive validity is the pinnacle of all validation. In the broadest sense, we like to know if this instrument can predict the actual outcome as postulated in a longitudinal design. For instance, children from vulnerable families who stay in schools will receive more education and, thus, empower them with better employment opportunities. As such, predictive validation is established when the child's past attendance in school predicted their future quality of life.

Reliability and validity are two important methodological and analytical concepts in social sciences. Just like the similarity between reliability and precision, "validity" in the social sciences is akin to "accuracy" in the "hard" social sciences. In other words, "precision-accuracy" is used in "hard" social sciences such as statistics and geography, while psychology (and possibly when examining social policies in social work and/or

Table 6. Potential Types of Data that Measure Quality of Life

Individual Level	Group Level
• Personal income	• National income
• Education	• Employment rate
• Health status	• Home ownership
• Marital status	• Education/Literacy rate
• No. of children	• Life expectancy
• Civic participation	• Crime rate
• Attendance in programmes	• Philanthropic donations
• Family relations	• Opinion polls, surveys
• Life satisfaction	
• Socio-economic security	

sociology), on the other hand, speaks of "reliability-validity", as it measures latent constructs.

To give a more concrete example on reliability-validity, supposing we want to develop a measure on "quality of life", what data should we consider? In this case, there are several types of data (individual-level and group-level data) and measurement issues (reliability & validity, objective vs subjective, sample vs population) — the former include questions on personal income, education, health status and other subjective ratings on well-being; the latter include indicators on national income, literacy, crime rate and national opinion polls (see Table 6).

Hence, as we attempt to answer the empirical question, it is essential to ensure that the research data obtained are reliable and valid, and ascertain whether objective, subjective or both types of data are being utilised. Measurable, objective data are favoured over subjective evaluation for greater reliability.

Sampling and participant recruitment

As it is very costly and challenging to collect data from all members of a population, random samples that are representative of the research population are more often utilised in data collection. However, data collected from a random sample of individuals in a targeted population are often contaminated with some form of biasness that is often hard to detect.

Individuals from vulnerable families, for instance, may be reluctant to share with the investigators out of concern for privacy and for fear of retribution.

For some research, a convenient sampling approach is adopted due to limitations in resources or other constraints — a convenient sample is collected using the most accessible method. It is a form of non-random sampling. The external validity of the study would be limited, as the characteristics, experience and sentiments of the non-random sample might not be representative of the general populace or target group the study hopes to reach out to. For instance, in public opinion studies conducted prior to the 2020 U.S. general elections, Joe Biden was in the lead by about five to 10 percentage points. However, when it came to the actual results of polling day, it was revealed that only 2% more Americans had voted for Joe Biden than Donald Trump. This shows that the pre-voting public opinion survey had garnered responses from a convenience sample of the population that was not representative of all Americans. It might be inferred that Donald Trump's supporters might have abstained from taking the pre-voting survey, in fear of being stigmatised or criticised for their political opinions.

In order to ensure sample biases are minimised, we typically aim to collect a larger sample and from a wide range of sources as much possible. In general, the size of the random error variance will decrease as sample size increases; moreover, a large sample offers researchers the option to weight specific cases that are under-represented. The investigators can assign greater importance to certain characteristics that are disproportionately less than what they should be, i.e., fewer respondents with these characteristics took part in the research.

Supporting Data from Multiple Studies and Levels

We have discussed the different types of data, such as objective–subjective measurements, individual- and group-level data, and analytical considerations such as sampling and reliability-validity. Hence, a question that one may ask is as follows: Why do we need to measure different levels of data?

Social science research that is both robust and insightful tends to be measurable and replicable. In fact, it is useful to measure different levels of data as confidence in research is enhanced when different databases and different levels of analysis produce the same conclusion. In addition, multi-level and multi-site studies enable us to examine possible interaction effects between individual-level and group-level data — which means that individuals from different backgrounds react differently depending on the external environment. In this case, interaction is said to exist and this signifies that a one-size-fits-all policy may not work well.

Such interaction effects are exemplified in a study by Roy *et al.*, which examines the impact of neighbourhood relative income and subjective social status on one's physical and mental health.[6] Both individual-level and group-level data on income were obtained, which helped identify the interaction effect between the two.

From Figure 5, we can observe that lower-income families generally reported lower physical and mental health compared to higher-income families, i.e., the twin bars on the left of each diagram are consistently lower compared to the twin bars on the right of each diagram. A closer examination however, suggests that lower-income families demonstrate better physical and mental health when they live in higher-income neighbourhoods. In other words, it is better to be a poor man in a rich neighbourhood than a poor man in a poor neighbourhood.[7] Hence, in this example, family/household income (individual-level data) interacted with neighbourhood income (group-level data) to influence one's physical and mental health (outcomes), and similar trends were observed in Singapore.[8] Interventions can be targeted in vulnerable neighbourhoods to serve the needy families.

---

[6] Roy, A. L., Godfrey, E. B. and Rarick, J. R. D. "Do We Know Where We Stand? Neighborhood Relative Income, Subjective Social Status, and Health," *American Journal of Community Psychology*, 57, 2016, 448–458.
[7] *Ibid.*
[8] Leong, C. H., Tan, S. J., Minton, E. A. and Tambyah, S. K. "Economic Hardship and Neighbourhood Diversity: Influences on Consumer Well-being," *Journal of Consumer Affairs*, 55(4), 2021, 1226–1248.

Physical Health

4.00

3.80

3.60

3.40

3.20

3.00

A   B   C   D

Low family income   High family income

■ Low NH income   ■ High NH income

Mental Health

4.00

3.80

3.60

3.40

3.20

3.00

A   B   C   D

Low family income   High family income

■ Low NH income   ■ High NH income

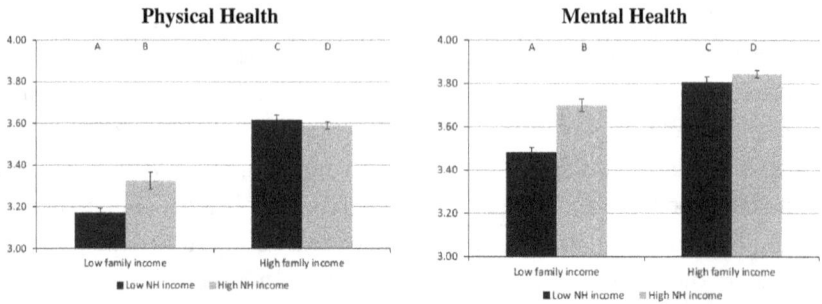

Figure 5.   Physical and Mental Health Among Low- and High-income Families

Source: Roy, A. L., Godfrey, E. B., and Rarick, J. R. D. "Do We Know Where We Stand? Neighborhood Relative Income, Subjective Social Status, and Health," *American Journal of Community Psychology*, 57, 2016, 448–458.

Key Attention by Agency on Data Management

Taking an overarching view, what are the key takeaways for social service agencies on data management? First, programme evaluation is an integral aspect of social service delivery to ensure sound corporate governance, strategic planning and accountability. By extension, data management — which is the pillar for impact evaluation and assessment — is a part of the larger analytical framework. Relevant data should be meticulously collected and maintained with a longer-term goal in mind. Social service agencies commonly operate with limited finances and an operational workload that offers little allowance for administrative tracking. This political reality and constraints should be addressed at the start of the programme, and the cost of impact assessment and data collection should be considered at the planning stage.

Second, a programme may be designed to reach out to a specific local community but the impact could have a wider repercussion that goes beyond the targeted beneficiary. For instance, a Child Aid initiative to provide food and allowance to children from low-income families in one school could have galvanised a regional support for similar causes in other neighbourhoods. The broader impact should therefore be assessed at the provincial level. In this case, a more comprehensive impact evaluation would require data at the regional level, information that may be otherwise not accessible to the social service agencies.

Lastly, robust data management and analysis and the appreciation for social impact evaluation would require multi-disciplinary knowledge in statistics, research methods, corporate governance and public policies. Practitioners in social service agencies will need support and encouragement from academia, social service regulatory authority and the civil societies to ensure that the evaluations and analyses are performed to most rigorous standards.

Conclusion

This chapter offered an overview on data management and analyses for social impact analysis. We introduced the different genres of databases (e.g., individual- versus group-level data, objective versus subjective data, sample versus population data) and other conceptual and measurement-related considerations such as reliability, validity and research designs (e.g., cross-sectional versus longitudinal). In the increasingly complex and interwoven climate, the social service sector will need to fall back on evidence-based empirical research to fine-tune their professional development and service delivery. The types of data, methodology and the analytical approach are the tools to achieving this purpose and to ensure there is robust policy formulation and deliberation. This chapter does not cover the full range of methodological and data analytics, but instead, it is written with the aim to inspire social service practitioners to be cognisant of their own environment and the potential to continually enhance their programmes and services through social impact evaluation.

Chapter 11

Ageing in Singapore and the Asian Context

Srinivasan Chokkanathan

Abstract

Population ageing is an important demographic feature in Asia. Different regions of Asia exhibit different rates of ageing. Nonetheless, no Asian region is immune to population ageing. Singapore in Southeast Asia is ageing rapidly. Increase in older adults aged 85 years and above, diminishing old-age support ratio, low labour force participation and increasing chronic illness are some challenges associated with the unprecedented growth of older adults in Singapore. Increase in retirement age, non-discriminatory work environment, equitable access to the healthcare system, and creating a favourable social environment devoid of ageist attitudes are some measures to create an age-inclusive society in Singapore and in other Asian countries.

Ageing is a global phenomenon. In 2020, there were 727 million older adults aged 65 years and above worldwide. In 2050, the elderly population is projected to increase more than twofold, reaching about 1.5 billion. By 2050, one in six persons in the world will be 65 years and above, as compared to 1 in 11 in 2019.[1] Ageing once widespread in developed western countries is currently occurring at a relatively faster rate in Asian countries. Ageing does not occur in a silo. Instead, it occurs alongside broader socio-economic and demographic changes encompassing both intra- and inter-country contexts. Therefore, a nuanced exemplification of ageing demands a context-specific discourse. The current chapter focuses on ageing trends in Asia with a special focus on Singapore. Specifically, the ageing scenario and the challenges that ageing poses to the socio-economic landscape in Asia including Singapore will be elucidated. First, this chapter describes ageing trends in different parts of Asia and Singapore, following which the micro and macro socio-economic environments that shape and in turn are shaped by population ageing will be expounded. In this chapter, the ageing scenario in Asia is limited to East/Northeastern, Southeastern and South/Southwestern Asian regions (see Table 1).

Asia is ageing rapidly. Population ageing, i.e., the increase in the number of older adults due to longer life expectancy and decreasing fertility rates, is occurring at a faster rate in Asia than in Europe and North America.[2] On one end of the continuum is East Asia with the highest proportion of older people and on the other end is South Asia with the lowest proportion of older adults (Table 1). Within these regions, there are wide inter-country variations. In East and Northeast Asia, Japan ranks first in terms of the proportion of the aged population. In Japan, older people aged 60 years and above and 65 years and above form 34.3% and 28% of the population, respectively. However, in Mongolia, the corresponding figures are 7.3% and 4.3%. Even though China has 12% of older people, in terms of absolute numbers of older people, it ranks first in the world. In the Southeast Asia region, Singapore with 13.4% of older people aged 65 years and above tops the list. Indonesia, Thailand, Vietnam and Myanmar are at a vital transitional

---

[1] United Nations, Department of Economic and Social Affairs, Population Division, World Population Prospects 2019, custom data acquired via website. https://population.un.org/wpp/DataQuery/.

[2] Smith, J. P. "Preparing for Population Aging in Asia: Strengthening the Infrastructure for Science and Policy," in J. P. Smith and M. Majmundar (eds.), *Aging in Asia: Findings from New and Emerging Data Initiatives*, (Washington, D.C.: National Academies Press, 2012).

Table 1.   Proportion of Older Adults in Asia

	60 Years and Above (% of population)		65 Years and Above (% of population)			
			2020		2050	
	Total	Female%	Total	Female %	Total	Female %
East and Northeast Asia	18.8	52.8	13.3	53.9	27.1	53.7
China	17.4	52.1	12.0	53.1	26.1	53.3
Democratic People's Republic of Korea	15.1	60.5	9.3	65.2	19.7	59.7
Hong Kong China	26.1	52.5	18.2	53.4	34.7	62.2
Japan	34.3	55.3	28.4	56.4	37.7	55.2
Macao China	18.9	51.4	12.0	52.1	28.9	58.2
Mongolia	7.3	57.9	4.3	58.9	12.0	60.1
Republic of Korea	23.2	54.9	15.8	56.8	38.1	54.7
Southeast Asia	11.1	55	7.1	56.5	16.7	56.1
Brunei Darussalam	9.5	50.2	5.6	51.2	21.7	50.1
Cambodia	7.6	60.9	4.9	60.8	11.7	57.3
Indonesia	10.1	52.9	6.3	54.3	15.9	55.2
Laos	6.8	53.5	4.3	55.4	10.4	55.4
Malaysia	11.0	50.7	7.2	51.3	17.0	51.1
Myanmar	10	58.6	6.2	59.8	13.2	59.2
Philippines	8.6	56.1	5.5	58.2	11.8	58.8
Singapore	20.9	49.8	13.4	51.8	33.3	50.9
Thailand	19.3	55.4	13.0	56.4	29.6	56.7
Timor-Leste	6.6	52.3	4.3	53.5	6.5	54.2
Vietnam	12.3	57.9	7.9	60.4	20.4	56.7
South and Southwest Asia	9.6	51.1	6.3	51.8	13.5	52.4
Afghanistan	4.2	52.3	2.6	53.6	5.4	52.6
Bangladesh	8.0	48.8	5.2	49.6	15.8	53.3
Bhutan	9.0	45.9	6.2	45.2	15.8	46.1
India	10.1	50.9	6.6	51.7	13.8	52.1

(*Continued*)

Table 1.   (*Continued*)

	60 Years and Above (% of population)		65 Years and Above (% of population)			
			2020		2050	
	Total	Female%	Total	Female %	Total	Female %
Iran	10.3	49.5	6.6	49.0	20.2	51.5
Maldives	5.7	49.6	3.6	48.8	20.9	41.1
Nepal	8.7	54.2	5.8	54.6	12.8	60.7
Pakistan	6.7	49.3	4.3	49.2	7.9	51.2
Sri Lanka	16.4	56.5	11.2	57.7	22.6	57.5
Turkey	13.1	56.6	9.0	57.8	20.9	54.9

Source: United Nations ESCAP Population Data (2021).

stage where better average life expectancy and diminishing fertility rates have led to rapidly greying populations. In 2020, South and Southwest Asia were younger in comparison to the other East, Northeast and Southeast Asian regions. The ageing trend of 2020 appears to continue without much change till 2050. East and Northeast Asia will continue to have the highest proportion of older adults followed by Southeast Asia and South and Southwest Asia.

Several factors make Singapore stand out from the other Asian countries. Singapore is a small multicultural city-state in Southeast Asia. Singapore's total population grew by around 1.1% a year between 2010 and 2020. The resident population stood at 4,044,210 in the year 2020.[3] The citizen population increased from 3.23 million to 3.52 million over this period, while the permanent resident population remained stable at around 0.5 million. The ethnic composition of the resident population remained stable, with 74.3% Chinese, 13.5% Malays and 9.0% Indians in 2020. In the year 2011, the proportion of elderly persons was 9.3% and it increased to 16.0% in the year 2021, i.e., an increase by 7%.

---

[3] Department of Statistics, Census of Population 2020 Statistical Release 1: Demographic Characteristics, Education, Language and Religion, 2021. https://www.singstat.gov.sg/-/media/files/publications/cop2020/sr1/cop2020sr1.pdf.

The Chinese ethnic group had the highest proportion of older people, followed by the Malay and Indian ethnic groups with similar proportions.[4] An increasing median age, i.e., 38 in 2011 to 41.8 years in 2021, and a growing number of persons aged 75 years and above, i.e., from 3.7% in the year 2011 to 5.6% in 2021, indicate that persons who are old tend to live longer. Singapore is also ageing rapidly. A society where more than 7% of its total population is aged 65 years and above is considered as ageing, >14% as aged and >20% as superaged.[5] For a country to be ageing (between 7% to 14%), France took 115 years, and in Asia, the superaged country Japan took 26 years, whereas Singapore took a mere 15 years.[6] Indeed between 2019 and 2050, Singapore is projected to rank second among the top 10 countries in the world to register the largest percentage point increase in the share of older people.[7] Taken together, Singapore has to face unique challenges in designing culturally appropriate services for a rapidly ageing population in a shorter period.

Gender and Ageing

Irrespective of the Asian regions, older women outnumber older men (see Table 1) — a trend witnessed in Singapore as well, although the gender gap is on decline. In the year 2012, there were 802 males 1,000 females, and in the year 2022 there are 850 males per 1,000 females.[8] With few exceptions, the gender gap is likely to stay the same for most Asian countries, including Singapore, in 2050. Research has shown that the longevity advantage of women is nullified by their experiences of socio-economic

---

[4] SingStat, Key Indicators on the Elderly, 2022. https://tablebuilder.singstat.gov.sg/table/TS/M810611.

[5] United Nations, Department of Economic and Social Affairs, Population Division, World Population Prospects: The 2017 Revision — Special Aggregates, DVD Edition.

[6] Henning, S. Population Ageing in ASEAN Countries: Trends and Perspectives. 2019. https://www.unescap.org/sites/default/files/Population%20Ageing%20in%20ASEAN%20Countries%20%20by%20Sabine%20Henning%20ESCAP.pdf.

[7] United Nations, Department of Economic and Social Affairs, Population Division, World Population Prospects 2019, custom data acquired via website. https://population.un.org/wpp/DataQuery/.

[8] SingStat, Key Indicators on the Elderly, 2022. https://tablebuilder.singstat.gov.sg/table/TS/M810611.

and health disadvantages.[9] Consequently, there has been an increased call to situate older women at the centre of ageing policies.[10] On the other hand, authors have cautioned that undue focus on older women vs older men *per se* will render policies piecemeal and counterproductive to achieving the needs of the older adults.[11] Perhaps a viable option is to design policies that take a balanced position through accommodating both male and female vulnerabilities as well as age as central variables.

Living Arrangements and Older Adults

Living arrangements have been found to be positively associated with positive physical and mental health of older adults.[12] Older adults living alone or in an institution as opposed to those living with their family members are at a greater mortality risk.[13] Living arrangements also have crucial macroeconomic implications by impacting the demand for housing, retirement homes, respite care services and social services.[14]

Co-residence continues to be a predominant form of living arrangement in Asia (see Table 2). With regard to regional variations, Southern Asia (73%) and South-central Asia (73.3%) with a similar proportion top

[9] Chen, C., Maung, K. and Rowe, W. J. "Gender Differences in Countries' Adaptation to Societal Ageing: An International Cross-sectional Comparison," *The Lancet,* 2, 2021, E460–E409.

[10] Mehta, K. *Untapped Resources: Women in Ageing Societies*, (Singapore: Times Academic Press, 1997); and UNECE, Gender Equality in Ageing societies, 2020. https://unece.org/fileadmin/DAM/pau/age/Policy_briefs/ECE_WG-1_34.pdf.

[11] Knodel, J. and Ofstedal, B. M. "Gender and Aging in the Developing World: Where Are the Men?" *Population and Development Review*, 29, 2004, 677–698.

[12] Chou, K. L., Ho, A. H. Y. and Chi, I. "Living Alone and Depression in Chinese Older Adults," *Aging Men Health,* 10, 2006, 583–591; Hwang, E. J. and Sim, I. O. "Association of Living Arrangements with Happiness Attributes Among Older Adults," *BMC Geriatrics*, 21, 2021, 100; and Matsuura, T. and Ma, X. "Living Arrangements and Subjective Well-being of the Elderly in China and Japan," *Journal of Happiness Studies*, 2021.

[13] Feng, Z., Falkingham, J., Liu, X. and Vlachantoni, A. "Changes in Living Arrangements and Mortality Among Older People in China," *SSM — Population Health*, 3, 2016, 9–19.

[14] United Nations, Department of Economic and Social Affairs, Population Division, *Living Arrangements of Older Persons: A Report on an Expanded International Dataset* (ST/ESA/SER.A/407), 2017.

Table 2.   Old-age Support Ratio in Asia

	Number of Persons Aged 15–64 per Persons Aged 65 Years or Over		Number of Persons 80 Years or Older per Number of Older Adults 65 Years or Over (2021)
	2012	**2021**	
East and Northeast Asia	6.0	5.0	18.6
China	8.3	5.6	15.6
Democratic People's Republic of Korea	7.0	7.3	19.2
Hong Kong China	5.5	3.6	26.8
Japan	2.6	2.1	32.3
Macao China	10.2	5.7	16.6
Mongolia	16.6	14.4	14.8
Republic of Korea	6.1	4.3	23.2
Southeast Asia	10.0	9.2	17.2
Brunei Darussalam	18.1	12.1	13.8
Cambodia	16.3	12.9	12.1
Indonesia	11.7	10.4	14.3
Laos	15.8	14.6	13.1
Malaysia	12.6	9.3	16.0
Myanmar	13.2	10.6	12.3
Philippines	16.2	11.3	15.3
Singapore	7.3	5.1	16.8
Thailand	7.5	5.2	21.3
Timor-Leste	17.3	13.7	14.1
Vietnam	11.4	8.4	23.4
South and Southwest Asia	11.0	10.3	15.6
Afghanistan	23.7	20.9	10.7
Bangladesh	14.2	12.8	20.5
Bhutan	13.6	10.9	21.6
India	12.7	10.0	14.9

(Continued)

Table 2.   (*Continued*)

	Number of Persons Aged 15–64 per Persons Aged 65 Years or Over		Number of Persons 80 Years or Older per Number of Older Adults 65 Years or Over
	2012	2021	(2021)
Iran	13.3	10.1	16.0
Maldives	13.3	20.1	23.0
Nepal	14.2	11.2	13.8
Pakistan	14.2	13.9	15.3
Sri Lanka	7.6	5.6	15.2
Turkey	10.8	7.2	19.7

Source: Data compiled from United Nations, Department of Economic and Social Affairs, Population Division (2017); United Nations ESCAP Population Data (2012; 2021).

the list followed by Southeast Asia (65.9%) and Eastern Asia (57.4%).[15] Although co-residence is the norm, the increasing number of older adults and decreasing family sizes are exacerbating families' caregiving burden. The old-age dependency ratio (OADR) represents the number of persons aged 65 years or over per 100 persons of working age (aged 20–64 years). OADR is increasing in all countries.[16] In Eastern and Southeastern Asia, the OADR is expected to rise from 18 older adults per 100 workers in 2019 to 43 in 2050, whereas in Southern Asia it is expected to rise from 10 per 100 in 2019 to 22 per 100 in 2050. In contrast, the old-age support ratio represents the number of persons 20–64 years per person over 65 years. Across all regions, the old-age support ratio has declined from 2012 to 2022 (see Table 2).

---

[15] United Nations, Department of Economic and Social Affairs, Population Division, *Living Arrangements of Older Persons: A Report on an Expanded International Dataset* (ST/ESA/SER.A/407), 2017; United Nations, Ageing in Asia and the Pacific: Overview, 2017. https://www.unescap.org/resources/ageing-asia-and-pacific-overview.

[16] United Nations, Department of Economic and Social Affairs, Population Division, World Population Prospects 2019, custom data acquired via website, 2019. https://population.un.org/wpp/DataQuery/.

In Singapore, the changes in OADR and old-age support ratio are more drastic and pronounced.[17] Old-age dependency almost doubled in a decade, i.e., from 13.5 in 2010 to 23.5 in 2020. The old-age support ratio has also declined by almost half within a decade. In 2010, there were 8.2 persons aged between 15–64 years for every older adult and in the year 2020 there were a mere 4.6 persons per older adult. Similarly, persons aged 20–64 years also declined from 7.4 in 2010 to 4.3 in 2020. One important consequence of the increase in OADR and decrease in the old-age support ratio is the increase in the number of older adults living alone, both in Singapore and in the other parts of Asia. In Asia, the proportion of elderly people living alone registered an increase from 18 percentage points in 1990 percentage points to 27 percentage points in 2010, i.e., an increase by 9 percentage points.[18] Among aged households in Singapore, the proportion of single-person household increased from 10.1% in 2010 to 13.5% in 2020.[19] However, the proportion of older adults living alone is lower than those in other Asian territories such as Japan, Taiwan and South Korea.[20] Living alone need not necessarily mean low family support. Research indicates that family members do continue providing support even when living away. In Singapore, the prevailing norm appears to be "living away but living together".[21] In Asia, with the

---

[17] Department of Statistics, Indicators on Population, 2021. https://tablebuilder.singstat. gov.sg/table/TS/M810001.

[18] United Nations, Department of Economic and Social Affairs, Population Division, *Living Arrangements of Older Persons: A Report on an Expanded International Dataset* (ST/ESA/SER.A/407), 2017; United Nations, Ageing in Asia and the Pacific: Overview, 2017. https://www.unescap.org/resources/ageing-asia-and-pacific-overview.

[19] Ministry of Social and Family Development, Ageing Families in Singapore 2010–2020. Insight Series paper January 2022. https://www.msf.gov.sg/research-and-data/Research-and-DataSeries /Documents/Ageing_Families_in_Singapore_2010-2020.pdf.

[20] Yeung, J. W-J. and Cheung, A. K-L. "Living Alone: One-person Households in Asia," *Demographic Research*, 32, 2015, 1099–1112.

[21] Chan, A., Malhotra, C., Malhotra, R. and Østbye, T. "Living Arrangements, Social Networks and Depressive Symptoms Among Older Men and Women in Singapore," *International Journal of Geriatric Psychiatry*, 26, 2011, 630–639. https://doi.org/10.1002/gps.2574.

rural–urban divide, even when younger family members from rural areas migrate to urban areas, they continue taking care of their parents.[22]

Given the below replacement fertility rates in countries such as Singapore, South Korea and Japan, technology-assisted living is widely promoted to ensure independent living within one's home environment.[23] In addition, in Singapore incentives and housing subsidies are provided to family members to stay in close proximity with their older family members to facilitate ageing in place.

Labour Force Participation and Old Age

An ageing population impacts economic growth. Asian countries' economic affluence in part could be attributed to their ample labour force and this shrinkage in demographic dividend will impede sustained economic growth. The contraction of the labour force may intensify labour costs and the increase in the older adult population will reduce levels of savings, resulting in low capital accumulation.[24] Contrarily, the ageing labour force may also indicate accumulated experience that may not derail economic productivity. In countries such as Japan and South Korea, technological upgrading has led to productivity gains among older adults.[25] Encouraging

---

[22] Knodel, J. and Ofstedal, B. M. "Gender and Aging in the Developing World: Where Are the Men?" *Population and Development Review*, 29, 2004, 677–698; and Teerawichitchainan, B., Knodel, J. and Pothisiri, W. "What Does Living Alone Really Mean for Older Persons? A Comparative Study of Myanmar, Vietnam, and Thailand." *Demography Research*, 32, 2015, 1329–1360.

[23] Lai, O. "The Enigma of Japanese Ageing-in-place Practice in the Information Age: Does Digital Gadget Help the (Good) Practice for Inter-generation Care?" *Ageing International*, 32, 2008, 236–255; and Goonawardene, N., Lee, P., Tan, H. W. X., Valera, A. and Tan, H. P. "Technologies for Ageing-in-place: The Singapore Context," in T. Menkhoff, S. N. Kan, H. D. Evers and Y. W. Chay (eds.), *Living in Smart Cities: Innovation and Sustainability*, (Singapore: World Scientific, 2017, 2018), pp. 147–174.

[24] Bloom, D. E. and Lucas, D. L. "The Global Demography of Aging: Facts, Explanations, Future," in *Handbook of the Economics of Population Aging*. Elsevier, pp. 3–56.

[25] Kim, J., Park, D. and Estrada, R. A. M. "Population Aging Economic Growth and Old Age Income Support in Asia," 2020.

people to work as long as possible ensures non-shrinkage of the workforce and enables individuals to be self-reliant.

Much of the pro old-age legislations appear to be confined to formal sectors in economically advanced Asian countries. In developing Asian countries, more than half of older adults continue to work, but in informal sectors characterised by low income and poor work environment.[26] This trend in part indicates that labour force participation need not necessarily be a sign of wellness. In fact, some research has shown that older adults, especially in developing countries such as India and Thailand, engage in productive activities due to economic compulsion.[27] Older working males outnumber older working females in almost all the Asian countries. The gender gap is glaring in countries such as Bangladesh (50.3% males vs 16.1% females) and India (41.5% vs 10.7%).[28] Irrespective of age, women's labour participation is lower than that of men. Moreover, women in general tend to get paid lower than men. All these factors combine to place women at a greater economic instability than men during old age. Given that older women outnumber older men (see Table 1), and that older women are at an economic disadvantage, income security measures are more vital for older women than for older men. Engaging in economically productive activities may trickle during old-old age (80 years and above). In such instances, there is a need to tailor and implement effective social protection programmes targeting economic independence during old age. Myriad but interconnected measures such as increasing retirement age,

---

[26] United Nations, Department of Economic and Social Affairs, Population Division, *Living Arrangements of Older Persons: A Report on an Expanded International Dataset* (ST/ESA/SER.A/407), 2017; and United Nations, "Ageing in Asia and the Pacific: Overview." 2017. https://www.unescap.org/resources/ageing-asia-and-pacific-overview.

[27] Singh, A. and Das, U. "Increasing Compulsion to Work for Wages: Old Age Labor Participation and Supply in India over the Past Two Decades," *Population Ageing*, (8), 2015, 303–326; and Paweenawat, S. W. and Liao, L. "Labor Supply of Older Workers in Thailand: The Role of Co-residence, Health, and Pensions," ADBI Working Paper 1224, (Tokyo: Asian Development Bank Institute, 2021). https://www.adb.org/publications/labor-supply-olderworkers-thailand-role-co-residence-health-pensions.

[28] United Nations ESCAP. 2016 ESCAP population data sheet, 2016. https://www.unescap.org/sites/default/d8files/knowledge-products/SPPS%20PS%20data%20sheet%202016%20v15-2.pdf.

flexible working environments, lifelong learning, promoting human capital investment, and liberalising immigrant and labour flows should be implemented to prolong the productivity of older adults.[29]

In Singapore, the re-employment age (post-retirement employment) is currently 67 and is expected to extend to 70 years by 2028. Singapore has implemented a slew of policies to enable older Singaporeans to engage in work well past their retirement. The Retirement and Re-Employment Act supports older Singaporeans who prefer to continue working post retirement.[30] Progressive employment practices support employers in redesigning workplace processes to create an older-person-friendly work environment. Through subsidising courses for all residents including older adults, the SkillsFuture initiative provides an optimal platform to upgrade skills and enhance employment readiness. The National Silver Academy initiative encourages lifelong learning for eligible seniors through a network of education institutions and community organisations.[31] The old-age labour force participation has increased from 17.6% in 2010 to 32.9% in 2021. Despite the increase, there is a need for age-inclusive work policies in Singapore. Although both male and female older employees continue to increase, there is a vast gender discrepancy with older men outnumbering older women significantly.

Informal and Formal Income Sources

To date, families remain the main source of financial support during old age in most parts of Asia.[32] In essence, families are informal pension

[29] Borsch-Supan, A. H. *Global Ageing: Issues, Answers, More Questions*, Michigan Retirement Research Center Research Paper No. 2004-084, 2004; and Menon, J. and Nakamura, A. *Ageing in Asia Trends, Impacts and Responses*, (Asian Development Bank, 2009).

[30] Singapore Government, Retirement and Re-employment Act (Revised ed. 2012). https://sso.agc.gov.sg/Act/ RRA1993.

[31] Council for Third Age, National Silver Academy, 2018. http://www.nsa.org.sg/index.php.

[32] United Nations, Department of Economic and Social Affairs, Population Division, *Living Arrangements of Older Persons: A Report on an Expanded International Dataset* (ST/ESA/SER.A/407); and United Nations, "Ageing in Asia and the Pacific: Overview," 2017. https://www.unescap.org/resources/ageing-asia-and-pacific-overview.

systems during old age, especially in rural areas where three-generation family systems provided succour and care for their older adult family members. However, a constellation of socio-economic changes character-ised by low fertility rates, increased urbanisation and changing family values have led to smaller nuclear families which are straining to provide inter-generational support.[33] In most parts of Southern Asia and Southeastern Asia including Singapore, public transfers are low and fami-lies experience greater financial pressure to sustain their older adult fam-ily members. Households with older adults, only in comparison to households without older adults and households with older adults and younger family members, report greater economic deprivation and higher monthly expenses.[34]

Although major strides have taken place in terms of pension coverage, there is still a long way to go.[35] In countries where a pension system exists, it is limited by its adequacy (coverage and range of risks), affordability (individual, organisational and societal), sustainability, robustness (with-stand macroeconomic shocks) and its capacity to provide adequate retire-ment income and form a safety net for the elderly poor. There are wide variations in pension coverage, both between and within Asian regions.[36] The percentage of persons above statutory pensionable age receiving pen-sion is the lowest in Southern Asia (23%) followed by Southeastern Asia

---

[33] Park, D. and Estrada, G. "Introduction: Why Does Asia Need Well-functioning Pension Systems," in Park, D. (ed.), *Pension Systems in East and South East Asia: Promoting Fairness and Sustainability*, (Philippines: Asian Development Bank, 2012), pp. 1–5. https://www.adb.org/sites/default/files/publication/29954/pension-systems-east-southeast-asia.pdf.

[34] Bakshi, S. and Pathak, P. *Aging and the Socioeconomic Life of Older Adults in India: An Empirical Exposition*, (Sage Open, January–March 2016), pp. 1–17. DOI: 10.1177/2158244015624130.

[35] International Labour Organization [ILO]. *Social Protection for Older Persons: Policy Trends and Statistics 2017–2019/International Labour Office, Social Protection Department*, (Geneva: ILO, 2018). https://www.ilo.org/wcmsp5/groups/public/---ed_protect/---soc_sec/documents/publication/wcms_645692.pdf.

[36] International Labour Organization [ILO]. *Social Protection for Older Persons: Policy Trends and Statistics 2017–2019/International Labour Office, Social Protection Department*, (Geneva: ILO, 2018). https://www.ilo.org/wcmsp5/groups/public/---ed_protect/---soc_sec/documents/publication/wcms_645692.pdf.

(74.1%) and Eastern Asia (77.3%).[37] In Southeast Asia, Cambodia with 3.2% ranks the lowest and Singapore ranks the highest on the number of persons receiving pension. In Southern Asia, on the lower end of the continuum is Pakistan (2.3%) and at the highest end is Maldives (99.7%). In Eastern Asia, pension coverage ranges between 77.6% in South Korea and 100% in Japan. A perennial problem that runs through Asian countries with the urban–rural divide is to provide pension to older adults in rural areas and to those who are employed in informal sectors.[38] In China, Pakistan, Sri Lanka and Malaysia, a combination of early retirement age and high pension might render financial sustainability of the pension system infeasible. Early withdrawals in Singapore and lump-sum payments in India severely threaten adequacy.[39] There are no easy solutions to the problems posed by pension. A dual system involving private and public contribution is being increasingly preferred by most countries.

Similar to other Asian countries, in Singapore, families continue to be the primary source of support.[40] From 2010 to 2020, the number of aged resident households with at least one older adult in Singapore increased from 275,500 (24.0% of all resident households) to 472,800 (34.4% of all resident households). Older adults rely on their married and unmarried children for their physical, emotional and financial support. Singapore has a well-established multi-pillar pension system. The Central Provident Fund (CPF), a mandatory employment pension system involving

[37] International Labour Organization [ILO]. *Social Protection for Older Persons: Policy Trends and Statistics 2017–2019/International Labour Office, Social Protection Department*, (Geneva: ILO, 2018). https://www.ilo.org/wcmsp5/groups/public/---ed_protect/---soc_sec/documents/publication/wcms_645692.pdf.

[38] Brustad, D. O. "Thailand. Pension System Overview and Reform Directions," in Park, D. (ed.), *Pension Systems in East and South East Asia: Promoting Fairness and Sustainability*, (Philippines: Asian Development Bank, 2012), pp. 99–115. https://www.adb.org/sites/default/files/publication/29954/pension-systems-east-southeast-asia.pdf; and Kim, C. and Bhardwaj, G. "South Asia Pension Forum Fostering Inclusive and Sustainable Pension Systems in the Region," 2011. See http://www.iopsweb.org/resources/48210556.pdf.

[39] OECD, "Pensions in Asia/Pacific," 2018. See https://www.oecd.org/finance/private-pensions/46260941.pdf.

[40] Ministry of Social and Family Development, Ageing Families in Singapore 2010–2020. Insight Series paper, January 2022. https://www.msf.gov.sg/research-and-data/Research-and-DataSeries/Documents/Ageing_Families_in_Singapore_2010-2020.pdf.

contributions from the employee and employer, is the main pillar, and the Workfare Income Supplement Scheme (WISS), the Supplementary Retirement Scheme (SRS) and the Housing Pension System (HPS) form the supplementary pillars. In general, the CPF has been considered sustainable and worthy of adaption by other countries.[41] However, the CPF is not without its limitations. The CPF is not limited to pension and can be used for housing, education and healthcare needs. Therefore, pre-retirement withdrawals are common, restricting adequacy of pension. Moreover, older women who were not employed are at an increased risk of economic vulnerability due to non-contribution from self and employer.[42]

Health of Older Adults

Healthy Life Expectancy (HALE) refers to "average number of years that a person can expect to live in 'full health' by taking into account years lived in less than full health due to disease and/or injury".[43] The increase in life expectancy has not witnessed a parallel increase in HALE (see Table 3). Across all countries and over the two periods, the rise in HALE is lower in comparison to rise in the life expectancy — living longer but not healthier. In 2017, in Japan, the life expectancy at 65 years was 22.2 years; however, the HALE was 16.9 years, i.e., about 5.2 years lived in poor health. HALE is lowest in Afghanistan (8.6 years) and highest in Singapore (17.3 years). Life expectancy and HALE at birth and at 65 years are higher in high socio-economic countries such as Singapore, Japan and the Democratic People's Republic of Korea in comparison to low socio-economic countries such as Pakistan, Afghanistan and Nepal. Fewer years of HALE have grave implications for healthcare planning,

---

[41] Xiao, J. and Dong, K. "Research and Inspiration on the Reform and Innovation of Singapore Central Provident Fund Pension System to Cope with the Aging Population," *Journal of US-China Public Administration*, 17(5), September–October 2020, 229–238.

[42] Koh, K. S. B. "Singapore's Social Security Savings System: A Review and Some Lessons for the United States," 2014. https://pensionresearchcouncil.wharton.upenn.edu/wp-content/uploads/2015/09/WP2014-18-Koh.pdf.

[43] World Health Organization, "Healthy Age Life Expectancy at Birth," 2003. See https://www.who.int/data/gho/indicator-metadata-registry/imr-details/66.

Table 3.   Life Expectancy and HALE in Asia

| | Life Expectancy | | | | HALE (Healthy Life Expectancy) | | | |
| | 1990 | | 2017 | | 1990 | | 2017 | |
	Birth	65 Years	Birth	65 Years	Birth	65 Years	Birth	65 Years
East and Northeast Asia								
China	68.7	14.2	77.1	17.1	60.9	10.9	68	13.1
Democratic People's Republic of Korea	72.2	14.8	82.6	20.8	63.1	11.1	71.7	15.6
Japan	79.3	18.6	84.2	22.2	69.7	14.3	73.1	16.9
Republic of Korea	71.8	15.3	72	15.4	63.4	11.6	63.5	11.5
Southeast Asia								
Brunei Darussalam	70.5	13.1	75.3	16.6	62.1	9.8	66.2	12.6
Cambodia	57.6	11.8	69.9	14.7	49.9	8.5	60.7	10.6
Indonesia	63.9	13.7	71.5	14.8	55.9	10	62.7	10.9
Laos	51.9	11.2	67.6	14.5	45.8	8.5	59.5	10.9
Malaysia	71.3	14.2	74.7	15.8	63	10.7	66	12.0
Myanmar	53.3	11.5	68.5	14.7	48.2	8.3	59.9	10.7
Philippines	67.9	15.3	69.7	14.4	58.9	11.2	67.9	13.5
Singapore	76.1	16.5	84.8	22.5	67.1	12.7	74.2	17.3
Thailand	70.7	15.9	78.1	20.2	62.2	12	68.5	15.3
Timor-Leste	60.2	13.5	70.8	15	51.7	9.7	61.2	10.8

Vietnam	68.9	14.7	74.5	16.6	60.5	11.1	65.8	12.5
South and Southwest Asia								
Afghanistan	52.6	10.6	63.4	12.3	43.5	7.5	53	8.6
Bangladesh	58.2	13.2	73.1	16.8	50.4	9.8	63.1	12.3
Bhutan	59.9	13.5	74	16.6	51.5	9.9	64.1	12.5
India	59.6	12.3	69	14.5	51.1	8.8	59.4	10.4
Iran	68.1	15.7	77.4	18	58.2	11.6	65.7	13.2
Maldives	65.1	13	81.4	20.3	56.7	9.6	71.7	15.2
Nepal	58.3	12.7	70.9	14.8	49.8	9.1	61.1	10.7
Pakistan	61.7	14.1	66.8	14.7	53.4	10.3	58	10.7
Sri Lanka	69.7	14.8	77.4	17.9	61.1	11.2	67.9	13.5
Turkey	68.6	15.6	78.9	19.1	59	11.4	67.9	14.1

Source: Data compiled from GBD 2017 DALYs and HALE Collaborators (2018).

strain healthcare expenditures and impact retirement policies such as determining retirement ages.

Singapore ranks first in HALE, globally — the result of a life course health approach involving primary prevention (National Steps Challenge, EatDrinkShop Healthy Campaign, National Senior's Health Programme for stroke and fall prevention, active ageing programmes, etc.), secondary prevention (Screen for Life and Project Silver Screen) and tertiary prevention (care close to home, home- and community-based care, etc.).[44] In Singapore, although most older adults continue to live healthily, chronic illnesses are on the rise. With more older adults living beyond 80 years (Table 1), the susceptibility to myriad neuro-cognitive and physical health issues increases manifold requiring specialist care. Therefore, not only does overall demand increase but the range of needs grows as well. Increasing prevalence rates of chronic diseases and multi-morbidity in ageing societies necessitate the transformation of healthcare service delivery systems that were principally intended for acute illnesses.[45] Health screening, health promotion and illness prevention activities will increasingly need to focus on cognitive and functional decline, including frailty and falls. In Singapore, a spectrum of long-term and intermediate care services exists.[46] At one end of the continuum are the costliest care services such as Nursing Homes, skilled nursing services and Hospice care facilities. Community-based services involve day-care and respite care facilities. In-home services take the form of meals on wheels and home healthcare facilities.

Service presence does not translate into service use. Healthcare services are plagued by several limitations. In Singapore, increasing chronic

[44] Ministry of Health, "Speech by Health Minister Gan Kim Yong at the G20 Side Event by International Longevity Centre UK Prevention in an Ageing World," October, 2019. https://www.moh.gov.sg/news-highlights/details/g20-side-event-by-international-longevity-centre-uk-prevention-in-an-ageing-world.

[45] Noda, S., Hernandez, R. M. P., Sudo, K., Takahashi, K., Woo, E. N., Inaoka, K., Tateishi, E., Affarah, S. W., Kadriyan, H. and Kobayashi, J. "Service Delivery Reforms for Asian Ageing Societies: A Cross-country. Study Between Japan, South Korea, China, Thailand, Indonesia, and the Philippines," *International Journal of Integrated Care*, 21(1), 2021.

[46] Chan, A. "An Overview of Singapore's Long-term Care System: Towards a Community Model Care," in O. Komazawa and Y. Saito (eds.), *Coping with Rapid Population Ageing in Asia*, (Jakarta: ERIA, 2021), pp. 28–35.

disease burden, long waiting time for nursing home beds and high health-care costs despite subsidies are major challenges. In developing Asian countries, geriatric services are lacking, much more so in rural areas. In rural India and Cambodia, the shortage of affordable transportation to medical services primarily concentrated in urban areas is a major impediment to service use.[47]

Health occurs at an intersection of diverse individual, familial, social and cultural factors. Therefore, the health sector should advocate for a whole-of-government and whole-of-society approach to integrated health.[48] With a heterogenous older adult population, the healthcare system should strive to align with the diverse needs of older adults. Investment in integrated and individualised services, designing effective financial policies and development plans for healthcare professionals with a positive attitude towards older people and with the right skills to work with older adults are some ways to deliver optimal health services.[49] In the long run, taking health to the home and community will gain prominence. In Japan, the Community-based Integrated Care System aims to provide up to end-of-life care in one's residence. Self-help, mutual aid, social solidarity and government help are the four pillars of the system.[50] In Singapore, through the "many helping hands approach" involving the individual, voluntary welfare organisations (VWOs), community and government, an optimal platform is provided for ageing in place. To this end, innovative

[47] Banerjee, S. "Determinants of Rural-urban Differential in Healthcare Utilization Among the Elderly Population in India," *BMC Public Health,* 21, 2021, 939. https://doi.org/10.1186/s12889-021-10773-1; and Jacobs, B., de Groot, R. and Fernandes Antunes, A. "Financial Access to Health Care for Older People in Cambodia: 10-year Trends (2004–2014) and Determinants of Catastrophic Health Expenses," *International Journal of Equity Health*, 15, 2016, 94. https://doi.org/10.1186/s12939-016-0383.

[48] World Health Organization, "Governance Snapshot: Whole of Society Approach," The coalition of partners for strengthening public health services in the European Region, 2019. WHO-EURO-2019-3475-43234-60595-eng.pdf.

[49] World Health Organization, "World Report on Ageing and Health," 2015. https://apps.who.int/iris/bitstream/handle/10665/186463/9789240694811_eng.pdf?sequence=1&isAllowed=y.

[50] Song, P. and Tang, W. "The Community-based Integrated Care System in Japan: Health Care and Nursing Care Challenges Posed by Super-aged Society," *Biosci Trends*, 13(3), 2019, 279–281.

and technology-based home and community care for older adults is needed.

Conclusion

Ageing in Asia is a heterogenous phenomenon. Countries across the different regions of Asia have reached different stages of population ageing, leading to intra- and inter-country ramifications. For instance, Singapore, in addition to dealing with the challenges of its ageing population, might also be impacted by the ageing population of other developing Asian countries. Singapore depends, in part, on other Asian countries for its manpower needs. Given that other Asian countries are ageing, labour migration will be constrained, and Singapore might have to explore alternate avenues in the near future. Therefore, forward-looking policies that consider current and future population ageing dynamics are necessary to create an optimal environment for ageing in Singapore and other Asian countries. Through policies and programmes that aim to create a "society for all ages", greater social integration and economic participation of older adults can be achieved. Contrary to the popular misconception that population ageing constricts labour and economic production, countries such as Singapore provide evidence for channelising older adults to spur greater labour participation and economic growth. Labour participation policies should aim to increase women's participation at all working ages in the labour force, enhance pay and working conditions in informal sectors and implement age-friendly work policies to promote self-reliance during old age. For productive participation, health is vital. Healthy ageing and prolonging HALE will undoubtedly form the central focus of health policies in Singapore and in other parts of Asia. Developing age-integrated health services that emphasise prevention of chronic illness, neuro-cognitive problems and ensuring equal access to affordable health service will be the focus of future policies in Asian countries including Singapore. Socio-economic and health policies should be designed and implemented to enable older adults to be equal partners in growth. To this end, more important is the need for a positive societal attitude towards older adults and non-discriminatory ageing policies. With dwindling traditional support system and challenges associated with formal support, needless to say, in the future the responsibility of ageing will continue to increasingly rest on the individual. To this end, policies should strive to enable people to plan to age successfully from their earlier stages of life. Successful policies among other factors rest on empirical data. Asian nations need to invest in and develop appropriate research capacity to monitor and comprehend multi-dimensional factors that shape ageing experiences. Cross-national studies on ageing, longitudinal studies on life span effects on ageing and evaluation studies on efficacy of interventions during old age might yield empirical findings that inform ageing policies and interventions.

Chapter 12

Every End Requires Planning — End-of-life Issues Among Older Adults

Lee Geok Ling and Chee Wai Yee

Abstract

While not much is usually discoursed about the end of one's life, there is an increasing need and importance to plan for end-of-life care and death. The critical need to live until death and die with dignity requires a range of decisions to deal with issues involving hospice and palliative care, a patient's right to self-determination of life and treatment, and the ethics and efficacy of medical interventions. As Singaporeans are ageing fast and the silver community forms a rising proportion of the population, fundamental questions, such as access to old-age healthcare, healthcare financing and legislations dealing with end-of-life care with all the ethical and social aspects, need to be borne in mind and addressed.

Introduction

Since young, emphasis has been laid on the importance to plan for our life, be it education, employment, courtship, marriage or family planning.

However, we are seldom introduced to the idea to plan for end-of-life care and death. End-of-life care is generally defined as care and support provided for patients who are very ill and who have stopped receiving curative treatment, with the aim to enable them to live as well as possible until death and to die with dignity.[1] End-of-life care can be provided in the form of acute care in days or months, as well as in years to improve the quality of life prior to death. A range of decisions is required pertaining to issues related to hospice and palliative care, patient's right to self-determination (of life and treatment), and the ethics and efficacy of (extraordinary or routine) medical interventions. In one local study with more than 60 Singapore citizens and residents aged 50 years and above, eight components of good end-of-life care were identified. These included having physical comfort at the end of life, avoiding an unnecessary prolonged dying process, maintaining sensitivity towards religious and spiritual beliefs, avoiding burden on family, avoiding expensive care, being cared for by a trustworthy doctor, maintaining control over decisions and achieving a sense of completion.[2]

With Singapore moving towards a demographic of ageing or in fact super-ageing population, there will be increased stress placed on the current healthcare system. Therefore, it is pertinent to start considering end-of-life issues that are commonly asked among the older adults: What type of care do I want? What types of service and support can I get access? How not to burden my family financially, physically and even mentally because of my illness? How can I prepare myself and my family for the final days? These questions are often interlocked with moral, ethical or legal difficulties, if not dilemmas.

This chapter aims to describe and discuss in depth three key issues faced by the older adults ("elderly patients" may be used interchangeably), in the context of end-of-life care. They are (1) access to hospice and

---

[1] NCI Dictionary of Cancer Terms (n.d.). *End-of-life Care.* https://www.cancer.gov/publications/dictionaries/cancer-terms?cdrid=774823.

[2] Malhotra, C., Chan, A., Do, Y. K., Malhotra, R. and Goh, C. "Good End-of-life Care: Perspectives of Middle-aged and Older Singaporeans," *Journal of Pain and Symptom Management,* 44, 2012, 252–263.

palliative care services,[3] (2) healthcare financing in hospice and palliative care, and (3) legislative events in addressing end-of-life care. Ethical and social issues or dilemmas faced at the end of life and the implications for the older adults and their families are embedded in the discussion, when relevant.

Historical Development of Hospice and Palliative Care in Singapore

Singapore saw the humble beginning of palliative care in 1985 with 16 inpatient beds at the St. Joseph's home. A newspaper report in 1986 on the visit to Singapore by Dr. Tetsuo Kashiwagi, a renowned Japanese advocate for palliative care, brought a group of medically trained professionals together and started the first volunteer-based home hospice care programme in 1987. Currently, the community-based and hospital-based approaches are the two main palliative care practice models in Singapore. The community-based palliative care practice model includes inpatient hospice care, home hospice care and day hospice care.

In 2014, the *National Strategy for Palliative Care* was formulated and adopted, which played a significant role in taking stock and as a roadmap for future palliative care development. This was followed by the development of sector-wide guidelines for all types of palliative care services.[4] Subsequently, the guidelines were implemented in the form of a self-assessment workbook, which the palliative care service providers undertook annually and voluntarily as part of the assessment and quality improvement through benchmarking initiative.[5] At the time of this writing, the quality improvement team of Singapore Hospice Council (SHC) was working on the fourth edition of the Self-Assessment Workbook of National Guidelines for Palliative Care, with greater emphasis put on psychosocial care of patients and caregivers.

---

[3] In Singapore, the terms "palliative care" and "hospice care" are used interchangeably (SHC, n.d.).

[4] Singapore Hospice Council, *Self-assessment Workbook*, 2nd draft edition, (December 2015). https://singaporehospice.org.sg/site2019/wp-content/uploads/National-Guidelines-for-Palliative-Care-Self-Assessment-Workbook-2nd-Draft-Edition-Dec-2015.pdf.

[5] *Ibid.*

Access to Hospice and Palliative Care Services

Hospice and palliative care is a form of compassionate and quality care for patients whose life expectancy can be anticipated in terms of months (usually less than 12 months of life) and who forgo curative care for supportive care as they enter the terminal phase. However, controversies are observed in the service delivery landscape. It will be discussed by examining the following issues: Who receives hospice and palliative care? Who receives better hospice and palliative care? What happens to those who outlive the prognosis?

Who receives hospice and palliative care?

As observed in the current hospice and palliative care landscape, such services have mainly been provided and met the needs of patients with cancer, even though cancer constituted less than 29% of the deaths in 2019.[6] This can be seen in the number of patients admitted in the inpatient care and home hospice care programmes (personal communications, Dover Park Hospice, 2020). Fewer non-cancer patients, such as those having organ failure (for example, congestive heart failure and chronic obstructive pulmonary disease) or frailty (such as dementia), receive hospice and palliative care service. The nature of disease trajectories could be a possible reason. The course of dying and the duration are more predictable and identifiable for patients having cancer but the prognostication for patients having non-cancer diseases is not so straightforward.[7] As a result, referral to palliative care may be delayed, even though medical treatment continues to be provided to patients with non-cancer diseases in the face of uncertain prognosis.

Who receives better hospice and palliative care?

There is a recent movement towards ageing and dying in place. A local study found that there was a greater preference for terminal care at home

---

[6] Ministry of Health, "Principal Causes of Death," 20 August 2020. https://www.moh.gov.sg/resources-statistics/singapore-health-facts/principal-causes-of-death.

[7] Lunney, J. R., Lynn, J., Foley, D. J., Lipson, S. and Guralnik, J. M. "Patterns of Functional Decline at the End of Life," *The Journal of the American Medical Association*, 289(18), 2003, 2387–2392.

among the patients with cancer.[8] Prior studies also reported that more than 80% of patients with advanced cancer prefer to die at home.[9] Yet, our local statistics indicate that the proportion of death occurring at home had been hovering at 26% in 2014 and a slight dip in 2019 at 22.9%, with most deaths occurring in hospitals, 62.2% in 2019 from 60.6% in 2014.[10]

One key contributing factor to the observed phenomenon could be due to the discrepancies in the resource allocation to the inpatient hospice care and home hospice care programmes. While those with a higher need for symptom management may be admitted for care compared to those being cared for at home, the latter are less resourced in supporting the psychosocial and spiritual care of the elderly patients and their family caregivers. In inpatient hospices, patients have access to designated social workers, creative arts therapy, physiotherapy, occupational therapy, social engagement with volunteers and medical staff who work three shifts in a day. This is downright different for patients who are receiving home palliative care service, who do not have these services provided as the "standard suite". The palliative care team may visit the elderly patient at home once or twice a week, depending on the patient's condition. What the elderly patients have at home are their individual family caregivers, who have to play multiple roles and work 24 hours, seven days a week. This leaves a question of whether elderly patients truly have the choice to age, be cared for or die in place.

What happens to those who outlive the prognosis?

While palliative care does not aim to prolong life, it helps to reduce symptoms, thus improving the quality of life of the patients compared to those

---

[8] Lee, A. and Pang, W. S. "Preferred Place of Death — A Local Study of Cancer Patients and Their Relatives," *Singapore Medical Journal*, 39(10), 1998, 447–450.

[9] Vidal, M., Rodriguez-Nunez, A., Hui, D., Allo, J., Williams, J. L., Park, M., Liu, D. and Bruera, E. "Place-of-death Preferences Among Patients with Cancer and Family Caregivers in Inpatient and Outpatient Palliative Care," *BMJ Supportive and Palliative Care*, 2020.

[10] Registry of Births and Deaths, *Report on Registration of Births and Deaths 2014*, (Singapore: Immigration and Checkpoints Authority, 2015); and Registry of Births and Deaths, *Report on Registration of Births and Deaths 2019*, (Singapore: Immigration and Checkpoints Authority, 2020).

who receive standard medical care. As such, some hospices may see their patients enjoying improvement in their health condition and even outliving the prognosis. This potentially raises some ethical dilemmas as inpatient hospice care is planned for patients who are expected to live for three or fewer months. In this situation, an elderly patient who is not dying "as expected" may be considered for discharge back to his own residence or a nursing home as part of right placement of care. The act can be seen as a form of abandonment by the patient and family, which in turn adversely affects the working relationship with them.

This also gives rise to contentious issues between the patient's family members and the healthcare team: Should the patient be transferred to a nursing home when he is already receiving professional and better care in a hospice? Should a patient be asked to return home when there are empty beds in the hospice? How do service providers come to a balance between meeting existing patients' needs and being prepared to attend to or have beds available for the next needy patients? What are the psychological and emotional costs to the elderly patient and the family caregivers whenever there are transitions to the place of care and the care team in the last one year of the patient's life? Situations may be trickier for an elderly patient living with progressive chronic illness, who is likely to be cared for at home with episodes of care provided in acute hospitals, and who may later transit from community medical/nursing care to end-of-life care. Every change of service provider may require added adjustments from the older adult and his caregiver(s). Withdrawal of established services from earlier providers may also have an impact on the well-being of the elderly patient and his caregiver(s). Moreover, recurring care transitions that may happen could tax the elderly patient, caregiver, healthcare providers and the healthcare system.

Healthcare Financing of Hospice and Palliative Care

The hospice and palliative care services started as volunteer home-based programme in the 1980s and were charity-funded and the services were provided free to end users. Till today, a majority of the community-based organisations and hospices continue to provide free home hospice care services to elderly patients. Only a few of the organisations began to charge according to means testing in recent years. Free services are possible with the government subventions and from public donations. However, this also implies that services have been provided based on equality rather than equity or justice. That is, free services may be provided to those who are resourceful and rich rather than those who are poor or are needy of such services. It may be worthwhile to note too that when a patient is already receiving a subsidy in palliative care, the same patient is unable to seek another subsidy. For example, a patient who is receiving home hospice care is not able to get subsidised home nursing services such as management of wounds or change of catheter, especially if such services are not provided by the palliative care team. This leaves a question on whether the elderly patient is truly receiving quality and dignified end-of-life care.

One significant milestone that led to positive developments in hospice and palliative care services in Singapore was the use of Medisave for general/specialist palliative care since 1994. The Medisave claimable limits have been raised to $250/$350 per day for general/specialist palliative care from April 1, 2020. More recently, the use of Medisave has been expanded to hospice home care and hospice day care. This is another significant milestone, especially when most elderly patients prefer to be cared for and die at home. In addition, the scheme was extended to include the Medishield Life coverage for inpatient hospice stay in 2020.[11] This is seen as a major leap from the past; dying older adults are more likely to get access to professional care in a hospice by their families because of the feasibility to tap into their Medisave or Medishield Life. In turn, this also reduces the bottleneck at the acute care hospitals.

However, it is worthy to note that the Medisave and Medishield Life claims are only up to three months of stay in the hospice. If the elderly patient outlives the prognosis, a request for an extension is required for the patient to continue with the claims, if it is deemed needed. Moreover, the cost of family caregiving is not included in the healthcare financing model when families are integral to care at the end of life; their care is often

---

[11] Ministry of Health, *New Inpatient Palliative Care Service from 1 April 2020*, 31 March 2020. https://www.moh.gov.sg/news-highlights/details/new-inpatient-palliative-care-service-from-1-april-2020.

ongoing, routine care, whose commitment is likely to continue throughout the dying trajectory. The absence of family caregivers can be a barrier to hospice home care delivery. Out-of-pocket expenses, such as purchase of adult diapers, transportation fees incurred for hospital consultations and the overall increase in the daily living expenses, may further aggravate the loss of income of the primary caregiver.

Legislative Events Concerning End-of-life Care

Several key legislative events over the last two decades have shaped the current situation in end-of-life care and the way care is delivered for older adults. The developments include introduction of the Advanced Medical Directive (AMD) in 1997, the Mental Capacity Act (MCA) that was passed by Parliament in 2008 and came into effect in 2010, and Advance Care Planning (ACP) intended as a national programme in 2011. These legislations were implemented in relation to the new advances in medical knowledge and technology that potentially created more and new choices for patients at the end of life and the healthcare service providers, as well as to ensure the quality of care of the dying elderly patients.

AMD is a legal document that is signed by a competent person, aged 21 years and above, in advance to inform the physician of a decision made pertaining to a specific medical situation or when death is imminent — the use of any extraordinary life-sustaining intervention.[12] The completed AMD is registered and kept confidential with the Registrar of Advanced Medical Directives. The attending physician is required to check with the Registrar on whenever an AMD has been signed when such a need arises. However, the AMD Act does not apply to patients who are receiving palliative care.

The MCA works on the principle that a person, even for an older adult, can make decisions for himself if he is given sufficient information, support and time. Five statutory principles are enforced to ensure that the person who lacks capacity is protected. These include the need to establish that the person lacks capacity; the need to take all practical steps to

---

[12] Ministry of Health, *Advanced Medical Directive*, n.d. https://www.moh.gov.sg/policies-and-legislation/advance-medical-directive.

help him make a decision; the need to respect the decision made even if it is an unwise decision; the need to act under this Act for or on behalf of the person in his best interests; and the need to ensure the act or decision made is less restrictive of the person's rights and freedom of action.[13] Lasting Power of Attorney (LPA) is a statutory mechanism through which a trusted individual (known as "donee"), who is appointed by an elderly person (known as "donor"), can make decisions on the elderly person's behalf on issues related to his property and financial affairs, personal welfare and healthcare if he loses the mental capacity in the future. Similar to AMD, LPA is also a legal document.

While AMD allows the older adult to underwrite their decision for a specific medical situation and LPA focusses on the appointment of decision makers with general power to act in the event that an older adult becomes mentally incapacitated, ACP documents the evolving care preferences, values and beliefs of an older adult to guide future health and personal care. ACP is an ongoing process of communicating a person's beliefs and values that inform future health and personal care preferences, after-death wishes and having a healthcare spokesperson nominated by the person.[14] As such, opportunities must be created to integrate the ACP conversations early into the ongoing dialogue with elderly patients when they have the capacity to discuss about their current health status and preferences for future care. There are three different stages of ACP, and preferred-plan-of-care ACP is usually used with patients who are referred for end-of-life care.

Characteristics and potential limitations of AMD, ACP and LPA at end of life

One common goal shared by the AMD, ACP and LPA is the goal to empower the dying elderly patients with the right to exercise their autonomy over the preferred medical treatment or even quality of life at the

---

[13] Singapore Statutes Online Plus, *Mental Capacity Act (Chapter 177A), Revised Edition 2020*, 31 March 2020. https://sso.agc.gov.sg/Act/MCA2008.
[14] Agency for Integrated Care, *Advance Care Planning*, n.d. https://www.aic.sg/care-services/advance-care-planning.

time of a critical illness. This is to ensure that they are able to make decisions that reflect their personal values and beliefs even when they are incompetent or in the final stage of their terminal illness. The exercise of autonomy not only enables the elderly patients not to have prolonged pain and suffer unnecessarily, and maintain their dignity, but also reduces conflict and anxiety among family members and relieves the family members from the emotional burden, particularly when they need to decide without knowing if the decisions take into consideration the wishes of the elderly patients.

However, the uptake rates are rather low. According to the publicly available data, an accumulative total of 24,682 Singaporeans had registered for AMD as of 2015, 43,000 people have submitted their LPA applications as of March 2018[15] and only 4,500 instances of ACP were completed in 2018.[16] A scrutiny of the nature of the Acts may shed some light on the low uptake rates. Firstly, AMD, LPA and ACP are anticipatory acts, which are likely to be made without considering the possible changes that may happen between the signing of the document and its execution, such as the course and prognosis of the disease, advancement of the medical knowledge and technology, and opinions of the physician, patient and primary informal caregivers, that will be specific to the future episodes of care. Thus, they may be different from an informed decision made by a patient at the time of treatment. Take, for example, an older adult who at age 65 years could live up to at least 85 years old.[17] However, the gain in the number of years of life expectancy does not necessarily match gains in the number of years of good health. Occurring alongside the increasing life expectancy in Singapore is the increasing prevalence of chronic non-communicable diseases. According to the Singapore Burden of Disease study, an older adult could have at least 10 years of disability adjusted life

[15] Lai, L. "IPS Report Urges Better End-of-life Planning," *The Straits Times*, 13 July 2019. https://www.straitstimes.com/singapore/report-urges-better-end-of-life-planning.

[16] Ministry of Health, "Tools Available to Encourage Discussions About End-of-life care," 18 July 2019. https://www.moh.gov.sg/news-highlights/details/tools-available-to-encourage-discussions-about-end-of-life-care.

[17] Department of Statistics Singapore. *Population Trends 2020*, (Singapore: Ministry of Trade & Industry, 2020).

years before the eventual death.[18] The findings imply that an older adult will experience physical loss, limitation in daily activities and perhaps even diet as they age. The decision made 10 years prior to disability-adjusted life years might be different from that 10 years later.

Secondly, the three documents are administered and come under the jurisdiction of different Ministries and Acts: AMD is administered directly by the Ministry of Health (MOH), LPA is administered by the Ministry of Social and Family Development (MSF) and ACP is administered by a statutory board of MOH, the Agency of Integrated Care (AIC). This may create difficulties or even confusion among older adults who may not be knowledgeable enough to navigate the various systems. They may also not be able to tell the utilities and relationships among the documents. Thus, the older adults may be fearful that by signing the documents, they may receive less-than-desired treatment or that their physicians might abandon them. It is thus important to have mechanisms put in place to assist the older adults gain a totality view and make informed decisions in the use of the different planning documents.

Thirdly, one potential challenge that may arise out of these different administrative tracks is when the spokesperson nominated for ACP and the donee appointed for LPA are two different persons. Given that LPA is a legal document, the donee's decision will supersede that of the spokes-person of ACP, even if the spokesperson may be following the older adult's wishes. In cases when both donee and spokesperson perceive that they are each acting in good faith for the best interest of the elderly person, this may give rise to conflicts within the family and in turn hurt the family relationships.

On the other hand, there is a sub-population in which many older adults face difficulties in identifying a donee or nominating a healthcare spokesperson. This includes those who are childless, single or have a distant relationship with relatives. Fortunately, an amendment has been

---

[18] Ministry of Health, *The Burden of Disease in Singapore, 1990–2017: An Overview of the Global Burden of Disease Study 2017 Results*, Singapore: Institute for Health Metrics and Evaluation (Seattle, WA: IHME, 2019). https://www.moh.gov.sg/docs/librariesprovider5/default-document-library/gbd_2017_singapore_reportce6bb0b3ad1a49c19ee6e-badc1273b18.pdf.

newly made to MCA, introducing the provision of licenced professional donees and deputies. However, the new changes may not cater to the poor older adults as the current scheme is not under regulation for pricing of professional fees. There is a possibility that those older adults who only require donees for personal welfare and healthcare but with very little assets and property to be managed may not be offered such a professional service because they do not have enough to use as payment.

Fourthly, there are differences in opinions in the patient–family–healthcare provider unit on the preferred type(s) and extent of care. For example, patients were often found to be more likely to opt for less costly high-technology treatment in the terminal phase of illness; family members were more hesitant to withhold or withdraw life-sustaining treatment than the patients themselves, probably because of the cultural interpretation of filial piety; and healthcare providers were more likely than family members and patients to withhold or withdraw life-sustaining treatment.[19]

In summary, the concepts of AMD, LPA and ACP are potentially useful in the care of elderly patients, particularly in the terminal stage of diseases and when they no longer have the mental capacity. However, the execution of the concepts is not easy or simple. To better execute the advantages of the AMD, LPA and ACP, the following are suggestions for consideration. Firstly, there should be public education on end-of-life issues or even health and death literacy. Secondly, a clinical approach which focusses on understanding what matters to the older adults, rather than an administrative approach (when completing the form is the goal), should be adopted when administering the legislations. For example, a dying elderly patient may want to be sedated most of the time to be pain

---

[19]Ellis, E. M., Orehek, E. and Ferrer, R. A. "Patient-provider Care Goal Concordance; Implications for Palliative Care Decisions," *Psychology and Health*, 34(8), 2019, 983–998; Trarieux-Signol, S., Bordessoule, D., Ceccaldi, J., Malak, S., Polomeni, A., Fargeas, J. B., Signol, N., Pauliat, H. and Moreau, S. "Advance Directives from Haematology Departments: The Patient's Freedom of Choice and Communication with Families. A Qualitative Analysis of 35 Written Documents," *BMC Palliative Care*, 17(1), 2018, Article number 10; and Torke, A. M., Sachs, G. A., Helft, P. R., Montz, K., Hui, S. L., Slaven, J. E. and Callahan, C. M. "Scope and Outcomes of Surrogate Decision Making Among Hospitalized Older Adults," *JAMA Internal Medicine*, 174(3), 2014, 370–377.

free, but another elderly patient may forgo optimal pain control to stay alert as much as possible and be involved in family activities. The essential task is to enable the choice made by the patient and family members, allowing them to be heard and respected, with services or interventions designed and made available to mitigate the trade-offs from those choices.

Thirdly, ACP discussions may be promoted early in the community where the older adults can be given more time and space to discuss with someone knowledgeable about the legislations and the impact on their preferred care, possibly in the presence of supportive family member(s). Community is perceived as a better setting than a hospital as the competing demands to meet the immediate needs of patients in the hospital setting may make ACP seen as a non-urgent task. Fourthly, multiple conversations should be encouraged to seek understanding of the beliefs and values that informed the choices. This way, the physicians can be more certain about how to execute the patients' wishes when needed. Lastly, efforts should be made to periodically revisit the ACP documentation as it allows the ACP to be updated as and when the patients have a change of mind. This is particularly important when current ACP documents focus mainly on care decision and appointment of spokesperson, usually associated with end of life. The above suggestions would greatly enhance patient–family–physician communication and partnership in care. The utility of ACP would be higher if it could also encompass discussion and documentation on long-term care preferences and planning of the funeral (an area older adults are more adept to discuss).

Implications for Practice in End-of-life Care

With the advancement in medical science and technology, the quality of care of the dying has improved. Yet, the course of dying of older adults is also said to be more "medicalised' rather than "normalised" as part of life where the psychosocial and spiritual meanings of dying for both the elderly patients and their families are recognised as integral to the whole experience. The key to providing good end-of-life services is to adopt a person-centred approach which gives patients and their family control, respect, dignity and adequate decision-making power, with availability of options in the healthcare system being the pre-requisite condition.

The current healthcare landscape has much to achieve to be closer to this desire state.

One possible implication for practice is the need for end-of-life care policies to be designed with better understanding of the needs and cultural preferences of dying elderly patients and the impact on family caregivers. This may include understanding where and how caregiving takes place within domestic settings. To illustrate, potential tensions between the notions of home and care may fundamentally disrupt the physical and socio-emotional relationships between elderly patients and family caregivers, thus impacting the care experiences of both elderly patients and family caregivers and the subsequent bereavement experiences of the caregivers.

At the macro level, the above understanding is important for public health planning, with the intention to match needs and resources based on where services have to be provided, without depriving the needy elderly patients who may require palliative care or even long-term care. Introducing general palliative care in the community could be an approach, through which the needs of the elderly patients and their families could be better identified and addressed in a timely manner within the community. Specialist palliative care may be introduced when the patients are in the terminal phase or when care needs are more complex.

The other possible implication for practice is the need to reexamine the role of social workers in hospice and palliative care service. Social workers can play a central role in promoting respectful treatment at the end of life by performing a comprehensive assessment that addresses the psychological, social, emotional, spiritual, cultural, environmental, financial and even practical aspects of care.[20] Performing a comprehensive assessment takes time and effort but the subsequent interventions by the multi-disciplinary team can be enhanced in significant ways. First, social workers can help elderly patients and their family members examine the changes and needs related to the illness or find meanings in the dying process. Second, social workers can partner with the family, patients and

---

[20] Howe, J. L. and Daratsos, L. "Roles of Social Workers in Palliative and End-of-life Care," in B. Berman (ed.), *Handbook of Social Work in Health and Aging*, (Oxford: Oxford University Press, 2006), pp. 315–323.

even others to navigate the changes, empowering them by connecting them to internal resources within themselves besides communicating among the family members. Third, social workers can intervene outside the family system, such as advocating for the elderly patients and families with specific healthcare service providers or even advocating for policy changes at a macro level, to support a more caring approach to end-of-life care for both patients and families.

Currently, elderly patients and families are made known to social workers through referrals by the medical team and not necessarily at the early phase in the care continuum. One possible change is thus to introduce psychosocial-spiritual care to the elderly patients early in the disease trajectory so that the psychosocial-spiritual aspects related to coping with the disease could be better managed. As the disease progresses, there may be more emphasis on the medical treatment by the medical team. Simultaneously, more psychosocial care could be provided to the family caregivers as the disease progresses, particularly at the later phase and after the death of the elderly patient.

Conclusion

End-of-life care represents a complex interaction between the care issues and the partners involved in care. There is no "one formula" that can meet all the needs of the older adults. Instead, each of their personality, life experiences and social support must be considered and appreciated when understanding their decisions with respect to end-of-life care. Thus, communication regarding end-of-life care plans is of importance to both the older adults and their families. Over the years, more attention has been drawn to the sector on end-of-life care for terminal illness and life-limiting conditions. This is reflected in the introduction of an overarching end-of-life care strategy, legislation measures for advance directives, legal basis for mental incapacity and public–people partnerships to investigate knowledge, training and resources for end-of-life care. However, care must still be taken to translate the policies and the legal decision-making framework into more effective and comprehensive executions, with the older adults feeling supported, dignified and having a good quality of life. The attributes of the older adults and the dying experiences require a different conceptualisation of end-of-life care, which underscores the importance of paying attention to a range of ethical and policy issues (including personal choice, cost and quality of care), as well as challenges and opportunities for quality assessment, measurement and improvement in service delivery. Social work has an important role in this specialised field's ongoing developments; social workers can work with dying elderly patients and families on their psychosocial-spiritual issues along the care continuum.

https://doi.org/10.1142/9789811265198_0014

Conclusion: Addressing Some Critical Concerns

S. Vasoo

Singapore Ageing will become a critical societal concern as our population is not rejuvenated and in a danger of shrinking further. With the increase in life expectancy and lower fertility rates of about 1.2, societal ageing will be accelerated and about a third of the population will be 65 years and above.[1] For such a high silver population, the old-age support ratio is 1 elderly person above 65 years old being supported by 4 between 20 and 64 years of age in 2021. This dependency burden will increase with a reduction of the ratio to about 2 persons when the total fertility rate falls further if not mitigated by selective immigration of younger families without which the Singaporean community will be less versatile and vibrant. Renewal and rejuvenation of the population will be essential to

---

[1] Institute of Policy Studies, *Scenarios of Future Population Growth and Change in Singapore*, (2011); Teng, Y. M. and Gee, C. *Population Outcomes: Singapore 2050*, (Singapore: Institute of Policy Studies Exchange Series); Rangaswamy, E., *et al.* "A Study on Singapore's Ageing Population in the Context of Eldercare Initiatives Using Machine Learning Algorithms," *Big Data Cognitive Compututing*, 5(51), 2021, 1–17; and Hirschmann, R. *Aging Population of Singapore: Statistics and Facts*. Stastista.com., 2022.

keep the society going and sustainable.[2] Singapore must face the silver tsunami social landscape squarely and think about proactive and creative solutions to tackle the various social situations confronting an ageing society. Such a greying demographic profile cannot be wished away but must be tackled head on in a few selected areas which require close attention besides those recommended by the Committee on Ageing Issues.[3]

With a projected increase in the population of the elderly who are 65 years and above from one- to three-fold by 2030 to 900,000, there is a need to plan for the future including the need for employment of the elderly for the workforce.[4] There will be a surplus of silver workers with varying work skills who will meet the depleting young labour force due to reduction in the number of children born because of the lower fertility rate in the preceding decades. Singapore policy makers and corporations will have think of various options including ways to incentivise young families to have two or more children with improved childcare allowances and support. Steps that are more active can be initiated to help Singapore's population build up, although it is indeed trying. Aside from this action, more flexible approaches need to be utilised to retain and re-employ elderly workers beyond their retirement age or alternatively recruit foreign workers in place. This will be a touchy issue and will precipitate more public debate, criticisms and resentment unless there are more job openings than can be filled by the ageing workforce.

However, there will be work in the labour-intensive sectors that local and particularly the elderly workers of the post-*Merdeka* Generation will not want to take up and as such there needs to be more flexibility for these employment sectors to employ foreign workers. As can be seen, the future labour requirements will face a crunch in light of a reduction of the younger working population and a lack of elderly workers to meet the

---

[2] Teng, Y. M. and Gee, C. *Population Outcomes: Singapore 2050*, (Singapore: Institute of Policy Studies Exchange Series, 2014); and Goh, L. G., Kua, E. H. and Chiang, H. D. *Ageing in Singapore: The Next 50 Years*, (Singapore: Gerontological Society, 2015).

[3] *Report of the Committee on Ageing Issues*, (Singapore: Ministry of Social and Family Development, 2006).

[4] Rangaswamy, E. *et al.* "A Study on Singapore's Ageing Population in the Context of Eldercare Initiatives Using Machine Learning Algorithms," *Big Data Cognitive Computing*, 5(51), 2021, 1–17.

demands of the employment market. With the steep decline expected in the old-age support ratio from 4.5 in 2019 (Residents Aged 20–64 years per resident aged 65 years and over) to 0.8 in 2030 (Residents Aged 20–64 years per resident aged 65 years and over),[5] it will inadvertently add pressure on Singapore society to take urgent steps to consider toping up the population through selected immigration and employ foreign skilled and semi-skilled labour force to preempt Singapore from declining socially and economically.

Any miss-action or inaction due to negative sentiments of a population sector can have long-term disastrous effects on the livelihoods of Singaporeans as a whole. Singapore will be no better and the welfare of its people will deteriorate, as its society will not be socially and economically viable. This will become a reality if policy makers, corporate leaders and key opinion leaders do not pull together to find innovative solutions which are objectively essential to keep Singapore society going for the coming generation. Having been a close observer of Singapore social development for the last 60 years, I must with all sincerity urge Singaporeans to think about enabling Singapore to be sustainable for generations to come by keeping their minds open to measures taken to increase the fertility rates and replace or top up the population by selective immigration of young foreign families who are bonded to Singapore and its survival. Based on various analyses, Singapore has been observed to have the lowest fertility rate in the world and the median age of the population will be estimated to increase from 39.7 in 2015 to 53.4 in 2050.[6]

Given that there will be a larger proportion of the elderly, the labour force must attract and absorb as many ageing workers into employment as possible. Although, the labour force participation rate of senior workers 65 years and above has increased from 27.6% (2019) to 28.5% in 2020, this rate has potential to improve further as there will be a requirement to meet financial needs after retirement age and to keep engaged in the work world due to a longer life span.[7] It is not surprising to note that slightly more than half of Singaporeans surveyed were not financially prepared to

---

[5] *Ibid.*

[6] Hirschmann, R. *Demographics of Singapore: Statistics and Facts*. Stastista.com., 2021.

[7] Leng, T. S. "On Employment of Older Workers," *Channel News Asia*, 5 October 2021.

retire and only a third could cope with retirement. In the future, there will be more heads of households aged 65 years and above and as such there will be a push to extend the retirement age to cope with their continued employability so that financial adequacy could be maintained.[8] To facilitate employability of the ageing population, more programmes will have to be implemented to reskill workers, in particular the elderly workforce whose digital literacy capability can be enhanced. Tomorrow's ageing workforce will have to possess sharpened IT skills to remain more employable. This will be a norm if one intends to continue working in a transformed work environment run by artificial intelligence systems.

Inevitably, there will be a significant increase in the number of single elderly persons who form 16% of the 1.3 million households and not including another 16.6% couple-based households without children.[9] A majority of such elderly people live in high-rise public housing flats. According to a recent newspaper report, about one in eight public housing households is made up of single persons.[10] The concern, which has been found to afflict such single households, is the issue of loneliness and this can have consequential effects on mental health.[11] Loneliness in old age can be dreadful, and worse still without social support and interaction with others, it does have a toxic effect on mental and social health. Often, the community may focus less attention on this group because they are often not seen or heard. They are not on the community radar because of privacy and confidentiality matters. This is indeed a sober picture, as the number of lonely elderlies will grow exponentially. It is projected that there will be about less than one million elderly aged 65 years and above in the population. Single, less mobile elderly persons will require someone to reach out to them to tackle the effects of loneliness and mental

---

[8] Hirschmann, R. *Aging Population of Singapore: Statistics and Facts.* Stastista.com., 2022; and Institute of Policy Studies, *Scenarios of Future Population Growth and Change in Singapore*, 2011.

[9] *Population Trend 2021.* Singapore Department of Statistics. Singapore.

[10] Wong, P. T. "Sharp Rise in Single Person Households, Accounting for 1 in 8 HDB Homes in 2018," *Today Online*, 10 February 2021.

[11] Liang, E. W., *et al.* "Loneliness amongst Low-socioeconomic Status Elderly Singaporeans and Its Association with Perceptions of the Neighbourhood Environment." *International Journal of Environmental Research and Public Health*, 19(967), 2019, 1–9.

problems.[12] As a compassionate Singapore, one cannot ignore the plights of these Singaporeans who may at one time or another need community support and care.

Moreover, closer attention will have to be paid to lonely elderly who are from the lower economic strata as they are likely to live in rental flats where their neighbours also have limited resources. Therefore, more attempts must be undertaken to mobilise residents who are living in better neighbourhoods with better endowment to support them. Non-profit groups may find it challenging to set up a social exchange bank where lonely elderly and needy residents could help each other by resource exchange through this support network social exchange bank. This is a doable proposition that can be established with least cost as there are many types of resources such as skills, physical resources, materials, man-power and monetary resources that can be pooled into the social exchange bank for deployment for those who need help to cope with their lives.[13] As mental health will be affecting the lonely elderly more, it will be a good move for the social exchange bank to deploy befrienders to follow up with those in despair and to explore various ways to help connect them to more endearing networks, which can support them in getting over their worries or despair.

Not all societies can avoid dealing with end-of-life course matters. Singapore must brace itself to prepare for issues related to death and dying, a heart-breaking concern that will be faced by all families. With increasing elderly persons in the community, one can expect to see more families having to manage the loss of their loved ones or relatives.

In 2020, it was recorded that there were 22,054 deaths and the crude death rate per thousand residents increased to 5.2 from 4.2 in 2015 (Macrotrend Singapore Death Rates 1950–2022), and this was due to the

---

[12] Teng, Y. M. and Gee, C. *Population Outcomes: Singapore 2050*, (Singapore: Institute of Policy Studies Exchange Series, 2014); Rangaswamy, E. *et al.* "A Study on Singapore's Ageing Population in the Context of Eldercare Initiatives Using Machine Learning Algorithms," *Big Data and Cognitive Computing*, 5(51), 2021, 1–17; and *Population Trend 2021, Population Projection 2020–2030*, (Singapore: Singapore Department of Statistics).

[13] Vasoo, S. "Some Challenges in Managing Volunteers and Enhancing Their Participation in the Social Service Sector," in S. Vasoo, B. Singh and X. J. Chan (eds.), *Singapore in Community Development Arenas in Singapore*, (Singapore: World Scientific Press, 2019).

increasing number of elderly persons in the population.[14] However, with better healthcare and nutrition, longevity has increased over time and the life expectancy at birth was 83.9 years in 2020. In the case of the elderly over 65 years of age, life expectancy has increased from 19.8 years in 2010 to 21.5.[15] The improvement in the life span of the elderly is a good indicator of healthy life support and care services available in Singapore, but families must be prepared to cope with the end-of-life issues. Some families are ill prepared as sudden or unexpected deaths happen to their elderly loved ones. For these families, they could face difficulty in accepting the demise of their elders or getting closure. Consequently, there could be post-traumatic depression facing those closely related and the loss will take a long time to heal, in some cases affecting the mental health of those surviving. There will be families who are better able to cope with the demise of their elderly as the members of these families have had a reasonable period to prepare for death and have knowledge of the events leading to the demise of their elderly loved ones. For such families, there will be satisfactory closure as all treatment efforts have been accorded but without lifesaving outcomes.

Starting from 2030, the number of elderly Singaporeans aged 65 and above is anticipated to be around 900,000.[16] This will account for one in four Singaporeans in that age group. Such a demographic shift to Singapore ageing, without attempts to tinker in the topping-up of the population, will see an increase in social and economic burdens facing families as the resident old-age support ratio will decline from 4.0 to 2.1.[17]

There will be more frail elderly requiring care and support. When there are limited family members available due to household shrinkage, the families of these elderly will have to count on aged care services

[14]*Population Trend 2021, Population Projection 2020–2030*, (Singapore: Singapore Department of Statistics).

[15]*Singstat 2020*. Singapore; *Population Trend 2021, Population Projection 2020–2030*, (Singapore: Singapore Department of Statistics).

[16]Trendspotting, 22 August 2016. Singapore; *Population Trend 2021, Population Projection 2020–2030*, (Singapore: Singapore Department of Statistics).

[17]*Population White Paper*, Singapore Government, 2013; Goh, L. G., Kua, E. H. and Chiang, H. D. *Ageing in Singapore: The Next 50 Years*, (Singapore: Gerontological Society, 2015); and *Population Trend 2021*, (Singapore: Singapore Department of Statistics).

offered by public and social service agencies. Looking ahead, it is necessary for public and non-profit sectors' policy makers to plan more community-based elderly care and support services to be implemented besides nursing homes, which require more resources and cater to a small number of elderly people. More emphasis and resources could be channelled on community-based services such as home help, healthcare, befriending, meal delivery and financial support. Closer attention could be given to neighbourhoods with more elderly needing care and support with efforts to encourage ageing in place. Policy makers in the delivery of social and healthcare services should try as far as possible to enable the elderly to remain in their homes and community. That is in my mind a right direction to take.

At the same time, the future death rate of those aged 65 years and over will increase from the current 26.7 per thousand, given the increase in the elderly population.[18] Many of these deaths will be due to cancer, pneumonia and heart diseases.[19] Terminal illnesses will commonly affect the elderly and some of these can be long-drawn.[20]

An increasing number of families will have an elderly who may be afflicted by chronic and life-threatening diseases, which raise end-of-life dilemmas and often address the questions about keeping life going or ending life. Elderly persons who are more enlightened may seek a compassionate way to end life, as they do not want to suffer further pain and be a greater burden to their surviving family members. Such a double-bind human dilemma will come up more frequently in all societies that are ageing like Singapore. We have to be prepared to see much controversies arising, particularly between "pro-lifers" and "pro-choicers". These heart-wrenching and emotionally charged matters could be dealt with gracefully if Singapore families are primed early to empathetically face issues on end of life. There will be no easy answers as we are likely to have more people who are "pro-choicers". If policy makers or key opinion leaders do not handle the matter carefully, our society may become socially fractured.

---

[18] Hirschmann, R. *Aging Population of Singapore: Statistics and Facts.* Stastista.com., 2022.
[19] Healthhub, Health-Statistics, "Principal Causes of Death," 2020.
[20] Key Indicators on the Elderly 2018, Annual Data.gov.sg.

Therefore, a way to find a resolution will be for family members to come to a consensus in finalising the end-of-life journey for their loved ones by such decisions as advanced directives, power of attorney, written will or any other ways acceptable to the dying person.

Finally, to confront the various social issues and challenges facing ageing Singapore, we must take proactive steps to ensure the regeneration of Singapore. We should be open to innovative solutions to ensure that there is population growth either by improving our replacement level or by topping up through selective immigration of younger families who can help to make Singapore more vibrant, robust and sustainable. We should not be resentful and reactive Singaporeans and assert by shaping Singapore to be an exclusive society as this could have serious negative consequences for the republic's future growth and development. Singapore will have more mileage as its society becomes more open and inclusive in sharing with immigrants who can contribute to the survival of Singapore. In being selectively open, we can see a better horizon in the future. Otherwise, Singaporeans will end up no better without longer plans to regenerate and make our place more attractive to live to the fullest potential. Finally, with the collective support of Singaporeans and good responsible leadership in governing Singapore, we will be able to see Singapore through the difficult challenging times ahead despite Singapore ageing.

Select Bibliography

AARP and NAC. *Caregiving in the United States 2020*, (AARP, 2020). https://doi.org/10.26419/ppi.00103.001.

AARP. *Valuing the Invaluable 2019 Update: Charting a Path Forward* (Insight on the Issues), (AARP, 2019).

Action for Successful Aging, (Singapore: Ministry of Health, 2018).

Agency for Integrated Care, (Singapore: Ministry of Health, 2018).

Agency for Integrated Care. *Advance Care Planning*. n.d. https://www.aic.sg/care-services/advance-care-planning.

Allen, J., Chavez, J., DeSimone, S. S., Howard, D. D. *et al.* "'Americans' Attitudes Towards Euthanasia and Physician-assisted Suicide, 1936–2002," *Journal of Sociology and Social Welfare*, 33(2), 2006, 5–23.

Anderson, N. D., Damianakis, T., Kröger, E., Wagner, L. M., Dawson, D. R., Binns, M. A., Bernstein, S., Caspi, E. and Cook, S. L. "The Benefits Associated with Volunteering Among Seniors," *Psychological Bulletin*, 140(6), 2014, 1505–1533. https://doi.org/10.1037/a0037610.

Arnalds, O. and Archer, S. (eds.) *Rangeland Desertification*, (Switzerland: Springer Nature, 2000).

Atchley, R. *Social Forces and Aging: An Introduction to Gerontology* (9th ed.), (Singapore: Wadsworth, 2000).

Atul, G. *Being Mortal: Medicine and What Matters in the End*, (UK: Large Print Press, 2017).

Austin, C. "Case Management in Long-term Care," in C. Meyer (ed.), *Social Work and Aging* (2nd ed.), (MD: National Association of Social Workers, Silver Spring, 1986).

Aw, T. C. and Low, L. "Health Care Provisions in Singapore," in T. M. Tan and S. B. Chew (eds.), *Affordable Health Care*, (Singapore: Prentice Hall, 1997), pp. 50–71.

Ayalon, L. "Volunteering as a Predictor of All-cause Mortality: What Aspects of Volunteering Really Matter?" *International Psychogeriatrics*, 20(5), 2008, 1000–1013. https://doi.org/10.1017/S1041610208007096.

Barbara, P., Greig, M., Throne, S. *et al.* "Nursing and Euthanasia: A Narrative Review of the Nursing Ethics Literature," *Nursing Ethics*, 27(1), 2020, 152–167.

Bass, S. A., Caro, F. G. and Chen, Y. P. (eds.) *Achieving a Productive Aging Society*, (Westport, CT: Auburn House, 1993).

Bédard, M., Koivuranta, A. and Stuckey, A. "Health Impact on Caregivers of Providing Informal Care to a Cognitively Impaired Older Adult: Rural Versus Urban Settings," *Canadian Journal of Rural Medicine: The Official Journal of the Society of Rural Physicians of Canada = Journal Canadien De La Medecine Rurale: Le Journal Officiel De La Societe De Medecine Rurale Du Canada*, 9(1), 2004, 15–23.

Bertrand, R. M., Saczynski, J. S., Mezzacappa, C., Hulse, M., Ensrud, K. and Fredman, L. "Caregiving and Cognitive Function in Older Women: Evidence for the Healthy Caregiver Hypothesis," *Journal of Aging and Health*, 24(1), 2012, 48–66. https://doi.org/10.1177/0898264311421367.

Blando, J. *Counseling Older Adults*, (Routledge, 2011).

Bom, J., Bakx, P., Schut, F. and van Doorslaer, E. "The Impact of Informal Caregiving for Older Adults on the Health of Various Types of Caregivers," *The Gerontologist*, 59(5), 2019.

Börsch-Supan, A., Brugiavini, A., Jürges, H., Mackenbach, J., Siegrist, J. and Weber, G. (eds.) *Quality of Employment and Well-being: First Results from the Survey of Health, Ageing and Retirement in Europe*, (Mannheim Research Institute for the Economics of Aging (MEA), 2005).

Bronfenbrenner, U. *The Ecology of Human Development: Experiments by Nature and Design*, (Cambridge, MA: Harvard University Press, 1979).

Brydges, C. R., Carlson, M. C., Andrews, R. M., Rebok, G. W. and Bielak, A. A. M. "Using Cognitive Intraindividual Variability to Measure Intervention Effectiveness: Results from the Baltimore Experience Corps Trial," *The Journals of Gerontology: Series B*, 76(4), 2021, 661–670. https://doi.org/10.1093/geronb/gbaa009.

Bureau of Labour Statistics, "Volunteering in the United States, 2015," *Economic News Release*, 25 February 2016. https://www.bls.gov/news.release/volun.htm.

Butler, R. N. "Living Longer, Contributing Longer," *The Journal of the American Medical Association*, 278(16), 1997, 1372–1374.

Butler, R. N. and Gleason, H. *Productive Aging: Enhancing Vitality in Later Life*, (New York: Springer, 1985).

Calvo, E., Haverstick, K. and Sass, S. A. "Gradual Retirement, Sense of Control, and Retirees," *Happiness Research on Aging*, 31(1), 2009, 112–135.

Cambell, A., Gilbert, G. and Jones, G. *Medical Ethics (4e)*, (South Melbourne, Australia: Oxford University Press, 2005).

Central Provident Fund Reports, (Singapore, 2020).

Central Provident Fund, *CPF Contribution and Allocation Rates*, 2020a. https://www.cpf.gov.sg/employers/employerguides/employer-guides/paying-cpf-contributions/cpf-contribution-and-allocation-rates.

Central Provident Fund, *Self-employed Matters*, 2020b. https://www.cpf.gov.sg/members/FAQ/schemes/Self-Employed-Scheme/Self-Employed-Matters/FAQDetails?category=Self-Employed%20Scheme&group=Self-Employed%20Matters&folderid=12405&ajfaqid=2188316.

Centre for Liveable Cities, *Towards Ageing Well: Planning a Future-ready Singapore. Urban Systems Studies Series,* (Centre for Liveable Cities, Ministry for National Development, 2021).

Challis, D. and Davies, B. *Case Management in Community Care: An Evaluated Experiment in the Home Care of the Elderly*, (Aldershot, UK: Gower Publishing, 1986).

Chan, A., Ostbye, T., Malhotra, R. and Hu, A. *The Survey on Informal Caregiving — Full Report*, (Singapore: Ministry of Social and Family Development, 2013).

Chew, H. M. "Singapore's Total Fertility Rate Falls to Historic Low in 2020," *Channel NewsAsia*, 26 February 2021. https://www.channelnewsasia.com/news/singapore/singapore-total-fertility-rate-tfr-falls-historic-low-2020-baby-14288556.

Cheung, P. L. "Population Ageing in Singapore," *Asia Pacific Journal of Social Work*, 3(2), 1993, 77–89.

Cheung, P. L., Ngiam, T. L., Vasoo, S. and Chan, Y. Y. "Social Support Networks for the Elderly in a High-rise Public Housing Estate in Singapore," in *Social Services and Aging Policies in the U.S. and Asia*, (International Exchange Center on Gerontology, University of South Florida, 1988), pp. 305–340.

Chia, K. S. and Chong, S. A. "Most Singaporean Are Living Longer — But Are They Ready for Old Age," 2017.

Chia, K. S. and Lim, M. K. *Healthcare Reforms in Singapore in Health Reforms Across the World*, K. Okma and T. Tenbensel (eds.), (World Scientific Press, 2018).

Chin, C. W. W. and Phua, K. H. "Long-term Care Policy: Singapore's Experience." *Journal of Aging and Social Policy*, 28(2), 2016, 113–129.

Cook, J. R. "Strategies for Building Social Capital. In Social Capital and Community Well-being," in A. G. Greenberg, T. P. Gullotta and M. Bloom (eds.), *The Serve Here Initiative*, (Switzerland: Springer International Publishing, 2016).

Corrine, N. and Sim, A. *Building Social Support Networks for Older Adults: A Nation-wide Initiative by the Singapore Silver Generation Office*, (Singapore: World Scientific Publishers, 2022).

Deborah, M. and Miller, B. "Space and Contentious Politics," *Mobilization: An International Journal*, 8(2), 2001, 143–156.

Department of Statistics. *Population Trends 2020*, (Singapore: Ministry of Trade and Industry, 2020).

Dover Park Hospice. *Annual Report 2019–2020*, (Dover Park Hospice, 2020).

Easwaramoorthy, R. *et al.* "A Study on Singapore's Ageing Population in the Context of Eldercare Initiatives Using Machine Learning Algorithms," *Big Data Cognitive Computing*, 5(51), 2021, 1–17.

Economic and Social Commission for Asia and the Pacific (1996*). Population Ageing in Asia and the Pacific*. ESCAP, Bangkok, with Japanese Organisation for International Cooperation in Family Planning, Inc., Tokyo. United Nations: New York.

Ellis, E. M., Orehek, E. and Ferrer, R. A. "Patient-provider Care Goal Concordance; Implications for Palliative Care Decisions," *Psychology and Health*, 34(8), 2019, 983–998.

Ewan, C. G., Ely, E. W., Sulmasy, D. P., Bakkar, J. *et al. Critical Care Medicine*, 45(2), 2017.

Fan, X., Zhang, H., Leung, C. and Shen, Z. "Robust Unobtrusive Fall Detection Using Infrared Array Sensors." *IEEE International Conference on Multisensor Fusion and Integration for Intelligent Systems (MFI)*, (Daegu, South Korea, 2017), pp. 194–199.

First Interactive Gaming Kiosk Equipped With Personal Wellness Analytics. 30 August 2015. Retrieved 11 January 2021, from Singapore Book of Records: https://singaporerecords.com/first-gaming-kiosk-equipped-with-wellness-analytics/.

Fisher, G. G., Chaffee, D. S., Tetrick, L. E., Davalos, D. B. and Potter, G. G. "Cognitive Functioning, Aging, and Work: A Review and Recommendations for Research and Practice." *Journal of Occupational Health Psychology*, 22(3), 2017, 314–336.

Flett, G. L. and Heisel, M. J. "Aging and Feeling Valued Versus Expendable During the COVID-19 Pandemic and Beyond: A Review and Commentary of Why Mattering is Fundamental to the Health and Well-being of Older Adults," *International Journal of Mental Health Addiction*, 2020.

Freedman, M. *The Big Shift: Navigating Midlife and Beyond*, (New York, NY: Perseus Books Group, 2011).

Fujiwara, Y., Sakuma, N., Ohba, H., Nishi, M., Lee, S., Watanabe, N., Kousa, Y., Yoshida, H., Fukaya, T., Yajima, S., Amano, H., Kureta, Y., Ishii, K., Uchida, H. and Shinkai, S. "Effects of an Intergenerational Health Promotion Program for Older Adults in Japan," *Journal of Intergenerational Relationships*, 7(1), 2009, 17–39.

Gao, S., Wang, D., Tan, A.-H. and Miao, C. "Progressive Sequence Matching for ADL Plan Recommendation," *IEEE/WIC/ACM International Conference on Web Intelligence and Intelligent Agent Technology (WI-IAT)*, (Singapore, 2015), pp. 360–367.

Goh, Y. H. "$100 Worth of CDC Vouchers for Each S'porean Household Available for Collection Online," *The Straits Times*, 23 December 2021.

Goins, R. T., Spencer, S. M. and Byrd, J. C. "Research on Rural Caregiving: A Literature Review," *Journal of Applied Gerontology*, 28(2), 2009, 139–170.

Gonzales, E., Matz-Costa, C. and Morrow-Howell, N. "Increasing Opportunities for the Productive Engagement of Older Adults: A Response to Population Aging," *The Gerontologist*, 55, 2015, 252–261.

Gordon, D. and Donald, S. *Community Social Work, Older People and Informal Care: A Romantic Illusion?* (Avebury: Aldershot, UK, 1993).

Greene, V. L., Ondrich, J. and Laditka, S. "Can Home Care Services Achieve Cost Savings in Long-term Care for Older People?" *Journal of Gerontology*, 53B(4), 1998, 228–328.

Gubhaju, B., Malhotra, R., Chan, A. and Ostbye, T. *Deteriorating Health but Still Working Very Long Hours — A Profile of Singapore's Older Family Caregivers*, (Singapore: Centre for Ageing and Research, 2017).

Halvorsen, C. J. and Chen, Y.-C. "The Diversity of Interest in Later-life Entrepreneurship: Results from a Nationally Representative Survey of Americans Aged 50–70," *PLOS One*, 14(6), 2019.

Hofäcker, D., Hess, M. and König, S. *Delaying Retirement: Progress and Challenges of 17 Active Ageing in Europe, the United States and Japan*, (London: Palgrave MacMillan, 2016).

Holstein, M. B. and Minkler, M. "Critical Gerontology: Reflections for the 21st Century," in M. Bernard and T. Scharf (eds.), *Critical Perspectives on Ageing Societies*, (Buckingham, UK: Open University Press, 2007), pp. 12–26.

Hong, S., Morrow-Howell, N., Tang, F. and Hinterlong, J. "Engaging Older Adults in Volunteering: Conceptualizing and Measuring Institutional Capacity," *Nonprofit and Voluntary Sector Quarterly*, 38, 2009, 200–219.

Horatio, C. *Heavy Light: A Journey Through Madness, Mania and Healing*, (London: Chatto Windus, 2021).

Hou, J., Zeng, Z., Miao, C. and Liu, Y. "Prospective Memory Aid: A Reminding Model Based on Fuzzy Cognitive Maps," *IEEE International Conference on Fuzzy Systems (FUZZ-IEEE)*, (Vancouver, BC, Canada, 2016), pp. 170–177.

Howe, J. L. and Daratsos, L. "Roles of Social Workers in Palliative and End-of-life Care," in B. Berman (ed.). *Handbook of Social Work in Health and Aging*, (Oxford University Press, 2006). pp. 315–323.

ILO, "What About Seniors? A Quick Analysis of the Situation of Older Persons in the Labour Market," 4 May 2018. https://www.ilo.org/global/statistics-and-databases/publications/WCMS_629567/lang--en/index.htm.

Institute for Health Metrics and Evaluation, *The Burden of Disease in Singapore, 1990–2017: An Overview of the Global Burden of Disease Study 2017 Results*, (Ministry of Health, 2019).

Jia, H. and Vasoo, S. "Housing as Asset Building in Singapore," in S. Vasoo and B. Singh (eds.), *Critical Issues in Asset Building in Singapore's Development*, (Singapore: World Scientific Publishers, 2018).

Johnson, R. W. and Schaner, S. G. *Value of Unpaid Activities by Older Americans Tops $160 Billion Per Year* (No. 4; The Retirement Project: Perspectives on Productive Aging). Urban Institute, 2005.

Jongenelis, M. I., Jackson, B., Warburton, J., Newton, R. U. and Pettigrew, S. "Improving Attitudes to Volunteering Among Older Adults: A Randomized Trial Approach," *Research on Aging*, 42(2), 2020, 51–61.

Kang, Y., Tan, A. and Miao, C. "An Adaptive Computational Model for Personalized Persuasion," *Proceedings of the 24th International Conference on Artificial Intelligence (IJCAI'15)*, (Buenos Aires, Argentina, 2015), pp. 61–67.

Khalik, S. "Singapore Tops in Life Expectancy at 84.8 Years," *The Straits Times*, 20 June 2019.

Kim, S. and Ferraro, K. F. "Do Productive Activities Reduce Inflammation in Later Life? Multiple Roles, Frequency of Activities, and C-reactive Protein," *The Gerontologist*, 54(5), 2014, 830–839.

Knodel, J. and Debavalya, N. "Living Arrangements and Support Among the Elderly in South-east Asia: An Introduction." *Asia-Pacific Population Journal*, 12(4), 1997, 5–16.

Ko, P.-C. and Yeung, W.-J. J. "Contextualizing Productive Aging in Asia: Definitions, Determinants, and Health Implications," *Social Science & Medicine (1982)*, 229, 2019, 1–5.

Kosloski, K., Schaefer, J. P., Allwardt, D., Montgomery, R. J. V. and Karner, T. X. "The Role of Cultural Factors on Clients' Attitudes Toward Caregiving, Perceptions of Service Delivery, and Service Utilization," *Home Health Care Services Quarterly*, 21(3–4), 2002, 65–88.

Kua, E. H. "Psychological Distress for Families Caring for Frail Elderly," *Singapore Medical Journal*, 3, 1987, 42–44.

Labour Force Report 2020, Ministry of Manpower, Singapore.

Lai, L. "IPS Report Urges Better End-of-life Planning," *The Straits Times*, 13 July 2019.

Lane, A. P., Wong, C. H., Mocnik, S., Song, S. and Yuen, B. "Association of Neighbourhood Social Capital with Quality of Life Among Older People," *Journal of Aging and Health*, 32(7–8), 2020, 841–850.

Lee, A. and Pang, W. S. "Preferred Place of Death — A Local Study of Cancer Patients and Their Relatives," *Singapore Medical Journal*, 39(10), 1998, 447–450.

Li, C.-Y. and Sung, F.-C. "A Review of the Healthy Worker Effect in Occupational Epidemiology," *Occupational Medicine*, 49(4), 1999, 225–229.

Li, Y.-P., Chen, Y.-M. and Chen, C.-H. "Volunteer Transitions and Physical and Psychological Health Among Older Adults in Taiwan," *The Journals of Gerontology: Series B*, 68(6), 2013, 997–1008.

Lim, J. "Health Care Reform in Singapore: The Medisave Scheme," in T. M. Tan and S. B. Chew (eds.), *Affordable Health Care*, (Singapore: Prentice Hall, 1997), pp. 277–285.

Liu, J., Lou, Y., Wu, B. and Mui, A. C. Y.-S. "I've Been Always Strong to Conquer Any Suffering:" Challenges and Resilience of Chinese American Dementia Caregivers in a Life Course Perspective," *Aging & Mental Health*, 2020, 1–9.

Liu, S., Shen, Z., Yu, H., Lin, H., Guo, Z., Pan, Z., ... Leung, C. "A Kinect-based Interactive Game to Improve the Cognitive Inhibition of the Elderly: (Demonstration)," *International Conference on Autonomous Agents & Multiagent Systems (AAMAS)*, 2016, pp. 1479–1481.

Low, D. "Mom-and-pop Shops and Coffee Shop Stalls in Yuhua Get Their Own Shopping Platform," *The Straits Times*, 31 October 2021.

Luborsky, M. and Sankar, A. "Extending the Critical Gerontology Perspective: Cultural Dimensions," *The Gerontologist*, 33(4), 1993, 440–444.

Lunney, J. R., Lynn, J., Foley, D. J., Lipson, S. and Guralnik, J. M. "Patterns of Functional Decline at the End of Life," *The Journal of the American Medical Association*, 289(18), 2003, 2387–2392.

Malhotra, C., Chan, A., Do, Y. K., Malhotra, R. and Goh, C. "Good End-of-life Care: Perspectives of Middle-aged and Older Singaporeans," *Journal of Pain and Symptom Management*, 44, 2012, 252–263.

Mastro, C. A. and Mason, S. E. "Ethical Issues and Attitudes Towards Euthanasia," *Modern Psychological Studies*, 22(2), 2017, 149–155.

Matz, C., Sabbath, E. and James, J. "An Integrative Conceptual Framework of Engagement in Socially-productive Activity in Later Life: Implications for Clinical and Mezzo Social Work Practice," *Clinical Social Work Journal* [special issue on productive aging], 48, 2020, 156–168.

McDermott-Levy, R., Kolanowski, A., Fick, D. and Mann, M. "Addressing the Health Risks of Climate Change in Older Adults," *Journal of Gerontological Nursing*, 45, 2019, 21–29.

Mehta, K. "Caring for the Elderly in Singapore," In W. Liu and H. Kendig (eds.). *Who Should Give Care to the Elderly? An East-West Social Value Divide*, (Singapore: Singapore University Press, 2000).

Mehta, K. "Stress Among Family Caregivers of Older Persons in Singapore," *Journal of Cross-cultural Gerontology*, Special Issue, 20, 2006, (Special on Aging in Asia) 319–334.

Mehta, K. and Thang, L. L. "Experiences of Formal and Informal Caregivers of Older Persons in Singapore," *Journal of Cross-cultural Gerontology*, 32(3), 2017, 373–385.

Mehta, K. and Vasoo, S. "Community Programmes and Services for Long-term Care of Elderly in Singapore: Challenges for Policy Makers," *Asian Journal of Political Science*, 8(1), 2000, 125–140.

Mehta, K. and Vasoo, S. "Organisation and Delivery of Long-term Care in Singapore: Present Issues and Future Challenges," *Journal of Aging & Social Policy*, 13(2/3), 2001, 187–201.

Mehta, K. K. "Social Integration and Creating an Age-inclusive Community in Singapore," *SUSS – Researchers @ Work, Issue 3*. https://www.suss.edu.sg/about-suss/centres/centre-for-applied-research/researchers-at-work/issue-3/social-integration-and-creating-an-age-inclusive-community-in-singapore.

Meng, L., Nguyen, Q. H., Tian, X., Shen, Z., Chng, E. S., Guan, Y., ... Leung, C. "Towards Age-friendly E-commerce Through Crowd-improved Speech Recognition, Multimodal Search, and Personalized Speech Feedback," *Proceedings of the 2nd International Conference on Crowd Science and Engineering (ICCSE'17)*, (Beijing, China, 2017), pp. 127–135.

Menon, M. "Close to 100,000 Residents Having Trouble with Basic Tasks," *The Straits Times*, 19 June 2021.

Ministry of Community Development. *Because We Care: Guidelines for Community-based Services for Elderly*, (Singapore: Ministry of Community Development, 1998).

Ministry of Community Development. *Report of the Inter-ministerial Committee on the Ageing Population*, (Singapore: Ministry of Community Development, 1999).

Ministry of Health, *Advanced Medical Directive*, n.d. https://www.moh.gov.sg/policies-and-legislation/advance-medical-directive.

Ministry of Health, *Annual Reports*, (Singapore, 1997, 1998, 1999).

Ministry of Health, *Beds in Inpatient Facilities and Places in Non-residential Long-term Care Facilities*, 2020. https://www.moh.gov.sg/resources-statistics/singapore-health-facts/beds-in-inpatient-facilities-and-places-in-non-residential-long-term-care-facilities.

Ministry of Health, *Blue Paper on the National Health Plan* (NHP), (Singapore, 1983).

Ministry of Health, *Frequently Asked Questions on Medifund,* 2020. https://va.ecitizen.gov.sg/CFP/CustomerPages/MOH/explorefaq.aspx?category=12667.

Ministry of Health, *Government Health Expenditure and Healthcare Financing*, 2020. https://www.moh.gov.sg/resources-statistics/singapore-health-facts/government-health-expenditure-and-healthcare-financing.

Ministry of Health, *Hospital Admission Rates by Age and Sex 2018*, 2020. https://www.moh.gov.sg/resources-statistics/healthcare-institution-statistics/hospital-admission-rates-by-age-and-sex/hospital-admission-rates-by-age-and-sex-2018.

Ministry of Health, Ministry of Community Development, Department of Statistics and National Council of Social Services. *National Survey of Senior Citizens in Singapore*, (Singapore: National Press, 1996).

Ministry of Health, *New Inpatient Palliative Care Service from 1 April 2020*, 31 March 2020. https://www.moh.gov.sg/news-highlights/details/new-inpatient-palliative-care-service-from-1-april-2020.

Ministry of Health, *Population and Vital Statistics*, 2020. https://www.moh.gov.sg/resources-statistics/singapore-health-facts/population-and-vital-statistics.

Ministry of Health, *Principal Causes of Death*, 20 August 2020. https://www.moh.gov.sg/resources-statistics/singapore-health-facts/principal-causes-of-death.

Ministry of Health. *Report of the Committee on the Problems of the Aged*, (Singapore: Ministry of Health, 1984)

Ministry of Health. *Report of the Inter-ministerial Committee on Health Care for the Elderly*, (Singapore, Ministry of Health, 1999).

Ministry of Health, *Singapore Annual Report 2020*.

Ministry of Health, *Tools Available to Encourage Discussions about End-of-life Care*, 18 July 2019. https://www.moh.gov.sg/news-highlights/details/tools-available-to-encourage-discussions-about-end-of-life-care.

Ministry of Health, *White Papers on Affordable Health Care*, (Singapore, 1993).

Moody, H. "Productive Aging and the Ideology of Old Age" in N. Morrow-Howell, J. Hinterlong and M. Sherraden (eds.), *Productive Aging: Concepts and Challenges*, (Baltimore: Johns Hopkins University Press, 2001), pp. 175–196.

Moody, H. "Toward a Critical Gerontology," in J. Birren and V. Bengston (eds.), *Emergent Theories of Aging*, (N.Y.: Springer, 1998).

Morrow-Howell, N. and Mui, A. C. "Introduction," in N. Morrow-Howell and A. C. Mui (eds.), *Productive Engagement in Later Life: A Global Perspective*, (Routledge, 2012).

Morrow-Howell, N. and Wang, Y. "Productive Engagement of Older Adults: Elements of a Cross-cultural Research Agenda," in A. C. Mui, N. Morrow-Howell and D. Peng (eds.), *Productive Aging in the World: Toward Evidence-based Practice and Policy*, (Beijing: Beijing University Press, 2012) (In Chinese).

Mui, A. C. "Productive Ageing in China: A Human Capital Perspective," *China Journal of Social Work*, 3(2–3), 2010, 111–123.

Munnell, A. and Sass, S. A. *Working Longer: The Solution to the Retirement Income Challenge*, (Washington, DC: Brookings Institute Press, 2008).

National Population and Talent Division, Prime Minister's Office, Department of Statistics, Ministry of Home Affairs, Ministry of Manpower, Immigration and Checkpoints Authority, *Population in Brief 2020*, (Singapore, 2020).

National Volunteer and Philanthropy Centre, *Issues in the Low Income Space in Singapore*, 2021. https://cityofgood.sg/sector-insights/low-income-families/?gclid=EAIaIQobChMIlcr9trS88QIVTn8rCh2ONwkcEAAYAiAAEgLdcPD_BwE.

NCI Dictionary of Cancer Terms, *End-of-life Care*, n.d. https://www.cancer.gov/publications/dictionaries/cancer-terms?cdrid=774823.

Nosek, B. A. and Banaji, M. R. "The Go/No-go Association Task," *Social Cognition*, 19(6), 2001, 625–666.

OECD, *Employment Rate by Age Group*. OECD Data, 2021. http://data.oecd.org/emp/employment-rate-by-age-group.htm.

Ong, E. S., Tyagi, S., Lim, J. M. and Chia, K. S. "Health Systems Reform in Singapore: A Qualitative Study," *Health Policy*, 122, 2018, 431–443.

Onwuteaka-Philisen, B. D., Muller, M. T., *et. al.* "Euthanasia and Old Age," *Age and Ageing*, 26(6), 1997, 487–492.

Pan, Z. "Information Technology's Role in Aging and Community Service," *Singapore Aging: Issues and Challenges*, (Singapore: World Scientific Publishers, 2022).

Pan, Z., Miao, C., Tan, B. T., Yu, H. and Leung, C. "Agent Augmented Inter-generational Crowdsourcing," *IEEE/WIC/ACM International Conference on Web Intelligence and Intelligent Agent Technology (WI-IAT)*, (Singapore, 2015), pp. 237–238.

Pan, Z., Miao, C., Yu, H., Leung, C. and Chin, J. J. "The Effects of Familiarity Design on the Adoption of Wellness Games by the Elderly," *IEEE/WIC/ACM International Conference on Web Intelligence and Intelligent Agent Technology (WI-IAT)*, (Singapore, 2015), pp. 387–390.

Pan, Z., Yu, H., Miao, C. and Leung, C. "Efficient Collaborative Crowdsourcing," *Proceedings of the 30th AAAI Conference on Artificial Intelligence (AAAI'16)*, (Phoenix, Arizona, USA, 2016), pp. 4248–4249.

Pan, Z., Zhang, H., Zhang, Y., Leung, C. and Miao, C. "A Goal Oriented Storytelling Model for Improvement of Health Game Experiences Among Older Adults," *Human Aspects of IT for the Aged Population. Supporting Everyday Life Activities (ITAP)*, (Cham: Springer, 2021), pp. 135–152.

Pan, Z., Zhang, Y., Zhang, H. and Miao, C. "Health Games Adoption Among Elderly: A Depiction of the Elderly Health Game Experience," *International Journal of Information Technology*, 2021.

Pan, Z., Zhang, Y., Zhang, H. and Shen, Z. "Coaching Older Adults in Health Games: A Goal Oriented Modelling Approach," *Social Computing and Social Media: Applications in Marketing, Learning, and Health (SCSM)*, (Cham: Springer, 2021), pp. 424–442.

Papa, R., Cutuli, G., Principi, A. and Scherer, S. "Health and Volunteering in Europe: A Longitudinal Study," *Research on Aging*, 41(7), 2019, 670–696.

Pelham, A., & Clark, W. (Eds.). *Managing Home Care for the Elderly*, (N.Y.: Springer Publishing, 1986).

Phua, K. H. *Privatization and Restructuring of Health Services in Singapore*, Occasional Paper No. 5; Institute of Policy Studies, (Singapore: Times Academic Press, 1991).

Pillemer, K., Wells, N., Meador, R., Schultz, L., Henderson, C. and Tillema Cope, M. "Engaging Older Adults in Environmental Volunteerism," *The Gerontologist*, 57, 2017, 367–375.

Population Census, (Singapore: Department of Statistics, 2020).

Prescott, N. (Ed.). *Proceedings of a Conference on Choices in Financing Health Care and Old Age Security.* World Bank Discussion Paper No. 2. (Washington, D.C., USA: World Bank, 1998).

Quah, S. *Study on the Singapore Family*, (Singapore: Ministry of Community Development, 1999).

Ratcliffe, J., Lester, L. H., Couzner, L. and Crotty, M. "An Assessment of the Relationship Between Informal Caring and Quality of Life in Older Community-dwelling Adults — More Positives than Negatives?" *Health & Social Care in the Community*, 21(1), 2013, 35–46.

Registry of Births and Deaths, *Report on Registration of Births and Deaths 2019.* Immigration and Checkpoints Authority, (Singapore, 2020).

Registry of Births and Deaths, *Report on Registration of Births and Deaths 2014.* Immigration and Checkpoints Authority, (Singapore, 2015).

Richards, M. *Community Care for Older People: Rights, Remedies and Finances*, (Bristol, UK: Jordans, 1996).

Rowe, J. and Kahn, R. *Successful Aging*, (New York, NY: Pantheon Books, 1998).

Roy, S. "Baby Boom Generation in Singapore and Its Impact on Ageing," *International Journal of Humanities and Social Sciences*, 8(3), 2014, 809–817.

Saleebey, D. *The Strength's Perspective in Social Work Practice*, 3rd ed. (Boston: Allyn and Bacon, 2002).

Schneider, R., Kropf, N., & Kisor, A. *Gerontological Social Work: Knowledge, Service Settings, and Special Populations*, (Australia: Brooks/Cole, 2000).

Seifert, A., Cotten, S. R. and Xie, B. "A Double Burden of Exclusion? Digital and Social Exclusion of Older Adults in Times of COVID-19," *The Journals of Gerontology: Series B*, 2020.

Shantakumar, G. "Aging and Social Policy in Singapore," *Ageing International*, 22(2), 1995, 49–54.

Shantakumar, G. *The Aged Population of Singapore.* Census of Population 1990, Monograph No. 1, (Singapore, 1994).

Sherraden, M., Morrow-Howell, N. and Hinterlong, J. "Productive Aging: Theoretical Choices and Directions," in *Productive Aging: Concepts and Challenges*, (Johns Hopkins University Press, 2001), pp. 260–284.

Siegel, J. S., & Hoover, S. L. "Demographic Aspects of Health of the Elderly to the Year 2000 and Beyond," *World Health Statistics Quarterly*, 35(3/4), 1982, 140–141.

Singapore Action Group of Elders (SAGE) *Case Management Service*, (Singapore: SAGE, 1998).

Singapore Department of Statistics, *Census of Population 2020*, (Singapore: Singapore Department of Statistics, 2021).

Singapore Hospice Council, *National Guidelines for Palliative Care*, 2nd ed., 20 January 2015. https://singaporehospicc.org.sg/site2019/wp-content/uploads/National-Guidelines-for-Palliative-Care-Revised-Ed.-Jan-2015.pdf.

Singapore Hospice Council, *Self-assessment Workbook*, 2nd draft edition, December 2015. https://singaporehospice.org.sg/site2019/wp-content/uploads/National-Guidelines-for-Palliative-Care-Self-Assessment-Workbook-2nd-Draft-Edition-Dec-2015.pdf.

Singapore Hospice Council, *What You Need to Know — Why the Need for Palliative Care?* n.d. https://singaporehospice.org.sg/palliativecare/.

Singapore Statutes Online Plus, *Mental Capacity Act (Chapter 177A), revised edition 2020*, 31 March 2020. https://sso.agc.gov.sg/Act/MCA2008.

Statistics Singapore, Singapore Department of Statistics, *Statistics on Marriages and Divorces,* (Singapore: Ministry of Trade and Industry, 2019).

Straits Times. *Committee's 21 Members Named.* Singapore, 15 November 1998.

Sun, J. "Chinese Older Adults Taking Care of Grandchildren: Practices and Policies for Productive Aging," *Ageing International*, 38(1), 2013, 58–70.

Tan, T. "Fewer Seniors Go to Authorities to Seek Maintenance from Children," *The Straits Times,* 14 June 2021.

Tan, T. H. *SG50 Wish*, 2015. Androidblip: https://www.androidblip.com/android-apps/com.LILY.MKrapid.html.

Tan, T. K. "How to Help Seniors be More Digitally Connected," *Today*, 8 December 2020. https://www.todayonline.com/commentary/how-help-seniors-be-more-digitally-connected.

Tan, T. K. "Humanising Technology for Older Adults," *Ethos,* Issue 20, 28 January 2019, Civil Service College Singapore. https://www.csc.gov.sg/articles/humanising-technology-for-older-adults.

Teo, P. "The National Policy on Elderly People in Singapore," *Ageing and Society*, 14, 1994, 405–427.

Teo, P., Mehta, K., Thang, L. L. and Chan, A. "The Journey After Widowhood," in P. Teo, K. Mehta, L. L. Thang and A. Chan (eds.), *Ageing in Singapore: Service Needs and the State,* (London: Routledge, 2006), pp. 134–146.

Teo, Z. W. and Zainal, K. "Successful Aging: Progressive Governance and Collaborative Communities," *Ethos*, 2018, Civil Service College, Singapore.

Tew, C. W., Tan, L. F., Luo, N., Ng, W. Y. and Yap, P. "Why Family Caregivers Choose to Institutionalize a Loved One with Dementia: A Singapore Perspective," *Dementia and Geriatric Cognitive Disorders*, 30, 2010, 509–516.

Thang, L. L. "Experiencing Leisure in Later Life: A Study of Retirees and Activity in Singapore," *Journal of Cross-cultural Gerontology*, 20(4), 2005, 307–318.

Thang, L. L. and Mehta, K. K. "Teach Me to be Filial: Intergenerational Care in Singapore Families," in J. Shea, K. Moore and H. Zhang (eds.), *Beyond Filial Piety: Rethinking Aging and Caregiving in East Asian Societies*, (Berghahn Books. Life Course, Culture and Aging: Global Transformations, 2020), pp. 142–165.

Torke, A. M., Sachs, G. A., Helft, P. R., Montz, K., Hui, S. L., Slaven, J. E. and Callahan, C. M. "Scope and Outcomes of Surrogate Decision Making Among Hospitalized Older Adults," *JAMA Internal Medicine*, 174(3), 2014, 370–377.

Trarieux-Signol, S., Bordessoule, D., Ceccaldi, J., Malak, S., Polomeni, A., Fargeas, J. B., Signol, N., Pauliat, H. and Moreau, S. "Advance Directives from Haematology Departments: The Patient's Freedom of Choice and Communication with Families. A Qualitative Analysis of 35 Written Documents," *BMC Palliative Care*, 17(1), 2018, Article number 10.

Tuomola, J., Soon, J., Fisher, P. and Yap, P. "Lived Experience of Caregivers of People with Dementia and the Impact on Their Sense of Self: A Qualitative Study in Singapore," *Journal of Cross Cultural Gerontology,* 31(2), 2016, 157–172.

Tur-Sinai, A., Teti, A., Rommel, A., Hlebec, V. and Lamura, G. "How Many Older Informal Caregivers Are There in Europe? Comparison of Estimates of Their Prevalence from Three European Surveys," *International Journal of Environmental Research and Public Health*, 17(24), 2020.

Ugargol, A. P. and Bailey, A. "Family Caregiving for Older Adults: Gendered Roles and Caregiver Burden in Emigrant Households of Kerala, India," *Asian Population Studies*, 14(2), 2018, 194–210.

United Nations Population Report 2019, United Nation Population Division.

United Nations Volunteers (UNV) programme, *The Scope and Scale of Global Volunteering: Current Estimates and Next Steps*, UNV, 2018.

Vasoo, S. *Community Development Arenas in Singapore*, (Singapore: World Scientific, 2019).

Vasoo, S. "Investments for the Social Sector to Tackle Some Key Social Issues," in *Collected Readings on Community Development in Singapore*, (World Scientific Publishers, 2019), pp. 601–617.

Vasoo, S. "The Social Work Profession in Response to Challeging Times: The Case of Singapore," *Asia Pacific Journal of Social Work and Development*, 23(4), 2013, 315–318.

Vidal, M., Rodriguez-Nunez, A., Hui, D., Allo, J., Williams, J. L., Park, M., Liu, D. and Bruera, E. "Place-of-death Preferences Among Patients with Cancer and Family Caregivers in Inpatient and Outpatient Palliative Care," *BMJ Supportive and Palliative Care*, 2020.

Vidovićová, L. "New Roles for Older People," *Journal of Population Ageing*, 11(1), 2018, 1–6.

Volandes, A. *The Conversations*, (London: Bloomsbury Publications, 2015).

Wang, D., Candinegara, E., Hou, J., Tan, A.-H. and Miao, C. "Robust Human Activity Recognition Using Lesser Number of Wearable Sensors," *International Conference on Security, Pattern Analysis, and Cybernetics (SPAC)*, (Shenzhen, China, 2017), pp. 290–295.

Wang, D., Subagdja, B., Kang, Y. and Tan, A. "Silver Assistants for Aging-in-place," *IEEE/WIC/ACM International Conference on Web Intelligence and Intelligent Agent Technology (WI-IAT)*, Vol. 3, (Singapore, 2015).

Wee, V., Harding, S. C., Geronimo, M. A. B. and Bezbaruah, S. "Singapore," in V. Wee, S. C. Harding, M. A. B. Geronimo and S. Bezbaruah (eds.), *Financial Security of Older Women: Perspectives from Southeast Asia*, (Singapore: Tsao Foundation, 2018).

Wickrama, K. (K. A. S.), O'Neal, C. W., Kwag, K. H. and Lee, T. K. "Is Working Later in Life Good or Bad for Health? An Investigation of Multiple Health Outcomes," *The Journals of Gerontology: Series B*, 68(5), 2013, 807–815.

World Health Organization (1995). *World Health Report, 1995. Bridging the Gaps*. WHO: Geneva.

Yap, M. T. and Gee, C. *Population Outcomes 2050*, (Singapore: Institute of Policy Studies, 2014).

Yu, H., Miao, C., Liu, S., Pan, Z., Khalid, N. S., Shen, Z. and Leung, C. "Productive Aging Through Intelligent Personalized Crowdsourcing," *Proceedings of the 30th AAAI Conference on Artificial Intelligence (AAAI'16)*, (Phoenix, Arizona, USA, 2016). pp. 4405–4406. https://dl.acm.org/doi/abs/10.5555/3016387.3016616.

Yu, H., Pan, Z., Miao, C. and Leung, C. "Crowd Computing for Population Aging Challenges," *Proceedings of the 1st International Conference on Crowd Science and Engineering (ICCSE'16)*, 2016.

Yu, X., Meng, L., Tian, X., Fauvel, S., Huang, B., Guan, Y., ... Leung, C. "Usability Analysis of the Novel Functions to Assist the Senior Customers in Online Shopping," *International Conference on Social Computing and Social Media (SCSM)*, (Cham: Springer, 2018), pp. 173–185.

Yuen, S. "Ramadan Free Meal Scheme in Woodlands Goes Digital. Singapore," *The Straits Times*, 18 April 2021.

Zayda, M. "From Visual Simulation to Virtual Reality to Games," *Computer*, 38(9), 2005, 25–32.

Zbyszewska, A. "Active Aging Through Employment: A Critical Feminist Perspective on Polish Policy," *International Journal of Comparative Labour Law & Industrial Relations*, 32(4), 2016, 449–472.

Zhang, F. and Kaufman, D. "Physical and Cognitive Impacts of Digital Games on Older Adults: A Meta-analytic Review," *Journal of Applied Gerontology*, 35(11), 2016, 1189–1210.

Zhang, H., Miao, C. and Yu, H. "Fuzzy Logic Based Assessment on the Adaptive Level of Rehabilitation Exergames for the Elderly," *IEEE Global Conference on Signal and Information Processing (GlobalSIP)*, Montreal, QC, Canada, pp. 423–427.

Zhang, H., Shen, Z., Liu, S., Yuan, D. and Miao, C. "Ping Pong: An Exergame for Cognitive Inhibition Training," *International Journal of Human–Computer Interaction*, 37(12), 2021, 1104–1115.

Zhang, Y., Qiu, Y., Pan, Z., Yu, X. and Miao, C. "Infusing Motivation into Reminders for Improving Medication Adherence," *Social Computing and Social Media: Applications in Marketing, Learning, and Health*, (Cham: Springer, 2021), pp. 456–471.

Index

www.ingramcontent.com/pod-product-compliance
Lightning Source LLC
Chambersburg PA
CBHW071733270326
41928CB00013B/2660